D0407981

The Library of Irish Studies

III
New Irish Writing

NEW IRISH WRITING

Essays in Memory of
Raymond J. Porter

Edited by
JAMES D. BROPHY
and
EAMON GRENNAN

Iona College Press
Twayne Publishers
A *Division of* G.K. *Hall &* Co. • *Boston*

New Irish Writing
James D. Brophy, Eamon Grennan

Copyright 1989 by G. K. Hall & Co.
All rights reserved.
Published by Twayne Publishers
A Division of G. K. Hall & Co.
70 Lincoln Street
Boston, Massachusetts 02111

Copyediting supervised by Barbara Sutton.
Book production and design by Patricia D'Agostino.

Typeset in 10 pt. Goudy Old Style
by Modern Graphics, Inc.

Printed on permanent/durable acid-free paper
and bound in the United States of America.

Library of Congress Cataloging-in-Publication Data

New Irish writing : essays in memory of Raymond J. Porter / edited by
    James D. Brophy and Eamon Grennan.
        p.   cm.—(The Library of Irish studies ; no. 3)
    ISBN 0-8057-9025-X
    1. English literature—Irish authors—History and criticism.
    2. English literature—20th century—History and criticism.
    3. Ireland in literature.   4. Ireland—Intellectual life—20th
    century.   5. Porter, Raymond J.   I. Porter, Raymond J.   II. Brophy,
    James D.   III. Grennan, Eamon.
    PR8754.N48   1988
    820'.9'89162—dc19   88–21207
                                                                         CIP

Contents

NEW IRISH WRITING

Preface

Raymond Porter died of heart disease on 6 March 1986 at the age of fifty-one. When later in that spring I participated in the memorial service at Iona College (where he had taught for twenty-five years), I read from Yeats's "The Tower," remarking that our colleague in his devotion to modern Irish literature might be considered one of those "outstanding men" to whom Yeats in that poem bequeathed his legacies of faith and pride. Ray indeed impressed all who knew him at Iona and in a number of organizations devoted to Irish literature as a scholar endowed with an inspiriting enthusiasm for Yeats, Joyce, Beckett, and similar gods of the Irish pantheon he worshiped. Ray was no "professional Irishman": he loved a joke, and very few "Irishisms" were spared his humor, but the subject of Irish literature was sacrosanct and paramount. *New Irish Writing* is a tribute to that extraordinary dedication.

Ray himself recognized the appropriateness of a memorial volume: it was he who took the initiative in planning the *festschrift* for William York Tindall (*Modern Irish Literature* [Twayne, 1972]), which we coedited. Ray wanted to celebrate not only Irish literature, but also those who celebrated it. I note a similar fitting loyalty in this volume where a number of contributors who joined Ray in that earlier volume and our subsequent *Contemporary Irish Writing* (Twayne, 1983) now return with memorial essays. Those of us who knew Raymond Porter acknowledge his studies of specific authors like Pearse and Behan, but we especially remember him as a person who was an indefatigable lover of the whole range of modern Irish literature. It is that lifelong commitment we honor in this volume.

James D. Brophy

Introduction

One should be wary of generalizations, especially in an Irish context, but since an introduction can hardly avoid them, I will hazard a few here by way of presenting and leading into the collection of essays that follows. They concern a number of elements that recur in interesting ways through the collection, inadvertent revelations—it may be—of the nature and meaning of the subject itself. (It is also worth remarking at the outset that James Brophy and I have arranged the essays in what we hope is a significant rather than a haphazard order, which may also help to illuminate the nature of the subject—new Irish writing, writing being done very close to the present moment by some of the most prominent, long-established, or recently emerged Irish poets, dramatists, and writers of fiction.)

Conor Cruise O'Brien has said that the "area where literature and politics overlap has to be regarded with much suspicion" ("Politics and the Poet: An Unhealthy Intersection," *Irish Times*, 21 August 1975). In Irish terms, however, this "area" is almost everywhere, so that the "overlap" and interplay of literature and social, cultural, and political reality is a feature common to many of these essays. Indeed, in the Irish context this is nothing new. Speaking of Irish poetry (in Irish) of the seventeenth, eighteenth, and nineteenth centuries, Thomas Kinsella has pointed out that "[a] great deal of it is political poetry or a response to social—and linguistic—injustice," and he refers to "the strong personal feeling that attaches itself to public issues" (*An Duanaire: Poems of the Dispossessed* [Philadelphia: University of Pennsylvania Press, 1981], xxii). And when, early on in the Irish Literary Revival, Yeats deliberately married politics, history, and society to minute questions of poetic form, he brought that traditional connection into the twentieth century and the English language: "We sought to make a more subtle rhythm, a more organic form than that of the older Irish poets who wrote in English, but always to remember certain ardent ideas and high attitudes of mind which were to our imagination the nation itself, as far as a nation can be summarized in the intellect" ("Poetry and Patriotism," in *Poetry and Ireland: Essays by*

NEW IRISH WRITING

W. B. Yeats and Lionel Johnson [Dublin: Cuala Press, 1908], 3). The essays in this volume show the various ways in which new Irish writing confirms, strengthens, and complicates this liaison. Whether the subject is contemporary Gaelic elegy, short stories by McGahern or Trevor, poems of distinctly feminist intention, a piece of radically innovative theater such as MacIntyre's *The Great Hunger*, or a postmodern philosophic novel like any of Banville's, our commentators have invariably located a site of creative tension between (in the broadest sense) social forces and the energies of articulate literary imagination. First to last the essays testify to the deep, shifting, complex ways these forces and those energies are richly implicated in one another. From the essays themselves, let a random sprinkling of quotations endorse my point:

> The debate contained by modern Irish poetry as a whole . . . . is indeed part of a larger discourse on cultural politics. (Bradley)

> [McGahern's] "High Ground," ostensibly a story in conflicting loyalties, scrutinizes the son–father relationship at a profound level and may even be an allegory of contemporary Ireland. (Kennedy)

> The final section [of Kinsella's *St. Catharine's Clock*] speaks directly and allegorically about what the poet has learned about his own and his country's fatal identity. (O'Hara)

> Contemporary Irish writing for the theater continues for the most part to mirror in realistic form Irish social life in its changing pressures, problems, and values. (Murray)

Given such a chorus, one might well pause over a remark made by Denis Donoghue in his introduction to *We Irish* (New York: Knopf, 1986): "Professionally, I am concerned with politics only when it invades literature and prescribes the gross conditions under which poems, plays, stories, and novels are written" (viii). This is, strictly speaking, proper, but in the Irish context (as so many of Donoghue's own essays show) a moot point. For there, such a prescriptive invasion seems always in full swing. And for this reason it seems fitting for Seamus Deane to claim as "one of the aims" of the recent *Short History of Irish Literature* (London: Hutchinson, 1986) "to show how literature has been inescapably allied with historical interpretation and political allegiance" (7). So Irish literary texts, it seems to me, are almost always, to one degree or another, "deconstructing" their own social, political, historical, and cultural contexts, while much of the further literary action of criticism and commentary—to judge by the sample in this volume—is an attempt to understand and give an adequately particular account of that creative deconstruction, to see clearly the complex relationship (often subtextual) between text and context.

With this relationship as the (perpetually shifting) ground of Irish literature and its criticism, the essays assembled here provide a few even more specific illuminations, revealing something of what the literary works let us know about their inevitable subject—the Irish psyche, public and private (or public / private). The specific recurring issues of particular interest to me were those of family, of multiplicity, and of faith (not explicitly "religious," but with something close to religious nuance and implication).

Family, multiplicity, faith: a compendious essay could be written on the way these figure—separately or together, explicitly or implicitly—in the following essays. A hint or two will serve to alert the reader to such telling presences. Family, for example, is the overt subject in the pieces on McGahern, Trevor, Durcan, Kinsella, Friel, and other dramatists, and in that on the enduring elegiac tradition in three contemporary poets who write in Irish. Family is masked and covert subject in the essays on "The Contemporary Fe / male poet" (the family of women), on Diarmuid Ó Suilleabháin (the Republican family), on John Banville (the artist as metaphysical orphan), or in that on "The Irishness of Irish Poetry After Yeats" (split affinities in the poetic family). In all cases, implicit and explicit, the use of the family is suggestive not only of wider allegorical connections, but of the way in which the country itself—small, insular, divided—can be thought of, *is felt,* in familial terms.

Multiplicity (in which I want to include the notions of plurality, of variety, of difference) naturally follows from this and is, I would imagine, a secret theme in all the "family" pieces just mentioned. In a more deliberate and obvious way it is also the theme of the wide-ranging account Christopher Murray gives of Irish theater since the 1950s (formal and substantive variety, playwrights from north and south of the border); of Anthony Bradley's essay on the different forms of "Irishness" Irish poets have or have not chosen; of John Engle's essay on the journey (multiple coverings of space, varying paradigms of home, the way the topos of travel helps the poets "move under a double load, the psychological and philosophical luggage borne by the modern writer and thinker, and the heavy pack of 'Irishness' with its strange gear"). One may even see a multiplicity of spiritual choices as part of John Mahon's theme when dealing with certain novels of Brian Moore; and certainly, in the deepest metaphysical sense, multiplicity is at the center of what George O'Brien discovers in the novels of Banville—multiplicity as a coded entrance into the problematic zones of history, science, and, especially, art. Even if one looks at how some of these essays relate to one another, again it is a sense of multiplicity that catches the attention: Protestant and Catholic, North and South, male and female, Irish language, and English language. In more definitively formal terms, multiplicity is suggested by the counterpoint between Richard Murphy's sonnet sequence as an alignment with a particular literary tradition, and Thomas Kinsella's enduring attempt to articulate idiosyncratic forms organic to his own individual and culturally collective exploration. Paul Muldoon's postmodern contortion of traditional forms suggests the same thing, as does, in the theater, the coexistence of realistic and nonrealistic modes. Multiplicity can also be detected in Harry Clifton's astringent anatomy of the ability of contemporary poets to deal with contemporary Irish actualities, the presence among the poets of different ideologies.

This accenting of multiplicity might be seen, I suggest, as a deep, unconscious response to what is, in an island of "great hatred, little room," the most pressing human need—the need for active and continued tolerance of difference. The literary arts themselves, that is, are a kind of conscious and preconscious embodying of the only quality that offers any true hope for survival as a (multiple, pluralist) community. And it is in this sense that I would take the statement of Derek Mahon's that a number of our contributors have cited—"a good poem is a paradigm of good politics"—the sense, that is, of multiple accepted possibilities of meaning, multiple minute shifts of tone attuned to a single civil utterance. The vivid statement John Banville gives to one of his characters could be seen in a similar light: "I am talking about the healing of wounds. I am talking about art."

Faith, odd enough word in the welter of contemporary literary "discourses," seems a natural enough accompaniment of family and multiplicity. Most overt in the essay on Brian Moore and in Dillon Johnston's discussion of the "otherworld"—that "significant location" continuous with and parallel to the one we normally inhabit—it is a distinct pressure to be felt in all the others. Where notions of family and multiplicity are firmly grounded in this world, faith fills out, even in agnostic terms, the abiding sense of a reality that will not be entirely confined within such borders. It is the mixture of such palpable and fraught earthly actualities with those other, maybe more enlarging, possibilities that makes a good deal of the literature discussed in these pages the strong, energetic thing it is. The fact of faith—in a form transcending any possible institutional version of it (versions that often provoke or stimulate literary creation in the northern and southern parts of the island, an imaginative source most influentially divined by Joyce)—wears a number of masks here. The essay on theater shows how alive the issue is in many of the playwrights, alive as "a famine of the spirit" (in Murphy or MacIntyre), or as a "sacral quality" in the feeling for place (in McGuinness). It intrudes into many of Trevor's "Irish" stories, is very much part, indeed, of "the news from Ireland." It is the tragic, often unspoken absence of some sort of consoling faith (countered at moments by an inexplicable "otherworld" awareness) that accounts for much of the existential bleakness and brilliance of McGahern's narratives. And even what John Engle calls Kinsella's "non-faith" can be described as "a craving for something like spiritual presence."

In more strictly political terms, faith (in a Republican ideal) is what animates the work of Diarmuid Ó Suilleabháin, whereas the hero of a Banville novel will authenticate himself, as George O'Brien reminds us, by keeping faith with his view of the world, which may be "an awful place, and yet, and yet a place capable of glory." All such manifestations of what I call faith establish a sort of family likeness under the skin (in the blood) of most of these subjects, linking even Paul Durcan's passionate affirmations or denunciations of his originally perceived world (our world, at curious angles of vision) with the wary, agnostic, cute-as-a-fox dodginess of Paul Muldoon, whose elusive poems—strongly there, yet hard to get a hold on—are informed by a sense of the world that acknowledges "an order" and "another dimension, something around us and beyond us, which is our inheritance" (in *Viewpoints: Poets in Conversation with John Haffenden* [London: Faber and Faber, 1981], 141). No matter what the stated subject of the essays that follow, some direct or tangential connection with faith is likely to be a qualitatively important part of the experience.

It seems apt, in a perverse sort of way, that one of the triggering devices for this introduction should be a moment of potential editorial censorship, disguised (understandably enough) as stylistic emendation. Coming across the phrase, "the unnatural division of the country," in one of the essays, I am stopped, blue pencil poised, over the adjective. At first it seems a question of rhythm: the sentence would read better without the epithet.

Then it is tone: "unnatural" suggests a series of assumptions that seem out of tune with the performative tone of the essay I have been reading, assumptions more in the grain of the essay's *subject*. At last, of course, I recognize that the word is alerting some undefined political (for want of a better, more accommodating word) wariness (can I say "belief") of my own. For what I find myself saying to myself is that the division of this island—disastrous and wretched as it is and has been in its consequences—is not so much "unnatural" (or "natural") as it is "historical." And so, in my view, the use of the word "unnatural" in this case is itself an unannounced entrance *on one side*, into the multifaceted political debate—a debate that works itself out in lives and the loss of lives, a debate about which the only sure thing one can say is that it cannot ever be resolved in the exclusive terms of any one side. "Unnatural," that is, is an exclusive term.

When I had reached this point in my (far from editorial) musing, then, I suddenly realized not only how volatile language was in this (Irish) situation, but also the degree to which a certain play and interaction between *nature* and *history* could be seen as the radical informing energy of much of the most alert, responsive, and responsible Irish literature written in this century. Indeed, the varying relationship between these forces of nature and history (broadly understood) might even be seen as a strong, deep undertow to those issues I have singled out as peculiarly pertinent to the present group of essays. (And surely it is this dynamic relationship that makes landscape such a potent presence in so much Irish literature: Brian Friel's *Translations*, to take only recent example, is merely the most thematically deliberate illustration of a pivotal encounter between history and nature.) Having gone through such a mental journey, I naturally left the word "unnatural" undisturbed, grateful both to it and to the writer of the essay for the timely reminder it provided of the degree to which our fate—natural, historical, political—is bound up in language, in the words we use and, in a sense, are used by. This is intensely, dangerously true in contemporary Ireland, and is a crucial source, I would say, for the peculiar vitality of new Irish writing.

Recently I asked a South African Xhosa oral poet, David Yali-Manisi (who normally lives in one of the "homelands"), what he thought "the poet's political responsibility" was. He picked his words with concentrated care: "The poet," he said, "must be . . . an agitator. He must agitate." A few years ago, after a public reading, I asked the Russian poet and Nobel laureate, Joseph Brodsky, the same question: "What is the poet's political responsibility?" Brodsky's answer was quick, marvellously simple. He said, "To the language." Separate as they might seem, I believe both poets, in their different ways and speaking out of their different needs and traditions, gave what is essentially the same answer. And I believe that that answer may be extended from the poet to other writers, and to the novelists, short story writers, and dramatists discussed in the following pages. Part of the writer's business must always be, through his or her own independent use of the language, to agitate us, shake up conventional assumptions, unsettle readers and listeners in those areas of the self where we reflect on being private humans, and in those areas of our selves where private and public borders cross, and cross-hatch. The writers of the essays in this collection reveal the many ways in which this agitating activity in language is exactly what new Irish writing does, and is about. And in the process, of course, they reveal how such writing is invariably "about" language, language that is always pausing at those borders to take stock of itself, see what it has, itself, to declare. "My soul frets," thinks the would-be Irish poet, Stephen Dedalus, when talking to the English dean of studies, "in the shadow of his language." Stephen's soul at that moment, like the language itself, is a site of both political and literary consciousness.

Finally, it is only right to say that, given such explicit and implicit concerns, the present collection seems a suitable memorial to a passionately engaged and active reader of Irish texts, a critic known professionally for his work on, among others, Pearse and Behan—the very conjunction of whose names in literary discussion is emblematic of how Irish writing is always crossing the (probably imaginary) border between literature and history. Raymond Porter's essay on Pearse (in *Modern Irish Literature,* one of two predecessors in the Twayne Library of Irish Studies to the present collection) contains the following quotation from Pearse, who (in 1908) is praising Yeats: "We cannot forget that he has spent his life in an endeavour to free our ideas of foreign thought, or that it was through his writings many of us made our first acquaintance with our early traditions and literature. He has never ceased to work for Ireland" (209). It is intriguing to consider, eighty years later and in an Ireland so different from what either Yeats or Pearse could have imagined (or hoped for), exactly what that last phrase ("to work for Ireland") would mean to the Irish writers whose work is the subject of the essays that follow. What *can* be said, I believe, is that these essays let us see that in every case, though in decisively different ways, the phrase continues to mean *something.* More than anything else, these essays show that Conor Cruise O'Brien's statement—"The area where literature and politics overlap has to be regarded with much suspicion"—formulates the issue (the "problem") in an unduly constricting way. New Irish writing, at its best, shows the inevitable nature of such overlap and the clear creative gains that can follow from it. If there is (and no doubt there should be) suspicion, let there also be celebration.

Eamon Grennan

The Irishness of Irish Poetry
after Yeats

Anthony Bradley

Derek Mahon once said that he looked forward to the day when the question "Is so-and-so *really* an Irish poet?" will clear a room in seconds.[1] The boredom and the horror induced even by the prospect of such a discussion arises from the presumably self-evident fatuousness of the question, from the insidious collocation of nationality with poetry. Mahon evidently feels that poetry should be beyond Irishness, that the intrusion of questions of political and cultural identity into art is spurious. Paul Muldoon's *Faber Anthology of Contemporary Irish Poetry* (1986) makes a similar point by reprinting a discussion between F.R. Higgins and Louis MacNeice in lieu of a preface. In this discussion, Higgins argues, basically, that there is some mystical attribute originating in race and blood that characterizes Irish poetry. No one would seriously make such an argument today, at least not in such essentialist and potentially fascistic terms. Yet one might acknowledge, without conceding anything to Higgins, that there are two very different traditions in modern Irish poetry, one of which is more obviously Irish than the other in its cultural values.

This difference corresponds, very broadly speaking, with a cultural pattern that has been, and continues to be, of great significance in shaping modern Ireland. In a recent book on the establishment of democracy in what is now the Republic of Ireland, Jeffrey Prager identifies the two poles of Irish political and cultural life as "Gaelic-Romantic" and "Irish-Enlightenment."[2] Stressing that these poles, in practice, are rarely exclusively definitive, Prager argues persuasively that it is between these complementary opposites that so much of the political culture of modern Irish life has been shaped. Prager sees the Gaelic-Romantic strand as preoccupied with the past, with Gaelic culture and language, with a definition

1

of Ireland as rural, its people as Catholic, its politics accepting of violence
and revolution as a justifiable response to oppression. The Irish-Enlightenment strand he sees as preoccupied with modernity, secularism, democracy, constitutionalism, rationalism.

Qualifications aside (and it should be pointed out that he does not
speculate about the contemporary period), Prager would seem to have hit
on a complementarity that has indeed shaped modern Irish life in a profound way.[3] If the labels Gaelic-Romantic and Irish-Enlightenment are
susceptible to misunderstanding, they are useful in indicating the differing
cultural values that inform modern Irish poetry as well as Ireland's political
culture. Thus the Gaelic-Romantic strand of Irish poetry assumes, broadly
speaking, a cultural identity based on the past, and especially the Gaelic
past and the Irish language, reflects an Ireland that is rural and agricultural,
in which the sense of place tends toward the atavistic, in which Catholicism is at some level a vital and defining force (even if its institutional
aspects are rejected); this strand is, moreover, engaged with public life in
Ireland, and implicitly accepts revolutionary violence as an inevitable
response to oppression. The other strand of modern Irish poetry (Irish-
Enlightment) assumes a different and broader concept of history and culture, one based in Europe rather than Ireland, includes but is not limited
to writers who come out of a Protestant background in the North, stresses
the inner life, is urbane rather than pastoral, secular rather than religious,
and is profoundly antagonistic to middle-class values.

I should acknowledge from the outset that much Irish poetry, like Irish
politics at their most successful in Prager's model, integrates elements of
both sets of cultural values. Also that poets writing in one tradition are
acutely conscious of those writing in the other (this is particularly true of
the contemporary situation): the consequence of the cultural politics of
modern Ireland. One might identify different manifestations of this dialectic in the Report of the Forum on a New Ireland, the Field Day
pamphlets and the multitude of essays and reviews in Irish journals and
periodicals such as the late lamented Crane Bag. Perhaps most important,
in this context, is the necessity to point out a certain self-consciousness
and artfulness in Irish poetry that, even where there exists an affiliation
with a generalized cultural tendency, safeguards the poetry from reduction
to mere ideology. To maintain this is not to retreat from the assumption
that Irish poetry (all literature, as such critics as Raymond Williams insist),
takes place in society, only to claim for the best of modern Irish poets the
function of artist as opposed to mouthpiece.

I should explain that this point of view is not shared by a leading critic
of contemporary Irish poetry: Edna Longley does not concede that most

Irish poetry has achieved the distancing I have described, but rather sees certain contemporary writers and some of their books in particular—Seamus Heaney's *North*, John Montague's *Rough Field*, Tom Paulin's *Liberty Tree*, Seamus Deane's *History Lessons*, Brian Friel's play *Translations* (and indeed the whole Field Day enterprise)—as politically tendentious in their rehearsal of nationalist mythology, and therefore not good literature (nor good politics, either).[4] My own conviction is that the art of these poems (and of Friel's play) makes them much more than the "old whines in new bottles" Longley suggests they are ("Poetry and Politics," 37). If there is an undeniable affiliation between the poetry just mentioned and Irish nationalism or republicanism, it is much more intelligent and complex in its possession of history and politics than previous Irish poetry. Indeed, I would argue that the poets in question write the kind of poetry that, in Reginald Gibbons's words, "*resists* ideology in favor of an insistence on the intrinsic value of life and the political value of life lived freely."[5] But my purpose in this essay is, however briefly and sketchily, to indicate what I take to be the two varieties of modern Irish poetry and to suggest their defining characteristics; readers may disagree on the value of the poetry and the politics, but will surely agree on their cohabitation in so much of modern Irish poetry.

Let me proceed, then, to describe the traits of what might be described as the Gaelic Romantic strand of modern Irish poetry. Even if the greatest accomplishment of modern Irish poetry is in the English language, there has always been a consciousness among Irish writers, most memorably articulated by Joyce's Stephen Dedalus in an oft-quoted passage (in *A Portrait of the Artist as a Young Man*), that English in Ireland is different.[6] It has been charged in a general way by the experience of colonialism, and the most obvious symbol of its difference lies in its perennial awareness of the Gaelic language and the residual Gaelic culture. Although Michael Hartnett's poem "A Farewell to English," in which he abjures English for Gaelic, is unique, and although Hartnett is again composing in English, the fact that an extremely talented poet can switch from English to Gaelic is a dramatic indication of the power of the residual culture in Ireland. One could also point, as evidence of the persistence of this residual culture in apparently incongruous circumstances, to another very talented younger poet writing in English, Ciaran Carson, whose first language, although he grew up in the industrial city of Belfast, was Gaelic.

The amount of translating from Gaelic poetry into English is a constant feature of modern Irish poetry: the major attempts at recovery of the older literature (in Kinsella's *Táin*, *An Duanaire*, and *New Oxford Book of Irish Verse*, Heaney's *Sweeney Astray*, Montague's anthology, Hartnett's *O'Bru-*

adair), coupled with translations from contemporary poetry in Gaelic (the poems of Nuala Ní Dhómhnaill have been translated by Hartnett, Muldoon, and Montague, among others) are clearly distinguishing features of one strand of Irish poetry in English. Moreover, modern and contemporary poetry in Gaelic is newly available in at least one bilingual anthology, not only making it more accessible but also implicitly recognizing, probably for the first time from the vantage point of Gaelic poetry, the symbiotic relationship of Gaelic and English as the languages of poetry in Ireland. [7]

Perhaps Austin Clarke's attempt to import technique from verse in Gaelic into his verse in English resulted in oddities and obscurities, especially for the reader coming from the tradition of English verse; yet Clarke's success (however one qualifies it) depends on just that capacity to write poetry in English that is demonstrably Irish, not merely in its content, but in its technique also. After Clarke, there are a large number of poems in English (by Kavanagh, Montague, Heaney, et al.), which, though they have a less conscious connection with Gaelic literature, correspond to the Gaelic genre of poems about place (*dinnseanchas*). One might also point to the use of such forms as the *aisling* (a political dream-vision poem) and the *immram* (a journey-quest poem) even when, as in Paul Muldoon's work, those forms are appropriated in a subversive or parodic way. Probably because of the persistence of the residual Gaelic culture and especially the Gaelic language, and because of the awareness that the English language in Ireland has been shaped by the history of colonialism, there is also in contemporary Irish poetry, most especially in poems by Heaney and Muldoon (and in Friel's play *Translations*), a sharp consciousness about the nature of language itself.

The affiliation with Gaelic in post-Yeatsian Irish poetry, however, does not, in my reading of that poetry, entail the romantic, cultural nostalgia it tended to enlist in the Irish Literary Revival: indeed, there is a much greater realism and irony in the style of translations from the Gaelic in post-Yeatsian poetry than in late-nineteenth- and early-twentieth-century versions. Of course, Prager's insistence on the complementarity of Gaelic-Romantic and Irish-Enlightenment cultural values can accommodate this realism; it can also accommodate the opposing argument, that the Gaelic-Romantic elements in contemporary Irish poetry and in the mentality of the population at large are, for the most part, unreconstructed in their romanticism and archaicism, and incapable of reconciliation with modern values.

For Irish poets in this Gaelic-Romantic mode, there is, to be sure, a preoccupation with the Irish past, but it is a preoccupation that probably

originates in an attempt to confront Ireland's turbulent present rather than
in some genetic coding that ensures the Irish will forever be addicted to
history. George Steiner's observations in another context are suggestive
not only of the cultural situation of the Ulster Catholic but of the whole
process of the making of modern Ireland: "A society requires antecedents.
Where these are not naturally at hand, where a community is new or
reassembled after a long interval of dispersal or subjection, a necessary
past tense to the grammar of being is created by intellectual and emotional
fiat."[8]

The images of the Irish past—the Famine, Cromwell, the Plantation
of Ulster, the Rebellion of 1798, even the archaeological past—are of
course not all treated in the same way; generally speaking, however, they
are not aestheticized and removed from actual history, but are seen to
bear in more or less oblique ways upon the present. If no great ingenuity
at discovering political subtexts in Irish poetry (especially in this vein) is
required, nonetheless the best of this poetry does not involve the poet as
spokesman for a particular ideological view, but rather as artist. I feel this
is especially true of Montague's *Rough Field*, where if the vision of history
is nationalist, the fluid, reciprocal relation between personal and family
history on the one hand and the history of Ulster on the other gives the
sequence its imaginative validity. It is also true of Heaney's *North*. While
deploring what he saw as the *"fixed and preordained" nationalism* of that
volume, Conor Cruise O'Brien also acknowledged that the poetry gives
us "the thing itself, the actual substance of historical agony and
dissolution. . . ."[9]

Edna Longley and others see in these books a tendentious projection
of time present onto time past. In finding metaphors for Ireland's violence
of the 1970s not only in other times, but in other cultures as well (especially
in his bog poems), Seamus Heaney in particular was accused of glamour-
izing barbarity and, essentially, endorsing republican violence. One could,
however, oppose a mirror to this reading of the poems, arguing that the
poems mask atrocity, aestheticize violence *against* the Catholic community
rather than by it. Heaney himself would seem to entertain the latter
possibility in "Station Island" when the ghost of a cousin, murdered in a
sectarian attack and elegized in a poem in *Field Work*, accuses Heaney of
having evaded the truth:

> 'You confused evasion and artistic tact.
> The Protestant who shot me through the head
> I accuse directly, but indirectly, you

who now atone perhaps upon this bed
for the way you whitewashed ugliness and drew
the lovely blinds of the *Purgatorio*
and saccharined my death with morning dew.'

All the poet can do when confronted by the ghost of another friend, also
a victim of sectarian murder, is beg forgiveness for his "timid circumspect
involvement" ("Station Island," VII). Once again, the term Gaelic-Romantic can accommodate different interpretations of the treatment of
history in this strand of Irish poetry.

If the landscape of modern Irish poetry is almost invariably Irish, it is
not the romantic West favored by the revival writers, however, but rather
the ordinary, often unpicturesque rural areas of Monaghan, Galway, Tyrone, and Derry (if we think of Kavanagh, Padraic Fallon, Montague, and
Heaney). Indeed, there is a kind of imaginative repossession of the unideal-
ized Irish landscape in modern Irish poetry, as opposed to the blurred
romantic scenery of earlier Irish poetry. This sense of place, moreover,
offers a setting for certain ideas and feelings associated with the antithesis
between nature and culture, an antithesis that is understandable in view
of personal gravitation of these writers from country to city and their
simultaneous allegiance to two different worlds. The poetry that gives us
a new sense of the Irish landscape also gives us, at the same time, a new
sense of Ireland's social organization, and of the social process and change
that characterize modern Ireland. Having said this, one might also argue
that certain place poems, especially by Heaney and Montague (as well as
Brian Friel's play *Translations*), amount, in addition, to a reclamation of
the Gaelic identity of Ulster and that these writings are infused by cultural
politics that are appropriately described by a fairly literal interpretation of
the term Gaelic-Romantic.

Catholicism is, of course, an essential part of Gaelic-Romantic cultural
values. Indeed, religion in Ireland, Catholicism or Protestantism, would
seem to permeate all social and political processes. This mixture of theology
and politics is certainly not unusual among the adherents of a fundamen-
talist Protestantism in the North: a prominent Ulster politician recently
announced to his constituents that they could not "work their salvation"
through the Anglo-Irish accord.[10] The extent to which life in the Republic
has been shaped by a rather narrow Catholicism has been evident in the
public debates over amendments to the constitution in recent years. While
there are many poems *about* Catholicism—poems that invariably resist
the oppressive aspects of the Church's social teaching and its function as

institution in Ireland—those same poems frequently manifest what is probably an unconscious absorption of ways of feeling deriving from Catholic belief. There are affinities here, however, with the sense of nature as sacramental, of poetry as a type of prayer, and of the artist as a sacerdotal figure that one finds in Gaelic poetry of the early period. One can find similar conjunctions of nature, art, and religion in poems by Clarke, Kavanagh, Montague, Heaney, and others. There is yet another type of poem that uses a practice of Irish Catholicism as a structure for poetry: Denis Devlin, Patrick Kavanagh, and Seamus Heaney all use, in different ways, the pilgrimage to Lough Derg as a literary structure and setting capable of accommodating the personal and the social in what seems a very natural way.

The critique of institutionalized Catholicism is an aspect of the role of Irish poets as unacknowledged legislators, a role it would be easy to overstate. Yet more than in most Western countries, Irish poets enjoy a certain respect, are listened to, and enjoy a certain public standing. If their role has frequently been one of opposition to a lack of consciousness and conscience in the social and political sphere, and has been pursued, at times, in obscurity, its value has been widely recognized, even if retrospectively. In modern Irish poetry there is a tradition of satiric and moral commentary on Irish social abuses and shortcomings which, following Joyce in *Portrait*, seeks "to forge . . . the uncreated conscience" of the Irish people. Austin Clarke's poems expose the complacency and bad faith of his times, and Kavanagh's *The Great Hunger* (the tradition spans both urban and rural experience) can be seen as a satiric commentary on the moral condition of rural Irish life, with pronounced analogies to Clarke's work and Joyce's *Dubliners*. More recently, the work of a whole range of poets from Thomas Kinsella to Paul Durcan has, in very different ways, sharply confronted the corruption of Irish society. This sort of poetry is not inhibited by the assumption that it makes nothing happen.

One can see in this aspect of modern Irish verse a correspondence with so much of the older Gaelic verse, which is similarly preoccupied, and unashamedly social and political. The Irish government's setting up of Aosdana, an academy of writers and artists who are supported by government fellowships, is a gesture, at least, intended to recognize the importance of the artist in modern Ireland and to parallel that importance with his role in the older, Gaelic culture.

In summary, what seems to me distinctive about the Gaelic-Romantic strand in modern Irish poetry is, essentially, that the lyric form should have assumed the job of expressing history, society, and culture, that it seems to fill the role elsewhere occupied by the novel, or at least, by poetry in non-European, Third World situations.[11] Traditionally, the lyric would seem like the most personal and individual form in literature, and the one least inclined to carry the burden of a social and historical consciousness; one tactical response of Irish poets (Yeats, Heaney, and Montague spring to mind) has been to write lyric sequences to gain the larger frame of reference. And there is a particularly piquant incongruity in the fact that the English lyric form characterized as "the well-made poem" has frequently borne the burden of expressing Irish culture and history. As Terence Brown has pointed out, the form of "the well-made poem" is subverted by the linguistic urgency of English in Ulster (I would say in Ireland generally, and add that the form is also distinguished by its non-genteel content).[12] So that not only does British Ulster, in Heaney's words, have "no rights on / The English lyric"—neither does Britain ("The Ministry of Fear").

Of course, there are many poems by writers I have consigned to this Gaelic-Romantic category that seem independent of the Irish cultural context—poems about art, love, childhood, the self, marriage, family, and work that do not seem conditioned by Irishness. Poems, too, that seek to transcend the worldliness that appears to be such a dominant feature of Irish poetry—"worldliness" here understood as the sense of social and political contingency Edward W. Said refers to in his book *The World, the Text, the Critic* (Cambridge: Harvard University Press, 1983). So there are the fabulous realities of Paul Muldoon's poems, or the allegories of Seamus Heaney's *The Haw Lantern* (1987)—"From the Republic of Conscience," "From the Canton of Expectation," "Parable Island," and "From the Land of the Unspoken." Yet one might say that the playfulness and imaginative freedom of these poems only serves as a deferring and complication of their relevance to the matter of Ireland. And one might also point out that the other world, imagined in despite of the actual, is a significant location in the old Gaelic poetry.

But the main opposition to the worldliness of the Gaelic-Romantic strand of modern Irish poetry comes from the large minority of Irish poets one might characterize, using Prager's label, as Irish-Enlightenment. As did Joyce, these writers contest the Gaelic-Romantic agenda of cultural identity, Irish history and society, the rural world and the Gaelic tradition. Irish-Enlightenment writers are committed to the idea of a pluralistic, modern world in which a concern with "Irishness" seems provincial and even, at times, dangerously tribal. Like Joyce, they refuse to be hamstrung by the idea of an art that is Irish. In an article on "Recent Irish Poetry" in 1934, Beckett categorically rejected the idea of "an accredited theme," proclaiming rather, with Thomas MacGreevy and the other signatories of the Vertical Manifesto, the importance of "self-perception" and "the hegemony of the inner life over the outer life."[13] A letter I received (6 November 1986) from Brian Coffey keeps the banner of modernity flying: he mentions that he hears he is "not much thought of by the Ourish or the Northern crowd," and defiantly proclaims, "Long live . . . Mac-Greevy, Devlin, Beckett and myself!" (Coffey's most recent book, *Chanterelles* (1985) is also defiantly modernist in style.)

That a number of these writers derive from a Protestant background, whether Anglo-Irish as in the case of Beckett and Richard Murphy, Ulster Protestant as in the cases of MacNeice, Rodgers, Hewitt, Mahon, Longley, Simmons, and Paulin, or just plain Irish Protestant like Hugh Maxton, is of some significance. The heritage of Irish Protestantism includes many notable proponents in the eighteenth century, especially in Ulster, of Enlightenment values and radical, Republican virtue. (For an interesting treatment of this topic, see Marianne Elliott's Field Day pamphlet, *Watchmen in Sion: the Protestant Idea of Liberty* [1985].) Tom Paulin's poetry sets forth the political orientation of Ulster Protestantism in the eighteenth century almost as a reproach to the political values it assumed in the nineteenth and twentieth centuries. If writers from Protestant backgrounds share a distaste for modern, political Protestantism in the Ulster context, preferring the secular, rationalist values inherited from the Protestant tradition, they have long been uneasy, very naturally, with a definition of Irishness based largely on Gaelic-Romantic values, and have been inclined to look to England and Europe as a larger cultural context, as a way of combatting a definition if Irishness that would marginalize their experience. The poetry of these Irish-Enlightenment writers, generally speaking, opposes the rural setting and feelings of the Gaelic-Romantic mode with an urban or rather cosmopolitan setting and feelings; Irish history with European; Irish literature with European (including English) literature; the Irish language with the European languages (including English); Irish themes with more personal and therefore more universal concerns. Their general attitude is to resist the tendency toward a limitation of self and art that they see as inherent in prevailing notions of Irishness. Although there are significant differences between the poetry of the European-Irish writers (which is inclined toward the hermetic) and that of those contemporary Ulster poets (who look to Louis MacNeice as examplar); both sets of writers have much in common in their opposition to "Irishness."

As in the case of writers from a Catholic background, though, the imagination of writers from a Protestant background can be seen to be colored in ways that do not imply dogmatic belief but rather, certain ways of seeing and feeling.[15] So, for example, as Terence Brown points out, the perceptive reader will register the "puritan's exactitude of definition and solemnity of judgement" in Derek Mahon's use of the word "foreknowledge" in his "Gipsies Revisited" ("An Ulster Renaissance?," 16).

Obviously, both sets of writers chafe against any sort of self-definition that would determine and limit their art. If the crossovers from one tradition to the other—Heaney's "Chekhov on Sakhalin," Mahon's self-reflexive *aisling* "Derry Morning," James Simmons's *From the Irish*, and place-poems by writers out of a Protestant background—are not always without a hint of incongruity, they are indicative of the struggle on the part of Irish writers to reach into the stock-in-trade of the *other* Irish tradition than the one to which they belong.

What is distinctive about modern Irish poetry taken as a whole, is precisely that it contains two modes of discourse that can usefully if only approximately be described as Gaelic-Romantic and Irish-Enlightenment, and that poets writing in one mode are conscious of those who write in the other. The debate contained by modern Irish poetry as a whole (between those committed to its Irishness and those committed to its non-Irishness) is indeed part of a larger discourse on cultural politics that can be seen in the pages of the various Field Day pamphlets, the periodical *The Crane Bag* and its successors, in anthologies as different as Kinsella's and Muldoon's, and in the fact that *literary* criticism as practiced by Ireland's leading critics (Seamus Deane, Declan Kiberd, Terence Brown, Edna Longley, and others) has become, in large part, cultural criticism. Even if there is, ultimately, some transcendent element in the best lyric poetry of modern Ireland that makes it *not* reducible to just another form of social expression, it is nonetheless one of the most salient attributes of the poetry that it offers a highly civilized and intelligent dialectic between the contested cultural values of modern Ireland. A similar debate over cultural values continues to be fought out in a much less rational and humane fashion in the streets and fields of Ulster. I began this essay with a quotation from Derek Mahon. Let me begin to end with another one: "A good poem is a paradigm of good politics."[16]

It may be easier to agree on what constitutes a good poem rather than on what constitutes good politics, but if Mahon means by this interesting categorical pronouncement that a good (Irish) poem should incorporate a certain dispassionateness, should get outside narrow historical or political loyalties—surely there are plenty of individual poems in modern Irish writing that fit the bill. Irish poetry, as a whole, indeed, would seem to be a model for good politics in its civilized argument between conflicting cultural values. More important, however, the totality of Irish poetry is not merely a model, but an inseparable part of the politics that continue to shape and to sunder modern Ireland.

Notes

1. Dillon Johnston, *Irish Poetry after Joyce* (Notre Dame: University of Notre Dame Press, 1986), 225.

2. Jeffrey Prager, *Building Democracy in Ireland* (Cambridge: Cambridge University Press, 1986).

3. In the Field Day pamphlet *Heroic Styles: The Tradition of an Idea* (1984), Seamus Deane argued that the two main ways of reading Irish literature and history can be characterized as "Romantic" and modern; in another pamphlet in the series, *Myth and Motherland* (1984), Richard Kearney argued that there is a basic polarity in Irish history and poetry between mythos and logos. That there is a broad congruence between the analysis of these critics and that of Prager strengthens the credibility of the idea that Irish culture may be defined between complementary opposites.

4. Edna Longley, "Poetry and Politics in Northern Ireland," *Crane Bag 9*, no. 1 (1985):26–40.

5. Reginald Gibbons, "Political Poetry and the Example of Ernesto Cardenal," *Critical Enquiry* 13, no. 3 (1987):661.

6. "He felt with a smart of dejection that the man to whom he was speaking was a countryman of Ben Jonson. He thought: The language in which we are speaking is his before it is mine. How different are the words *home, Christ, ale, master,* on his lips and on mine! I cannot speak or write these words without unrest of spirit. His language, so familiar and so foreign, will always be for me an acquired speech. I have not made or accepted its words. My voice holds them at bay. My soul frets in the shadow of his language."

7. *The Bright Wave / An Tonn Gheal: Poetry in Irish Now*, ed. Dermot Bolger (Dublin: Raven Arts Press, 1986) is the first bilingual anthology to appear, but there are a number of other collections and editions of modern poetry in Irish.

8. George Steiner, *In Bluebeard's Castle: Some Notes towards the Redefinition of Culture* (New Haven: Yale University Press, 1971), 3.

9. Edna Longley, *Poetry in the Wars* (Newcastle upon Tyne: Bloodaxe Books, 1986), 140.

10. Harold McCusker, cited in W.J. McCormack, *The Battle of the Books* (Mullingar: Lilliput Press, 1986), 71.

11. Anne McClintock points out the role of the black poet in contemporary South Africa as "lyric historian and political commentator" in "Black South African Poetry," *Critical Enquiry* 13, no. 3 (1987):616.

12. Terence Brown, "An Ulster Renaissance?" *Concerning Poetry* 14, no. 2 (1981).

13. "Recent Irish Poetry" is reprinted in Beckett's *Disjecta,* ed. Ruby Cohn (New York: Grove Press, 1984); "Manifesto: Poetry is Vertical," 1932, is reprinted in Thomas MacGreevy's *Collected Poems* (Dublin: New Writers' Press, 1971).

14. *Across a Roaring Hill: The Protestant Imagination in Modern Ireland,* ed. Gerald Dawe and Edna Longley (Belfast: Blackstaff, 1985), contains a number of valuable essays that are relevant to this discussion.

15. Longley, *Poetry in the Wars,* 185.

Friel and After:
Trends in Theater and Drama

Christopher Murray

In concluding his book on Brian Friel in 1973 D. E. S. Maxwell quoted him as saying: "I would like . . . to write a play that would capture the peculiar spiritual, and indeed material flux, that this country is in at the moment. This has got to be done, for me anyway, at a local, parochial level, and hopefully this will have meaning for other people in other countries."[1] Maxwell seemingly found this to be a "fair description" not only of Friel's plays up to 1973 but even of those written and staged in the 1970s and early 1980s, because he quotes the same words at the end of his *Critical History of Modern Irish Drama*, adding: "Friel's work is entirely compatible with that of his contemporaries considered here."[2] One may deduce from this repetition two things:[2] (1) Friel's work has remained consistent in its concentration on local affairs, construed as having general or universal implications; (2) Friel's approach to drama is representative of the approach of Irish playwrights in general. One might even fuse these two points into the single claim that new Irish writing for the stage is very much like the not-so-new, because it persists in mirroring actual experience in a style that seeks to adjust realism to symbolism or to some other form that implies the use of metaphor. In this essay I look at recent Irish drama in the light of such a claim.

I

The methodology used here craves the reader's indulgence. If he or she feels the need of a general survey of contemporary Irish drama he or she

13

will find one in Robert Hogan's *"Since O'Casey" and Other Essays,* and elsewhere.[3] What the reader will get in the present essay is a series of forays into theatrical and dramatic history aimed at supplying contexts for the understanding of developments since about 1960. Friel's work is commented on intermittently rather than given a comprehensive assessment. Yet Friel is the informing presence of the whole essay, just as he is one of the greatest Irish playwrights of this century. He is not dealt with comprehensively here because to do so would unbalance the essay; moreover, a considerable amount of good critical writing on Friel has been published in the past fifteen years or so, by people such as Seamus Deane, Ulf Dantanus, and D. E. S. Maxwell,[4] a factor that makes it more sensible here to pay attention both to other playwrights who have received less attention to date, such as Thomas Murphy and Thomas Kilroy, and to younger writers still making their way in the theatrical world, such as Bernard Farrell, Graham Reid, Martin Lynch, and Frank McGuinness.

In saying that Friel is the informing presence of this essay I refer mainly to the idea outlined in the first paragraph. But to what is stated there I would add another quotation from Friel that serves to clarify, and perhaps to validate, the methodology used in this essay: "A play offers you a shape and a form to accommodate your anxieties and disturbance in this period of life you happen to be passing through. . . . But you outgrow that and you change and grope for a new shape and a new articulation."[5] This means, in effect, that one cannot say that Friel's work, or, indeed, the work of any comparable playwright (Murphy, for example) forms a continuous line of development. It tends, rather, to be a formal response to what could loosely be called the Zeitgeist. Personal and public events interact to establish pressures on the dramatic artist to "speak out," but he does not so much speak out as find (in Eliot's phrase) an objective correlative for certain moods and feelings, or, as Friel put it above, "anxieties and disturbances." A major writer, however, like Friel or Murphy, actually articulates what is vaguely felt by the public as a mood or apprehension of reality. Other writers tune in to that mood and find their own images by which to give it dramatic form. Such is the latent thesis of this essay.

It must also be said that long before Friel first began to mirror Irish society in his plays the Irish drama had established as the norm the very ambition he set himself. One sees it embodied in the work of Synge. What else are *In Shadow of the Glen, Riders to the Sea,* and *The Playboy of the Western World* about but local affairs construed as having universal implications? What else are O'Casey's three Dublin plays but powerful attempts to capture what Friel calls above "the peculiar spiritual, and material flux" Ireland was in following the war of independence and the civil war? In other words, Friel is very much a traditional Irish playwright, in harmony with the aims and achievements of the first great exponents of modern Irish drama. The tension in his work, and the tension in contemporary Irish drama, is between the two fidelities, to tradition and to the living experience.

II

After World War II Ireland was slow to emerge from the isolationism that characterized both the culture and the arts from the late 1930s on. In the Dublin theater, the Gate compromised the daring independence of its earlier years (1928–40), and using the larger, commercial Gaiety Theatre MacLiammoir and Edwards provided productions of successful London and New York plays. When O'Casey's *The Bishop's Bonfire* was premiered in 1955 it caused a stir, to be sure, and was picketed by Catholic action protesters, but placed beside *The Plough and the Stars* (1926) O'Casey's later play is such a mild criticism of Irish self-deception and humbug that the opposition effectively measures the level of Irish conservatism at this time. One could also point to the well-documented treatment of O'Casey's *The Drums of Father Ned*, withdrawn from the Dublin Theatre Festival in 1958, or to J. P. Donleavy's victimization over the production in 1961 of the dramatic version of *The Ginger Man*, taken off after a few performances. Even though little experimental theaters such as the Pike (where Behan's *The Quare Fellow* was premiered in 1954) were sprouting out of Dublin basements in the 1950s the general theatrical atmosphere continued to be fatal to plays that were in any way iconoclastic. The Abbey Theatre was moribund. After a fire destroyed the theater in 1951 the company transferred to the larger Queen's Theater, home of nineteenth-century melodrama and variety, where box-office considerations ensured that plays of the least intellectually challenging kind dominated the repertory. The policy of fostering the Irish language, firmly supported by manager Ernest Blythe, received more attention than did theatrical or dramatic development. With very occasional exceptions, the Abbey repertory was safe, repetitive, and innocuous.

It is against this background that the dramatic revival of the mid-1960s must be seen. The pattern sketched above persisted until social and economic changes slowly moved Ireland from its earlier isolation into the era of television, the European Economic Community, jet travel, the civil rights movement, and Conor Cruise O'Brien, that is, a new liberalism and historical revisionism that made acceptable (for a time) the questioning and discussion of moral, ethical, historical, and religious matters. As Ireland changed so did the theater. In the early 1960s plays were still being rejected by the Abbey because they were too "strong." For example, Thomas Murphy's A Whistle in the Dark (1961); the Gate Theatre was on its last hinges; experimental work was seen only in theater clubs and basements. Then in 1966, to coincide with the golden jubilee of the 1916 rebellion, the new Abbey Theatre was opened on the site of the original (1904) building and the opportunity was created for the development of a new Irish drama. This is not to deny the impact made by the Dublin Theatre Festival (established 1957). Annually, this showcase encouraged new Irish playwriting in an atmosphere that, after the O'Casey row over The Drums of Father Ned taught a valuable lesson, commanded artistic rather than moral responses.

The Dublin Theatre Festival, in fact, hosted in the early 1960s plays that can now be seen as revolutionary. These include Friel's Philadelphia, Here I Come!, John B. Keane's The Highest House on the Mountain, Hugh Leonard's Stephen D, and Eugene McCabe's The King of the Castle. Such plays were significant because they challenged the conservative norms still rigorously upheld by the Abbey. They initiated a revival in Irish drama, strengthened as the 1960s advanced by such other new plays as Thomas Kilroy's The Death and Resurrection of Mr Roche and Thomas Murphy's Famine. Each of these deserves comment. Their thematic novelty lay in their breaching taboo areas of public discourse.

Whereas the theme of emigration found in Philadelphia, Here I Come! was not new and may be seen in Irish drama as early as Padraic Colum's Broken Soil (1905), the real concern of the play is with the private, unresolved suffering of the young man about to emigrate, Gar O'Donnell. The depiction of an isolated, alienated consciousness was new to Irish drama. In Philadelphia there is no real plot, something essential to Irish drama before 1964. Nothing happens to make any difference to Gar O'Donnell's last night at home: nobody dies, no last will suddenly allows the hero the financial resources to marry the girl of his dreams (for she's married before the play begins), no disclosures are made to alter his decision to leave. Instead, attention is directed to something negative: an emotional flaw, a gap in communication between father and son that cannot be bridged by either. The failure to communicate suggests a flaw in the society itself but it is not a flaw that has any clear cause; irremediable, it seems to suggest a flaw in life itself, in the nature of human relationships. When one attends to Friel's setting and the homely rituals surrounding the young hero's private suffering and fantasies one sees at first a deceptive traditionalism. Here, once more, is the familiar rural Irish kitchen, scene of so many Abbey plays. Here is the family rosary, image of so much that is orthodox and unwittingly sectarian in Irish life. Here, too, is the parish priest, stalwart of so many Irish stories and plays. But none of these features has any positive value here. All are, as it were, masks for the reality so painfully experienced by the main consciousness of the play, through which the "meaning," insofar as meaning is of interest to Friel, is communicated to the audience. The settled pastoral life is revealed not so much as a sham as offering no nurture to a spirit hungry for more than security, land, respectability: the things that preoccupied the characters in Irish drama of an earlier era. There is a critique of Irish society and culture here that goes deep (though not as deep as in several of Friel's subsequent plays). The ending, in particular, is a turning away from the securities and formal tidiness of Irish peasant drama. Private Gar demands of his other self, Public Gar: "why do you have to leave? Why? Why?" And the answer comes back, tentatively and despairingly, "I don't know. I-I-I don't know."[6] The inconclusiveness expresses an agnosticism impossible to earlier Irish drama. In the drama of the 1950s, for example, a plot had to have a definite ending: marriages had to take place or dead bodies had to be mourned. Characters, unless perhaps unhinged, didn't go around, Hamlet-wise, talking to themselves and saying they didn't know. Had they not the Church to tell them the answers? Was the country not itself as solid as a rock socially and spiritually, poor but happy, unlike pagan England (*The Righteous Are Bold*, 1946) or even America (*The Country Boy*, 1959)? Friel was the first playwright to give voice to the new Irishman, restless and discontent not because he is an artist figure being crushed by society (like Kavanagh's Tarry Flynn, for example) but simply because his is a modern sensibility discovering human isolation.

Hugh Leonard's Joyce adaptation, *Stephen D*, was new in 1962 because of its formal evasion of the well-made play, but like Friel's play it too articulated the consciousness of a discontented young hero, an archetypal figure in the Irish literary but not yet theatrical landscape. *Stephen D* could be described as the classic statement of Irish intellectual disaffection, which may explain its popularity in the early 1960s. Ironically, its success led,

Joyce-wise, to the exile of Leonard himself who went with the production
when it transferred to London, where he remained until 1970. He returned
with the punishing satire of the new bourgeoisie, *The Patrick Pearse Motel*
(1971)). Meanwhile, John B. Keane and Eugene McCabe were offering
their own versions of Irish pastoral and changing further the mold of the
Irish peasant play.

Notoriously, Keane's *Sive* had been rejected by the Abbey in 1959 and
had turned out to be one of the most popular plays ever to appear on the
amateur drama circuits. Keane, indeed, was to be the voice of the new
rural consciousness, hedged round by traditions and raging to be free. *The
Highest House on the Mountain* is by no means among Keane's best plays,
which include *The Field* (1965) and *Big Maggie* (1969), yet crude though
its dramaturgy may be the play is saying something new about the nature
of Irish country life. Had this play been written ten years earlier Sonny
Bannon would have been but a peripheral character, a foolish casualty of
life's stern realities. Here, this mentally damaged character is the moral
center of the action. Sonny has a house isolated on the Kerry mountains,
but he has come down to live with his brother Mikey because "the hurt"
he bears is too much for him. When Mikey's son brings home from England
his newly married wife, Julie, Sonny is drawn toward her and confesses
the source of his "hurt." Adrift in the city twenty years earlier he thought
he had overcome the loneliness of his mountain existence, but he confesses
"I was lonelier than ever there. Often I'd be walkin' the street and I'd
hear my name called—'Sonny! Sonny!—and my heart was fit to burst
thinkin' maybe 'twas someone that knew me. But when I'd look around
I'd find 'twas some other Sonny altogether."[7] One night at a bus stop he
makes a pass at a woman whose screams suddenly make him realize that
what he had in mind was rape, "and I stood there shamed for then and
forever." Julie is able to get him to forgive himself, and eventually the
plot so develops that she joins him in his high house on the mountain.
In subsequent plays down to *The Chastitute* (1980), Keane continued to
explore the frustrations of rural loneliness and the link between sexuality,
madness, and violence. Because he is a popular writer, in the sense that
he writes for a mass audience and seems to care little for the niceties of
dramatic art, Keane's work has not received its due of critical attention.

Eugene McCabe was similarly outspoken in his first and best play, *The
King of the Castle* (1964), tackling the theme of a childless couple on a
rich farm surrounded by malevolent neighbors. At harvest time, the husband, Scober McAdam, embittered by insinuations of impotence, tries to
persuade a laborer to impregnate his wife, Tressa. So badly has he misread

Tressa's feelings, however, and so crudely has he engineered the sexual encounter, that Scober succeeds only in destroying his marriage and in giving the neighbors even more to gossip about. McCabe's forthright handling of this subject demanded that audiences take an adult view of marital relations and of Scober's tragic situation. A similar purpose underlies Thomas Kilroy's *The Death and Resurrection of Mr. Roche*, although the main character, Kelly, is more akin to Keane's Sonny Bannon in his lonely, urban, deracinated state. Kilroy places Kelly in an all-male environment, the world of hard-drinking, bachelor aimlessness masquerading as freedom. The theme of homosexuality is raised when Mr. Roche enters the drinking circle, and at Kelly's basement apartment he is the scapegoat during the drunken revelry. Suddenly, however, the goading of Mr. Roche goes too far and he is killed. During the time when his body is being disposed of elsewhere, Kelly unburdens his sense of guilt. He confides to his friend the loneliness that led to an earlier encounter with Roche, a piece of news that so alarms his friend that he quickly deserts before the others get back from disposing of the body. This reentry is a fine coup de theatre, as Roche comes back from the grave, as in folk drama (or, indeed, in T. S. Elliot's *The Cocktail Party*, with which Kilroy's very sophisticated play has some affinity): *"They approach like figures in a dance, almost linked, partly to support one another, partly to catch the mood of delirious revelry that grips them. . . ."*[8] Kelly says, "Jesus!" and Mr. Roche replies drily: "Not quite, my dear chap, but I am flattered by your mistake." In the end, as Kelly runs off to early Sunday morning Mass, ironically still entrapped by rituals that fail to give either meaning or love to his life, Mr. Roche settles down in the apartment like one who has come to stay. As Kilroy depicts it, Kelly's life of drinking is a distraction from his essential (or is it existential?) plight. By extension, Kelly's sense of dislocation and fear is a critique of Ireland's pub culture. The play is a powerful metaphor of sterility. In this context, the real hero is the outcast Roche, an emphasis to be found in all of Kilroy's plays, notably *Talbot's Box* (1977), his play about Matt Talbot, and *Double Cross* (1986), his play setting the traitor William Joyce ("Lord Haw-Haw") as mirror image of Brendan Bracken.

Thomas Murphy's *Famine* (1968) is also a play in search of a hero. The people turn to their leader John Connor, descendant of kings, but he has no answer to their plea for action. Unhappy the land, indeed, that needs a hero. *Famine* is a history play as *Galileo* is: a means of coming to terms with and understanding forces that shaped contemporary conditions. As Murphy sees it, the famine of 1845–47 exposed the solitude of the Irishman, whom neither political nor religious institutions and orthodoxies preserved from starvation. Famine, like plague, is a modern image of self-discovery. It casts man back upon his primitive nature, the elemental passion to survive. It discovers to him the nature of evil, and the gods by which he lives. Connor's wife puts to him the question, when he tells her the only action he can take is whatever is morally right: "What's right? What's right in a country when the land goes sour?"⁹ He has no answer. He ends up killing her and their child. The consciousness the play dramatizes is agnostic, like Gar O'Donnell's in Friel's *Philadephia*, but also agonized and appalled by the terms of the human contract with a hidden god. Although Murphy based the play on Cecil Woodham-Smith's history, *The Great Hunger* (1962), he has said that he was not so much interested in the crisis as a historical fact as an event that left an awful legacy: "The castastrophe had stopped the Irish race in its tracks (as nothing else had done) and in the nineteen-sixties I was suffering a hangover that has lasted over a hundred years."¹⁰ In particular, poverty of thought and spirit persisted, "the natural extravagant vitality of youth being frustrated and made to feel guilty by the smell of too much history."

III

Looking back from the vantage point of just over twenty years one can now see that the new Abbey and Peacock came at a most opportune time in Ireland's theatrical history. The country was on the move for the first time in decades. The revolution in English drama, initiated at the Royal Court in 1956 with John Osborne's *Look Back in Anger*, had succeeded in enlivening theater and in extending horizons of expectation in Dublin as well as in London: Brendan Behan, after all, had won fame as part of this "new wave" of British drama, following Joan Littlewood's productions of *The Quare Fellow* and *The Hostage* in 1956 and 1958 respectively. The time was ripe for another Irish renaissance.

One can isolate three features of the new Abbey that were influential on the development of this renaissance. First, there is the structural question, which has (as it happens) two parts. The new Abbey and Peacock were structurally superior both to the Queen's and the old Abbey. The Queen's disallowed the sort of experimentalism that had intermittently been a feature of the old Peacock (opened 1927), where, after all, Mac

Liammoir and Edwards first launched their Gate Theatre productions and where, after April 1937, Ria Mooney directed the Experimental Theatre. Moreover, after the fire in 1951 Austin Clarke's Lyric Theatre Company, which had used the old Abbey to stage poetic drama, found a new home in Belfast and lent its name to the repertory theatre that grew there under the tutelage of Mary O'Malley. The new Peacock (opened 1967) was at first slightly compromised by Ernest Blythe's ambition that it should be used to foster Gaelic drama, but gradually this policy yielded to the more dynamic one of staging experimental work, whether from the Irish tradition or not. The theater itself seats only 157 but is a flexible area that can be used either in the round or with a conventional proscenium stage. In its first twenty years the Peacock has launched many new Irish playwrights working in various styles, including Neil Donnelly, Bernard Farrell, Tom McIntyre, Aodhan Madden, Heno Magee, Frank McGuinness, and Graham Reid. Of these, the most significant are Farrell, McGuinness, and Reid, working within the realist tradition, and Tom McIntyre, radically working outside and against it.

Bernard Farrell's first play, *I Do Not Like Thee, Dr. Fell* (1979), revealed both a good ear for dialogue and an unusual degree of craftsmanship, by Irish standards. Set in an encounter session that takes place over a weekend, the play by means of comic disclosures mounts an attack on the callousness and dishonesty that can permeate such commercialized soul-searching. There was nothing specifically Irish about this subject, but Farrell's subsequent plays (all staged on the Abbey's main stage) attempted to use comedy somewhat in the style of fellow-Dubliner Hugh Leonard as a means of simultaneously mirroring and criticizing Ireland's nouveaux riches. *Canaries* (1980), *All in Favour Said No!* (1981), *All the Way Back* (1985), and *Say Cheese!* (1987) have shown that Farrell has considerable talent. He has an eye for the absurdities of a society new to package holidays, industrial efficiency, and the vulgarities of high-powered salesmanship; yet he is also at pains to reflect the great economic disease of the 1980s, mass unemployment. Farrell's work is therefore not cocooned from contemporary realities, but tries to sharpen audience perceptions of these problems through use of farce. Here he differs widely from Graham Reid, who came to prominence at the same time.

A Belfast writer, Reid had his first play staged at the Peacock in the same year as Farrell's *Dr. Fell,* and their names tend to be coupled for that reason; indeed the two playwrights are friends, and coscripted a television series set in Belfast, *Foreign Bodies* (1986), for which one presumes Farrell did the funny bits and Reid the serious bits. Certainly, Reid is a grim, social-realist writer. *The Death of Humpty Dumpty* (1979) is a stark, depressing depiction of the effects on his family when a father is paralyzed from the neck down following an assassination attempt by paramilitaries. With merciless realism, Reid portrays the collapse of family love and ties, leading to the murder of the father by his son, arising from the bitterness of the father's refusal to accept his situation. A similar harshness pervades *The Closed Door* (1980), exploring the cowardice of a man who allows his best friend to be battered to death outside his house. At this point in his career Reid did not want to be labelled as a "Northern" playwright, and so these plays, while apparently set in Belfast, curiously avoided any kind of political statement. With *The Hidden Curriculum* (1982) Reid confronted some of the issues latent in the earlier plays, because sectarianism is unavoidable in a play about the relationship of education to society in modern-day Belfast. The success of this play (later televised) paved the way for Reid's career as television writer. At this point he became willy-nilly a "northern" writer, because he was now writing for BBC television and addressing a mass audience that was overwhelmingly British.

Equally, Frank McGuinness won fame through a play about the North. McGuinness began, however, as a writer of the well-made realistic play, *Factory Girls* (1982). Set in a Donegal shirt factory, it centers on a group of women workers who stage a sit-in and thereby come to some kind of feminist awareness. But McGuinness is not a political writer in the way that many contemporary British playwrights are, for example David Hare and Howard Brenton: no discernible ideology underlines his commentaries on Irish society. His other plays include *Baglady* (1985), a Beckettian piece for a solo actress, and *Observe the Sons of Ulster Marching Towards the Somme* (1985), his play about the North. More recently, McGuinness has written a play about Caravaggio, *Innocence* (1986), and has translated Lorca's *Yerma* (1987). McGuinness is a writer of great promise, a stylist who has not yet, however, articulated a vision of life.

Tom McIntyre, on the other hand, has found both a style and a vision in the theater. Neither came easily. A poet and writer of fiction, McIntyre first turned to the Peacock with a straightforward realistic play, *Eye-Winker Tom Tinker* (1972), concerning the psychological collapse of a revolutionary type, a latter-day Hamlet in khaki. It contained not the slightest hint of the kind of theater McIntyre was later to develop. Through the 1970s he studied modern European mime and dance and began to formulate an idea of Irish theater combining these arts with improvisational techniques. It wasn't until the early 1980s, however, that McIntyre had his first success with the kind of experimentalism he repeatedly tried without

much encouragement. *The Great Hunger* (1983), based on Patrick Kavanagh's poem, introduced to the Peacock stage a style of playing and
production soon to win a loyal Dublin audience. The actor Tom Hickey,
aided by several young performers trained in mime by Marcel Marceau,
and the director Patrick Mason were significant collaborators in the evolution of this style. Basic to the whole idea was the subordination of text
to the creation of effects through stage images. This was to be a theater
hostile to the literary tradition synonymous with the Abbey; this radicalism
is the core of McIntyre's energy. *The Great Hunger* abandoned narrative
for rituals and images of rural life, seen as repressed, repetitive, and boring.
The vision is steady, lyrical, and pessimistic. *The Great Hunger* won a
fringe First award at the Edinburgh Festival in 1986, but in the meantime
McIntyre gave to the Peacock two other plays, *The Bearded Lady* (1984),
based on *Gulliver's Travels*, and *Rise Up Lovely Sweeney* (1985), updating
the legend of mad Sweeney. These were followed by *Dance for Your Daddy*
(1986). All of these plays incorporate dance, mime, stage properties that
suddenly are transformed into images of states of feeling and of being, the
minimum of text and the maximum of unexplained, discrete, and surrealistic routines. Some observers dismiss all of this as self-indulgence on
the part of playwright, director, and loyal performers; others rejoice at
finding a kind of dream theater that tries to express breakdowns of various
kinds in modern Irish society.

Apart from the reintroduction into Irish theater of the Peacock, the
new Abbey had another structural feature. Whereas the capacity of the
theater is similar (628 as against 536), the stage of the new Abbey is far
bigger than that of the old.[11] Moreover, with the newest technical equip-
ment installed, the Abbey began after 1966 to pay more attention to
design and staging and soon established itself as the best in town for serious
theater. Consequently, although other reasons may also have been at work,
the new Abbey appropriated most of those playwrights who had revitalized
Irish theater in the 1960s, for with the new resources it developed also
the vision to bring into the repertory not only the great challenges offered
by the plays of Shakespeare, Ibsen, Chekhov, Wilde, Shaw, O'Neill, and
so on, but also the challenges to the Irish tradition offered by contemporary
playwrights. In particular, Friel and Murphy became "Abbey" playwrights,
and obtained the conditions that allowed the staging of some of the finest
Irish dramatic writing since O'Casey. All of the others mentioned earlier
also contributed: Eugene McCabe's *Swift* (1969) was followed by Thomas
Kilroy's *Tea and Sex and Shakespeare* (1976). Hugh Leonard, script editor
at the Abbey in the later 1970s, wrote *Time Was* (1976) and *A Life* (1979)

for the main stage. His *Stephen D* and *Da* were given Abbey productions around the same time. John B. Keane's *The Field*, *The Man from Clare*, and *Sive* won new audiences in imaginative productions (with revised texts) in the early 1980s. But it cannot be denied that Friel and Murphy made the greatest contribution, each creating a range of material of such complexity that only a theater fully up-to-date technically could have staged it.

There were four new plays from Friel (whose *Philadelphia*, of course, found its way into the repertory also): *The Freedom of the City* (1973), *Volunteers* (1975), *Living Quarters* (1977), and *Aristocrats* (1979), while *Faith Healer* (1979) received a powerful Irish premiere in 1980. Theatrically, these are very different sorts of plays, each taking risks with conventions, and each exploring in a different way Friel's enduring concerns: the tragedy of failure to communicate, the nature of identity, and accountability. The vision underlying these plays, with the exception of *Aristocrats*, is fatalistic, a mood quite in accord with that pervading Ireland in the 1970s. *Faith Healer*, a beautifully written play, is the portrait of the artist in a society that takes literally the claims of the imagination: the threat and eventual visitation of violence update, one may say, the history of Synge's playboy. Friel's concern with violence inevitably focused on the northern situation, however, and this aspect of his work will be discussed later.

Thomas Murphy, who was a member of the Abbey board of directors from 1972 to 1983, contributed six plays around this time: *A Crucial Week in the Life of a Grocer's Assistant* (1969), *The Morning after Optimism* (1971), *The White House* (1972), *The Sanctuary Lamp* (1975), *The Blue Macushla* (1980), and *The Gigli Concert* (1983). In these plays the "famine" of the spirit is probed and exemplified in diverse forms. Generally speaking, the plays divulge and intensify a mood, brooding, dark, and iconoclastic. The action, which is subordinated to the mood, tends to take the form either of baiting rituals ending in violence or of a truth game relentlessly pursued by a central, satiric figure. *The Gigli Concert*, however, one of his best plays, transcends these categories. In a series of consultations (rather than confrontations) between an unnamed, rich Irishman and a quack "dynamatologist," the play explores the theme of the sick soul in a materialist society. To some extent, also, it retells the Faust legend with music as the diabolic medium. When JPW King, the antihero as dynamatologist, finally manages to sing like Gigli something like a miracle occurs on stage. It is as if Friel's Faith Healer had managed to heal himself.

The arrival of the artistic director and the increased role of directors at the new Abbey also influenced the shape of new Irish playwriting. Hugh

Hunt was the first to insist on being designated artistic director of the Abbey, in 1969.[12] Prior to that time, neither Walter Macken nor Alan Simpson had sufficient power to control productions and influence artistic policy at the new Abbey. Once Hunt established the position it followed that a coherent artistic policy could be followed, without inordinate interference from the board of directors. As time went on, a liberal, imaginative policy was developed, allowing for the sort of productions just listed. When Joe Dowling resigned as artistic director in 1985, however, times had changed once again. By this time, economics had come to play a huge role in the Abbey's management, as the recession had bitten deeply into the Arts Council subsidy and the Abbey board was eager to return to the safety of box-office criteria in the mounting of productions. Dowling's resignation brought to an end an era of great artistic flowering at the Abbey. Similarly, the role of the director, which expanded at the new Abbey as it did elsewhere in postwar theater, made a considerable impact on the nature of Irish playwriting, The major playwrights just listed owed much to the imaginative collaboration of such directors as Tomas MacAnna, Hugh Hunt, Joe Dowling, and Patrick Mason. It is not now in the modern theater as it had been in the days of Synge or of the early O'Casey: nowadays, the semiotics of the stage are all-important, and nonverbal signs are as significant as the verbal, so that a play's success depends heavily on the orchestrating talents of the director. It is a mistake, therefore, to regard drama in the same way one regards poetry or fiction, as the product solely of an individual imagination. To judge rightly of new Irish drama one must see it in the context of the theatrical conditions of the time. Thus, for example, the published texts of Friel's *The Freedom of the City* or of Murphy's *The Gigli Concert*[13] should not be read as literary works but as evidence of powerful theatrical occasions, initially overseen by Thomas MacAnna and Patrick Mason.[14] Even more important, the earlier account of the new Irish writing that arose out of the Peacock conditions should be understood in the context of directorial encouragement and collaboration.

IV

Two implications of the account so far offered of Irish drama since the early 1960s are: (1) that it centered on Dublin, as if there were theaters no place else in Ireland; (2) that it merely continued in the 1970s and 1980s the style of drama that was revolutionary in the 1960s. It is as well to refine these implications here.

It is true that there are theaters outside of Dublin: it has been true since the eighteenth century. Since the 1960s, indeed, theater has become quite lively in Cork, Kilkenny, Galway, and Sligo, apart from the special case of theater in Northern Ireland. Yet even at the most dynamic of provincial theaters, the Druid Theater Company (established 1975) in Galway, no new playwrights have emerged. The Druid has established its reputation through the directorial work of Garry Hynes, heading a small but dedicated stock company that has won international acclaim with such classics as *The Playboy of the Western World*. The closest Druid has come to fostering new Irish drama was during 1984–85 when Thomas Murphy was playwright-in-association. For Druid he wrote *Conversations on a Homecoming* (a revision of his 1972 play on Ireland's "Kennedy children," *The White House*) and *Bailegangaire*, written with the late actress Siobhan McKenna in mind (she played Momino with the Druid company). Each of these plays extended Druid's reputation for strong, authentic Irish theater. They travelled to both the United States and Australia with one of these, *Conversations*, and to London with the other. But by 1986 Murphy was back at the Abbey, bringing with him not only the designation "writer-in-association" but a play arising out of *Bailegangaire* entitled *A Thief of a Christmas*. Irish playwrights cannot afford to stay long out of Dublin, where the bigger audiences obviously are. Likewise, the regional theaters, even though supported by Arts Council subsidies, cannot in the contemporary financial climate afford to take chances on staging the work of new, untried playwrights. There is thus the paradox of a lively provincial theater in Ireland that is failing to fulfill one of the basic functions of any community theater, namely to provide a forum for new plays.

As to the implication that recent Irish drama is a mere expansion of the repertory of the 1960s, the deprecating tone is misleading. Theater is in a continuum. A continuum becomes a rut only when plays are written to rule and audiences cease to be disturbed and refreshed. The Irish drama of the 1970s and early 1980s has built upon the courageous spirit of the 1960s, but it has manifested its own vitality. To be sure, one can say that the drama persists in mirroring society in a critical way, but one would also have to say that this way has become increasingly pessimistic. The mood of the early 1980s, being fraught with economic uncertainties, is vastly different from the brave new world of the 1960s.[15] Moreover, one theme has been quarried since that time, even though the drama in general has remained politically uninformed (i.e., it has not developed a left wing as in Britain): the situation in Northern Ireland.

There is already a long list to be compiled of plays dealing with the northern conflict since 1969. There is space here to mention only some of the most significant. John Boyd's *The Flats* (Lyric, Belfast, 1971) was the first of any consequence. Set in working-class Belfast it examined the beginnings of the rift between the British army and the Catholic community it came in to protect in 1969. Boyd is confessedly an admirer of O'Casey,[16] and *The Flats* shows the influence of *The Shadow of a Gunman* and *Juno and the Paycock* in characterization and plot. It is doubtless difficult for any modern Irish playwright who attempts to depict the relationship between working class and the British army to avoid echoes of O'Casey; in Boyd's play the echoes reverberate distractingly. Brian Friel's *The Freedom of the City* also shows the impinging of violence on ordinary civilians, but there are no discernible echoes of O'Casey, and the form of the play is more Brechtian than O'Caseyan. It is a play unified by its tone of anger at the crassness of officialdom that assaults the privacies of individuals and rationalizes its violence as rectitude. As has been shown,[17] Friel draws on the wording of the Widgery Report to indict British injustice on Bloody Sunday (30 January 1972); using irony as his weapon he turns a blistering eye also on the representatives of church, state, media, and social science, so that the three victims in the play appear to the audience publicly misrepresented, patronized, and intellectually reified. As in all of Friel's work, a gap is opened up between public and private experience: this time the gap is politicized, and the vacuum thereby dramatized is a national rather than a personal tragedy.

The controlled bitterness of this play slipped into indictment of southern indifference in Friel's *Volunteers*, which was not well received at the Abbey but stoutly defended by Seamus Heaney,[18] who clearly recognized in it affinities with his own preoccupations. If, as one reviewer at the time asserted, Friel had failed to make his "point" clear, this is because Friel is not a polemicist, or a didactic writer. (After all, he had learned a lesson with the ill-fated *The Mundy Scheme* [1969], which was political satire of an obvious kind.) *Volunteers* is a dance of death, a hollow laugh at man's imprisonment both in history and in language; the difficulty lies in its refusal to trust its audience, which Friel doubtless included in his contempt. Thus it is an inverted, self-mocking play, an uneasy attempt to confront the South with its complacency. Friel left the subject of Northern Ireland aside after this until he and actor Stephen Rea founded the Field Day Theatre Company in 1980, when he wrote *Translations*. This is primarily a history play, a study of cultural transformation at the time when the old hedgeschools were being replaced by the new national-school system, leading to the erosion of Gaelic as the language of the peasantry and the breaking up of an old order. On this level the play is Chekhovian elegy. But it is far more complex in structure than this outline suggests. Friel uses and combines with the language question the issue of map making, the ordnance surveys begun at roughly the same time, the 1830s. Drawing on John Andrews's A *Paper Landscape*, [19] he found in the ordnance survey an image of violation, a metaphor for (in its mythic sense) "obscenity," affront to a landscape. [20] But whereas *Translations* is rich in political implications, it is not a political play. It was perhaps out of impatience with the general perception of the play as a cryptonationalist petrol bomb that Friel wrote *The Communication Cord* (1982), a satire on nationalist attitudinizing, whether cultural or linguistic. *Translations* is a very subtle play, for it is a melodrama and a love story as well as a dramatization of the passing of an old order. It is a play, indeed, fluent with gestures, such as that suggested by Doalty's shifting childishly the survey poles of the sappers: "It was a gesture. . . . Just to indicate . . . a presence."[21] The presence throughout, in the background, of the Donnelly twins is a gesture of another kind: their absence from the stage gives the ending an unresolved quality. Friel, the dramatist as poststructuralist, refuses to end any other way. The reticence is all.

Such detachment as Friel's is understandably rare in plays about the northern situation. Martin Lynch, for example, is a playwright of passionate commitment to social revolution. His earliest work, as Hagal Mengel has shown, [22] was agitprop drama written for the Turf Lodge Community Fellowship, an amateur group he founded in Belfast in 1976 at age twenty-five. Once established at the Lyric Theatre, however, in 1981, Lynch had to translate his socialist views into dramatic art and at the same time, somehow, to make a statement about the northern political situation. These multiple aims have tended to weigh down a young and inexperienced playwright, so that his work to date, while energized by deep compassion (like that of his mentor John Boyd), is rather crude and overwritten. Yet *The Interrogation of Ambrose Fogarty* (1982) demands attention as a documentary about police methods in Belfast. A big success at the Lyric, it is among the few northern plays that transferred to Dublin in modern times. (Others include Patrick Galvin's *We Do It For Love* [1975] and Stewart Parker's *Northern Star* [1985].) The key to Lynch's attitude is contained in Fogarty's speech to the interrogator:

I've come this far because I believe in something. I had good job prospects before the Troubles started. Now I'm living on Social Security.

I wouldn't allow myself to go through this if I didn't believe in something. An ideal. Sergeant, I believe that the people of this place can live in peace and prosperity under a new social order.

They're my reasons. I'm not in this to buck my own goat. Those other guys [interrogators] lift a pay cheque at the end of the month. For what? For beating up people?

Christ, it's a sick society that can throw up police stations where people are beaten up systematically.

And a sick police force that carries it out.[23]

The problem with such speeches is their homiletic tone. Lynch follows in the footsteps of O'Casey and Brecht (he quotes the latter with approval in a subsequent play, *Castles in the Air* [1983]) in his attempt to combine protest drama and entertainment, but the very nature of his material—human bigotry, exploitation, poverty, despair—militates against cool, artistic detachment. Life, in short, is itself too intractable to yield to Lynch's imagination. It has to be added that the particular life Lynch documents is less than appealing to Southern audiences. From about 1980 on, or after *Translations*, Dublin audiences have virtually yawned in boredom at any further attempts to concern them with the northern question. Thus Parker's *Northern Star*, Graham Reid's *Remembrance* (1984), and Anne Devlin's *Ourselves Alone* (1985) each failed to make any impact. The problem perhaps is that people in the South no longer know what to think about the North: they are tired of it as an enduring drain on their sympathies, but they are also confused by the multiple intransigencies that offend a liberal outlook, and so they turn away.

Graham Reid's latest work is worth considering here. In between his *Hidden Curriculum* and *Remembrance* he won much acclaim with a trilogy of plays for the BBC, published as *Billy: Three Plays for Television* (London and Boston: Faber, 1984). These plays documented a working-class Protestant family's domestic conflicts in a style that had to call a spade a spade and an Orangeman an Orangeman: what Reid could cloak before while (as playwright in the Peacock) he concentrated on the horror of urban violence and avoided identification with political sources, he could no longer do if he was showing a parade in Belfast, for example, to which his characters must respond as either Catholics or Protestants. The *Billy* plays, then, brought Reid out of the political closet. His people are mainly working-class Protestants and it is from that point of view he writes. *Remembrance*, his next play, tried to comment on the sectarian divide in Belfast. Here Reid intertwines the stories of two families, one from each "community" (as the term is), each having lost a son in the violence. In a cemetery where they come to visit their dead Bert and Teresa, the father and mother of these victims, meet and fall in love. They are in their sixties. The relationship is violently opposed by their families and is eventually ended when Bert falls ill. The final image is of Teresa alone on the seat in the cemetery that was their rendezvous, reading a last letter from Bert. In future, her "remembrance" will be not just of the victims of sectarian violence but of the victims-of-victims also. This, in general is Reid's dramatic theme, clarified at last. Subsequently, in *Callers* (1985), staged at the Peacock, he tried to go beyond the characterization of a frightened RUC man introduced in *Remembrance* as Bert's surviving son, and showed on stage the assassination in his home of just such a figure. *Callers* tried to show both sides, literally. Using alternate sides of the stage, Reid presented the assassins in their preparation and the RUC man's family in their ordinary, if stressful, living conditions. The split stage images a split society. The final image, however, is of the victim's daughter assuming the role of avenger: nothing has been concluded.

That he is a playwright with a purpose is conclusively shown by Reid's return to the television medium with *Ties of Blood*, a series of six plays (published by Faber, 1986). Painstakingly, Reid explores in fictional form the effects of the British army on the lives of men and women in Northern Ireland. The concern is to show to a supposedly ignorant public the human drama behind the political fact of the army's involvement in the North. Within such a limited ambition Reid certainly shows "the pity of it," but these plays go no deeper than pathos, which is obviously what the public wants. Reid is himself a victim of the whole northern situation.

If a play such as *Remembrance* appealed little to southern audiences when taken on tour to the Project Arts Centre, Dublin, it is not surprising that the Irish premiere of Ron Hutchinson's *The Rat in the Skull* (1984, Royal Court) should have flopped at the same venue in May 1986. Peculiarly close to Lynch's *Ambrose Fogarty* in subject matter, *The Rat* is a rough presentation of the ambiguous hatred that subsists between Catholic and Protestant in the North. In the London police station where the play is set it is revealed that, for all their mutual opposition, the two Irishmen, the "bomber" Roche and his interrogator Nelson, share a common knowledge of history of which the English policemen are totally and willfully ignorant. The play laments the reluctance of each of the main opponents to allow the other's point of view to enter his consciousness: this is the "rat in the skull" that dare not be admitted. Ironically, the Dublin critics and audiences were as indifferent as the London policemen. One correspondent to the *Irish Times* (19 May 1986), deploring the fact that there were no more than fifteen people in the audience, at a production "as good if not slightly more gripping than its London counterpart," wondered if the play was not "just too close for critics to feel comfortable and objective. SHAME!"

Nevertheless, Frank McGuinness's *Observe the Sons of Ulster Marching Towards the Somme* (1985) proved very successful indeed in its production at the Peacock (and later had an award-winning production at London's Hampstead). It is worth considering why this play, in particular, should have been acceptable to Southern audiences where other plays were not. First, it is a history play (set in 1916) like *Translations*, and its relation to the contemporary Ulster situation is oblique rather than direct. Second, it focuses exclusively on Ulster loyalists, who have enlisted to fight in World War I, a subject in which Irish audiences have always been interested (cf. O'Casey's *The Silver Tassie*, 1929). Thirdly, it has no ax to grind but imaginatively, through the memory of one survivor of the group, enters the minds of eight enlisted men of contrasting (Protestant) backgrounds. The use of the survivor, Pyper, to summon up the past as in a dream is reminiscent of Friel's *Living Quarters* and *Faith Healer*. It works well to distance the action and allows the audience participation in the process of re-creation of experience. The result is a play that is neither antiwar nor anti-Unionist but humanist: one that shows men coming together to form a kind of solidarity that for them ultimately defines identity, in the face of certain death on the Somme. The pathos of the moment when Pyper makes a final prayer on behalf of the men carries a Shakespearean nobility. These men have rediscovered a kind of chivalry that transforms this nightmare of modern battle into another Saint Crispin's Day:

> God in heaven, if you hear the words of man, I speak to you this day. I do it to ask we be spared. I do it to ask for strength. . . . Let this day at the Somme be as glorious in the memory of Ulster as that day at the Boyne, when you scattered our enemies. Lead us back from this exile. To Derry, to the Foyle. To Belfast and the Lagan. To Armagh, To Tyrone. To the Bann and its banks. To Erne and its islands. Protect them. Protect us. Protect me. Let us fight bravely. Let us win gloriously. . . . Observe the sons of Ulster marching towards the Somme.

I love their lives. I love my own life. I love my home. I love my Ulster.
Ulster. Ulster. Ulster. Ulster. Ulster. Ulster. Ulster. Ulster.[24]

That final repetition, one cry of "Ulster" for each of the eight men, turns
into a battle-cry as the play ends. Its positive quality, its final up beat,
distinguishes this play from most of the others about Northern Ireland.
(A more recent exception is Stewart Parker's *Pentecost*, staged at the
Dublin Theatre Festival in October 1987, a play set during the Ulster
Workers' Council strike of 1974. Unlike his *Northern Star*, this play was
highly successful in the South, a major reason being that *Pentecost* is not
really a political but a deeply spiritual play.) McGuinness has succeeded
in seeing and in enabling the audience to see in the unionist tradition
something live and inspiring, even under sentence of death. One Dublin
reviewer saw the play as an attack on Northern unionists, but the opposite
is nearer the mark. There is a sacral quality to the final feeling for place
expressed by Pyper: that very sense of locale and *patria* that Friel saw
affronted in *Translations*. McGuinness's play thus dramatizes a notion all
too seldom appreciated in Ireland, that there is more than one kind of
patriotism. Of course, there is irony in Pyper's use of "Ulster" when he
seems to mean "the six counties" of Northern Ireland; but, after all, the
play is set at a time when partition was not yet an actuality. Identification
with landscape as a mode of establishing personal identity is a central
experience in *Observe the Sons of Ulster*. It is a concern that goes to the
root of the northern problem; it is also a concern, complicated by the
ironies of history, which lies at the heart of the Irish literary tradition.

Brian Friel left the local scene in 1987 when he wrote *Fathers and Sons*,
an adaptation of Turgenev's novel, for the National Theatre in London.
Enormously successful, the production ran in repertory from July 1987 to
March 1988. It would be a mistake, however, to view this event as an
indication that Friel is abandoning his Irish subject matter. On the contrary, *Fathers and Sons* has served to remove his writer's block and has
enabled him to write a new Irish play for Field Day in 1988, his first for
six years. As provider of dramatic images of Irish experience and history
Friel thus continues to represent the Irish playwright's preoccupation, if
not obsession, with matters of identity and fulfillment. Contemporary
Irish writing for the stage continues for the most part to mirror in realistic
form Irish social life in its changing pressures, problems, and values. It
continues also to be critical and satirical, in the tradition of Synge and
O'Casey. It tries to fuse together local and universal themes, but the

priority is always with the local: The gods, as Kavanagh reminds us, "make their own importance."

Notes

1. D. E. S. Maxwell, *Brian Friel* (Lewisburg: Bucknell University Press, 1973), 109. The quotation is from the *Irish Times*, 12 February 1970, 14.

2. D. E. S. Maxwell, *A Critical History of Modern Irish Drama 1891–1980* (Cambridge: Cambridge University Press, 1984), 212.

3. Robert Hogan, *"Since O'Casey" and Other Essays on Irish Drama* (Gerrards Cross: Colin Smythe; Totowa: Barnes and Noble, 1983), 119–54. See also Maxwell, *Critical History*, 158–212; and Christopher Murray, "Irish Drama in Transition 1966–1978," *Etudes Irlandaises*, n.s. 4 (December 1979):287–308, and "Recent Irish Drama," in *Studies in Anglo-Irish Literature*, ed. Heinz Kosok (Bonn: Herbert Grundmann, 1982), 439–46; also Murray, "Irish Drama: The Contemporary Scene," *Arbeiten aus Anglistik und Amerikanistik* 12, no. 1 (1987):27–40.

4. Seamus Deane, introduction, *Selected Plays: Brian Friel* (London and Boston: Faber and Faber, 1984), 11–22; also Deane, *Celtic Revivals* (London and Boston: Faber and Faber, 1985), 166–73; Ulf Dantanus, *Brian Friel: The Growth of an Irish Dramatist* (Göteborg: Acta Universitatis Gothoburgensis, 1985), Gothenburg Studies in English 59; D. E. S. Maxwell, as in notes 1 and 2.

5. Brian Friel in interview with Ciaran Carty, "Finding Voice in a Language Not our Own," *Sunday Independent*, 5 October 1980, 16.

6. Brian Friel, *Philadelphia, Here I Come!* (London: Faber and Faber, 1965), 110.

7. John B. Keane, *The Highest House on the Mountain* (Dublin: Progress House, 1961), 33–34.

8. Thomas Kilroy, *The Death and Resurrection of Mr. Roche* (London: Faber and Faber, 1969), 69.

9. Thomas Murphy, *Famine* (Dublin: Gallery Press, 1977), 33.

10. Thomas Murphy, "A Note by the Author," program note for the Tuam Theatre Guild production of *Famine*, 1984.

11. See Hugh Hunt, *The Abbey Theatre 1904–1979* (Dublin: Gill and Macmillan, 1979), 178, 196–97. Cf. Lennox Robinson, *Ireland's Abbey Theatre: A History 1899–1951* (London: Sidgwick and Jackson, 1951), 43–44.

12. Hunt, *The Abbey Theatre*, 207.

13. Brian Friel, *The Freedom of the City* (London: Faber and Faber, 1974); Thomas Murphy, *The Gigli Concert* (Dublin: Gallery Press, 1984).

14. See Patrick Mason, "Directing *The Gigli Concert*: An Interview," *Irish University Review* 17, no. 1 (1987):100–13.

34 NEW IRISH WRITING

15. See Terence Brown, *Ireland: A Social and Cultural History 1922–1985* (Glasgow: Collins / Fontana, 1985), 326–55: "Postscript: The Uncertain Eighties."

16. See Brian McIlroy, "An Interview with Playwright John Boyd," *Irish University Review* 17, no. 2 (1987):245. See also Heinz Kosok, "Juno and the Playwrights: The Influence of Sean O'Casey on Twentieth-Century Drama," in *Irish Writers and the Theatre*, ed. Masaru Sekine (Gerrards Cross: Colin Smythe; Totowa: Barnes and Noble, 1986), 80–81.

17. By Elizabeth Hale Winkler, "Reflections of Derry's Bloody Sunday in Literature," in *Studies in Anglo-Irish Literature*, ed. Kosok, 411–15.

18. Seamus Heaney, "Digging Deeper," *Times Literary Supplement*, 21 March 1975, 306. Heaney claimed that Friel had created a new dramatic *"kind"* that "involves an alienation effect but eschews didactic address." Cf. Ulf Dantanus, *Brian Friel*, 190; and Ruth Niel, "Digging into History: A Reading of Brian Friel's *Volunteers* and Seamus Heaney's 'Viking Dublin: Trial Pieces'," *Irish University Review* 16, no. 1 (1986):35–47. The Cork Theatre Company presented a new production of *Volunteers* at the Dublin Theatre Festival in October 1987.

19. John Andrews, *A Paper Landscape: The Ordnance Survey in Nineteenth-Century Ireland* (Oxford: Clarendon Press, 1975). Friel refers to this book in his "Extracts from a Sporadic Diary," in *Ireland and the Arts: A Special Issue of "Literary Review,"* ed. Tim Pat Coogan (London: Quartet / Namara Press, n.d.), 57. See also Brian Friel, John Andrews, and Kevin Barry, "Translations and A Paper Landscape: Between Fiction and History," *Crane Bag* 7, no. 2 (1983):118–24; and Anthony Roche, "A Bit off the Map: Brian Friel's *Translations* and Shakespeare's *Henry IV*, " in *Literary Interrelations*, ed. Wolfgang Zach and Heinz Kosok, 3 vols. (Tübingen: Gunter Narr, 1987), 2:139–48.

20. The notion of a god-haunted, sacral territory adumbrated by Robert Graves in *The White Goddess* (amended and enlarged edn., New York: Farrar, Straus and Giroux, 1966), is peculiarly apt to Ireland. See, for example, Seamus Heaney's "The Sense of Place," in *Preoccupations* (London: Faber and Faber, 1980), esp. 132–33; and his poem "The Toome Road," in *Field Work* (London: Faber and Faber, 1979), 15, where violation of the landscape is given a political gloss quite close to Friel's usage.

21. Brian Friel, *Translations* (London and Boston: Faber and Faber, 1981), 18.

22. Hagal Mengel, "What is the Point of Livin'—On Some Early Plays of Martin Lynch," *Etudes Irlandaises*, n.s. 8 (December 1983):145–63. Cf. David Ian Rabey, *British and Irish Political Drama in the Twentieth Century* (Basingstoke: Macmillan, 1986), 192.

23. Martin Lynch, *The Interrogation of Ambrose Fogarty* (Belfast: Blackstaff, 1982), 78–79.

24. Frank McGuinness, *Observe the Sons of Ulster Marching Towards the Somme* (London and Boston: Faber and Faber, 1986), 79–80, ellipses inserted.

"The Rest Is Silence": Secrets in Some William Trevor Stories

Robert E. Rhodes

Prior to the 1986 collection *The News from Ireland and Other Stories*, William Trevor had published five collections of short stories. The first collection (1967) contained a single Irish story, "Miss Smith." The four succeeding volumes had an average of four Irish stories each. In *News*, seven of the twelve are Irish: the title story, "The Property of Colette Nervi," "Bodily Secrets," "Virgins," "Music," "Two More Gallants," and "The Wedding in the Garden."[1] Published almost simultaneously in the *New Yorker* were two thus far uncollected Irish stories, "The Third Party"[2] and "Kathleen's Field,"[3] and not many months later, "Events at Drimaghleen" appeared in *Grand Street*.[4]

In these recent Irish works, Trevor has dropped a former major preoccupation, stories of the contemporary Troubles seen largely from an Anglo-Irish perspective, though the title story of *News* is an Anglo-Irish story, telling of the Great Famine and exploring something of the antecedents for the modern conflict. But for the most part these recent stories continue the types of settings, characters, and themes that are familiar to Trevor's regular readers: class and religious stress, rural isolation and loneliness, provincial drabness, thwarted love, the persistence of the past into the present, imaginations fed by films and shallow fiction, the vanity of human wishes.

On the whole, most reviewers of *News* found the collection admirable and frequently singled out one or more of the Irish stories for something that distinguishes them from the English stories. Virtually alone amongst the reviewers, John Dunne had serious reservations, noting that "generally [Trevor's] work ambles along in a pleasant nondescript manner which, for me at any rate, seldom elicits any emotional response at all."[5]

It is true that Trevor's stories are usually understated. For example, one will search in vain in *News* for striking or even memorable tropes, their stock being pretty much depleted by the following: "His hair was like smooth lead. . . ," ". . . his face . . . exploding like a volcano. . . ," "The moon that was Thelma's face. . . ," "his rounded hill of a stomach. . . ," and ". . . short hair as spiky as a hedgehog's." Nor is Trevor the exegete's dream in being a technical experimenter in point of view, for example. He's almost always in total charge as narrator and takes us where we need to go either through omniscience or through easy access to the consciousness of one character or another, with occasional irony deflecting a straightforward view of things. The reader seldom has problems with structure: Trevor stories ordinarily begin in a present and move without interruption to a conclusion; sometimes they open in a present and return to a past; sometimes they alternate between the present and the past; but very seldom do they give us difficulty in knowing where we are and when and why we are there.

But this very lack of difficulty—what Dunne calls "a pleasant nondescript manner"—a certain reticence on Trevor's part, leads, upon consideration, to an important motif that ties these several stories together—his use of secrets as a plot device and as a means of directing our attention to his most important fictional concern: the mystery of human personality, behind which may also preside some assumptions, conscious or otherwise, about dimensions of the Irish personality. Thus, "plot" and "character" and "style" are somewhat congruent and work together toward the presentation of theme. Secrets are of course not exclusive to Trevor, nor are they new to these stories; a quick review of Trevor's earlier Irish stories turns up, for example, "Autumn Sunshine," "Beyond the Pale," "Saints," "Attracta," "Mr. McNamara," "The Raising of Elvira Tremlett," "The Time of Year," "Miss Smith," "Death in Jerusalem," and "Teresa's Wedding," among others that are activated by secrets. But their persistence in the present set of stories finally claims extended attention and a firm reason for reading Trevor more carefully than may have been the case in the past.

On the face of it, "secrets" are basic to almost any story; indeed, simple plot hinges upon secrets—we keep reading because we want to know what happens next. Not every story has secrets—more ordinarily considered—kept or disclosed by characters. Those that do, however, probably involve readers more than those that do not; as insiders, when a secret is shared with a character or characters or the reader, there is compelling dramatic irony, and the tension that is part of the story communicates itself readily to readers. Certainly secrets in a story can generate tremendous energy by giving, for example, an added erotic charge to the secrecy of a love affair. And secrets may be part of the dramatization of deceit, discretion or indiscretion, the role of knowledge, the problem of communication, the conflict of illusion and reality.

To go an important step further, they add to the stories something of the mystery of human character, a quality that is at the heart of the two most important stories considered here, "The News from Ireland" and "Events at Drimaghleen," both works that probe the difficulty and perhaps the impossibility of one's ever truly penetrating the enigma of others, especially, perhaps, if the others are Irish. Thus, the title story, "The News from Ireland," about news that is only partially or imperfectly conveyed, serves admirably if ironically as a representative title for the seven Irish stories of the collection and the three additional stories; and "Events at Drimaghleen," the most recent of the stories, concludes the framing introduced by "News." Before turning to these two stories, a handful of observations on variations that Trevor has rung on the theme in the other stories will suggest its ubiquity and importance to Trevor.

Of the eight stories, four dramatize events in which secrets are kept. "Kathleen's Field," a title richly evocative of the possibilities of an allegorical reading for a story predicated on a characteristic Irish land hunger, tells of the innocent Kathleen, held hostage to the lechery of her employer by her fear that revelation of his lechery will mean that her father will forfeit the land he covets. The other three stories of this set have stories that end in marriages. In "The Property of Colette Nervi," Trevor reprises his familiar Irish rural isolation and emotional deprivation, and ends with a marriage under the shady circumstances of secrets kept about the stolen property of the French Colette Nervi, whose brief intrusion into an Irish backwater precipitates events. With a strong subtext of class and religious differences as the source for secrecy, "The Wedding in the Garden" sees maid Dervla remaining in the service of the family of her lost love after he marries another so that she may haunt his happiness with her daily presence and the secret of what had been between them. Like "The Wedding in the Garden," "Bodily Secrets" has deterrents to marriage in religious and class differences, but they are overcome by the middle-aged couple's maturity, intelligence, and determination, traits that also enable them to negotiate secrets and to secure a workable conspiracy of silence over the husband's hidden homosexuality and Norah, the wife's, unwillingness to expose her aging body's loss of beauty.

In all of these stories, by having secrets remain concealed, Trevor has sacrificed at least one dramatic confrontation scene in each that might have eventuated in climax, resolution, and easing of conflict. Instead, secrets—Kathleen's guilty one, for example, or Norah's vain one—remain intact; we share Kathleen's silent despair and perhaps Norah's relief, and whatever tension is generated by the secrets becomes all the more powerful for remaining untold.

"Two More Gallants," the first of four stories in which secrets are revealed—and Trevor's contribution to the James Joyce centenary observances—is perhaps the slightest of Trevor's recent Irish stories. It dramatizes the clandestine means by which a prideful student, Heffernan, exposes the pretensions of a Joycean scholar, Professor Flacks, himself hubris-ridden enough not to have penetrated the secret scheme against him. Given the love triangle suggested by its title, "The Third Party" is charged with secrets—the very conduct of the affair itself, the concealed natures of the lovers from one another, the revelation by the husband of his wife's true nature (or is it?) to her lover, the conundrum of the wife's ability to bear a child, for example—we are left pondering, even after certain revelations. In "Music" thirty-three-year-old Justin has built a fantasy life on the fiction of a musical talent fostered by a kindly surrogate mother, Aunt Roche, and father—a priest, Father Finn—as he in turn provides them with a surrogate son and pretext for a family, the existence of which has been kept secret from Justin's real family. When guilt drives Aunt Roche to confess the subterfuge to Justin, he pushes away her imploring hands and curses her as he leaves. In "Virgins" Trevor knits with elaborate care the friendship of two adolescent girls in a provincial Irish town. He then intrudes into their relationship the delicate but powerfully vain Ralph de Courcy, whose manipulation of the feelings of both girls causes them to keep secrets from one another, then to reveal them, and then, even forty years later, when they meet again, to part with wordless regret and "shrugging smile."

In these four stories where secrets are revealed, Trevor gains some of the dramatic confrontation scenes and sense of climax that he sacrifices when secrets remain concealed. For example, Heffernan's revelation of his manipulation of Professor Flacks results in Flacks's public disclosure and humiliation; and Aunt Roche's confession leads to Justin's private agony. Interestingly, revelation of secrets is no more of a guarantee of a happy ending than their being kept intact, a conclusion that accords with Trevor's persistent rueful appraisal of human affairs.

After several stories about the contemporary troubles in Ireland, very often told from an Anglo-Irish viewpoint, Trevor appeared to write a coda in the 1983 novel, *Fools of Fortune*, where the Anglo-Irish are anomalies in an Ireland they had ruled for 300 years, vestiges only, anachronisms,

but therefore all the more reason for them to have won Trevor's understanding, compassion, and even admiration. With "The News from Ireland," however, he again takes up their story, this time becoming more
judgmental of the Ascendancy Anglo-Irish and finding in their lives greater
responsibility for Ireland's present ills than he had earlier. Additionally,
the story provides Trevor with the opportunity to deploy subtly the uses
and effects of secrets in a more complex fashion than we have yet seen.

In "News," we are with the Pulvertaft family at an unnamed Anglo-
Irish Big House, one not much different in kind and significance from the
restored Glencorn Lodge of Trevor's "Beyond the Pale" or the Carraveagh
of his "The Distant Past" or the Kilneagh of *Fools of Fortune*, for example.
This is familiar territory to Trevor, except that it takes place in 1847–
48, near the end of the Great Famine, the single most important fact—
and source of the most important mystery—at the heart of the story.

The Pulvertafts of Ipswich had come to Ireland in 1839, on the death
of old Hugh Pulvertaft, to assume responsibility for the estate and to restore
the derelict house, symbol both of British dominance and British distance
from actual Irish circumstances. Relative newcomers to Ireland, the Pulvertafts have moved from "surprise and dismay at the Irish" to "making
allowances for the natives" to "coming to terms" and—a leitmotiv in the
story—"learning to live with things" (p. 10), stages more or less followed
by protagonist Anna Maria Heddoe, freshly arrived in Ireland in 1847 as
family governess on her own journey to accommodation with Ireland and
the Irish.

For the most part, the Pulvertafts, decent and wishing to be responsible
but undiscerning—much of the Irish situation is simply a closed case, a
"secret" to them—and therefore ineffective at relieving local distress, live
as if they were still in Ipswich. Indeed, much of the energy and tension
in the story are generated and sustained by the contrast between the naive
mentality of the Pulvertafts and the Irish realities outside. The contrast
is between what Mrs. Pulvertaft thinks of as "dear, safe, uncomplicated
England" (p. 26), reembodied in their Irish estate, and the physically
proximate but psychically remote, untidy, and very complicated mass
starvation outside the estate precincts.

A high stone wall surrounds Big House and grounds. A typical drawing-
room scene discovers the Irish maids fastening the shutters and drawing
the blinds, further isolating and insulating the family. Within, three mar-
riageable daughters ponder possible husbands. The sole son, young George
Arthur, considers an army career in distant India while innocently but
ignorantly wondering if the Irish "poor people," not far removed, eat their

babies. Mrs. Pulvertaft, "round and stout," has a daily nap. Mr. Pulvertaft, with gleaming boots, presides at table and painful piano recitals. And Trevor ironically limns starvation without by repletion within: Mrs. Pulvertaft's daily bouts of indigestion, for example, or the leftover food sometimes dispatched down the lavatory or the champagne at daughter Charlotte's wedding to Captain Roche.

Underpinning the essential uselessness of the Pulvertafts' role in alleviating famine starvation is the first of two major symbols in the story. Historically accurate in type, weaving its way throughout the story is a symptomatic and symbolic road under construction, the Pulvertaft contribution to the usually useless work projects under British aegis that proliferated by thousands throughout the Famine years. Its purpose (other than providing make-work) a mystery, it circles the estate within its walls, both further enclosing the Big House and replicating the circle that Anna Maria traces in moving from one kind of stranger in Ireland to another. This road that goes nowhere occupies the thoughts of the Pulvertafts as they plan scenic vistas and "ornamental seats" on its circular route. "What could be nicer," muses Mr. Pulvertaft, ". . . than a picnic of lunch by the lake, then a drive through the silver birches, another pause by the abbey, continuing by the river for a mile, and home by Bright Purple Hill? This road, Miss Heddoe, has become my pride" (p. 14). But Fogarty, the astute butler, knows the truth of it; "the useless folly of the road" (p. 18), he exclaims. And of Erskine, the one-armed former British army officer who hates the Irish but as estate manager has the job of overseeing the roadwork, we are told: "Leading nowhere, without a real purpose, the estate road is unnecessary and absurd, but he accepts his part in its creation. It is ill fortune that people have starved because a law of nature has failed them, it is ill fortune that he has lost a limb and seen a military career destroyed; all that must be accepted also" (p. 24).

Under all these circumstances, with a family nearly dedicated to not getting the truth, it would be difficult enough for anyone wanting to receive the real news from Ireland, and Anna Maria Heddoe wants to. To the difficult situation is added Fogarty, nearly the presiding genius in the story; more than a little sinister, moving always in secrecy and penetrating the secrets of others while husbanding his own; Protestant but still inimical to both the family and to Anna Maria. For example, he keeps from the Pulvertafts what he wishes he might say to them: "that their fresh decent blood is the blood of the invader though they are not themselves invaders, that they perpetuate theft without being thieves" (p. 10). Spying on the governess, he then keeps his thoughts about her from

his one confidante, his sister, the cook. After he has read some of Anna
Maria's own secrets about the family, her role in the house, Ireland and
the Irish, committed to her journal, and Anna Maria discovers that he
has, he asks her to keep his invasion of her privacy secret from the
Pulvertafts, to which she rejoins that she has no wish to share secrets with
him. And it is Fogarty, as we shall see, who mediates, only to confound
rather than to clarify, between both Pulvertafts and Anna Maria and the
key episode—and symbol—in the story, the Irish infant with Christ's
stigmata.

Governess Anna Maria Heddoe, twenty-five or -six, with "nervous"
features, "severe" hair, and "dowdy" clothes, is a "young woman of principle and sensitivity, stranger and visitor to Ireland" (p. 9), we are told
almost at once. That Anna Maria wants to learn—to hear and understand
the news from Ireland—is clear enough. That gimlet-eyed observer of her
life, Fogarty, tells her that her "fresh sharp eye has needled" (p. 43) things
out. But journal entries of 17 and 20 October 1847 suggest Anna Maria's
limitations and presage her eventual acceptance of enigma without understanding it. Her opening observation on 20 October is: "I am not happy
here. I do not understand this household, neither the family nor the
servants. This is the middle of my third week, yet I am still in all ways
at a loss" (p. 11). Yet later, under the same date, while reporting Mrs.
Pulvertaft's insistence that she get to know the family better, she confides
that, "I felt, to tell the truth, that I knew the Pulvertafts fairly well already"
(p. 13).

Anna Maria's unconscious confusion about what she does or does not
know establishes the context for introducing—in her journal entries for
both 17 and 20 October—the second major, much more ambiguous, even
mysterious, symbol, one that comes from beyond this local pale in a piece
of news from Fogarty. With "grisley smile" and seeming "faintly sinister"
to Anna Maria, he reports to her of an Irish child born with Christ's
stigmata on hands and feet; and he tells her the local priest's opinion is
that "so clearly marked a stigma has never before been known in Ireland.
The people consider it a miracle, a sign from God in these distressful
times" (p. 11). But a sign—a symbol—of what? "Stigmata" clearly suggests
one thing; the priest's word, "stigma," another. Have we a sign of God's
displeasure with the Irish or a mark of His benign concern for His Irish
children?

Anna Maria is "amazed" that the news does not even surprise Fogarty,
not because he believes in God's visitations to papists but because he
believes that the distraught parents, driven to blasphemy and barbarity

by the starvation deaths of their seven other children, have themselves inflicted the marks of the stigmata in the hope of obtaining food for themselves. Given its immense significance to Anna Maria, she is early on upset that the Pulvertafts never so much as mention the occurrence, and that when they do learn of it they are totally untouched and accept Fogarty's explanation of a hoax.

On the one hand, Anna Maria seems to accept the stigmata as a sign of God's presence; on the other, when the child dies and Fogarty reports that people in the soup line and on the road are "edgy" because they feel "that Our Lord has been crucified again," Anna Maria retorts "ridiculous!" (p. 30). Five months later, she thinks again of an "infant tortured with Our Saviour's wounds" (p. 37), a seeming acceptance of Fogarty's theory of cruel fraud. Wondering what the Irish have done to displease God— in a way she would not have done only months before—she admits to herself that the Irish have not been easy to rule, that they have not obeyed the laws, and that their superstitious worship is a sin.

These acknowledgments complete a desensitization process and ready Anna Maria to accept the marriage proposal of the insensitive Erskine, British estate manager, and to move closer to the company of the Pulvertafts. At the very end, bringing the story full circle in its language, within which are enclosed many mysteries—never mind "news"—Trevor writes: "Stranger and visitor, she has written in her diary the news from Ireland. Stranger and visitor, she has learned to live with things" (p. 46). Weeping and sick at heart because of her perceived loss of her sensitivity and, perhaps, the will to try to penetrate the mystery of the child and thus the mystery of her situation in Ireland; because of her compromise of principle by marriage to an unprincipled man; and because of her symbolic union with the Pulvertafts by an expected invitation to dine at their table as Mrs. Erskine, Anna Marie capitulates and rejects further pursuit of understanding.

Reminding us of "news," the "events" of "Events at Drimaghleen"— three violent deaths in the McDowd and Butler families and their discovery and first report—occur on the night of Tuesday and the morning of Wednesday, 21 and 22 May 1985. But the "truth" of them is ultimately as much a mystery, a secret, as the circumstances surrounding the infant bearing Christ's stigmata. As the local folks in "News" are seized by that confounding occurrence, the neighboring folks in "Events" find these three deaths more appalling and shocking and horrible than anything that has ever occurred in their area.

A newsworthy event in a sparsely populated area, one version of it is deduced by local garda Superintendent O'Kelly, supported by the people of Drimaghleen, and reported in the Irish media. A second, more lurid version later appears in an English newspaper's Sunday supplement. Both versions are suspect. Skeptical readers may well be meant by Trevor to ponder the truth of both versions, to examine the evidence themselves, and to ask, as the evidence or lack thereof suggests they should, what Trevor's reasons might be for continuing rather than revealing the mystery at the heart of events. The speed with which Superintendent O'Kelly reaches his conclusions is based on much less than complete observation and his reading of relatively simple personalities, this relative lack of complexity perhaps deepening the mystery rather than simplifying it. What we know of the three dead people is not complex: Mrs. Butler is fiercely possessive of her son, who is spoiled and weak and who has formed a relationship with the passive Maureen. The Sunday supplement version is based on new evidence, which may or may not be valid, some faulty observation, and a different rendering of personalities.

As Trevor lays out his story, personality and locale suggest something of the difficulty in getting at the truth. For example, in describing the unwillingness of Mr. McDowd, the father of one of the victims, to speak to an outsider photographer, Trevor provides much of the deterrence to arriving at the truth: "He lifted a hand and scratched at his grey, ragged hair, which was his way when he wished to disguise bewilderment. Part of his countryman's wiliness was that he preferred outsiders not to know, or deduce, what was occurring in his mind" (p. 46), and we as readers also remain outsiders in many ways.

McDowd's reticence, indeed, distrust—his wife shares it abundantly and, we may assume, the other countryfolk do as well—has been nurtured in his isolation from his neighbors. Trevor is on familiar and sure ground here and establishes it as firmly as he ever has: "Drimaghleen, Kilmona and Mountcroe," he writes, "formed a world that bounded the lives of the people of the Drimaghleen farms. Rarely was there occasion to venture beyond it to the facilities of a town that was larger—unless the purpose happened to be a search for work or the first step on the way to exile" (p. 43). Each area's particulars are set out to underscore isolation of families from one another and from the larger world of Ireland and beyond, isolation that creates wariness. Mountcroe, the largest, has the school, the creamery, the butcher shop, the hardware store and a grocery store, an abandoned cinema, and it is where the area men get drunk, though they may have a few bottles of stout in the bar adjoining the grocery in smaller Kilmona, where the church is also located. Drimaghleen itself is merely a townland marked only by a crossroads, and the small farms of the area are scattered miles apart over the boglands.

Wednesday, 22 May 1985, begins like most days for the sixtyish older McDowds. He dresses and goes out to fetch the cows for milking; she washes, puts on the kettle, and calls their twenty-five-year-old daughter, Maureen, the only one of five children still at home. Repeated callings jar McDowd into awareness that Maureen's bicycle is not in its usual place; and when his wife announces that Maureen's bed has not been slept in they know without saying so that she has not come back from the Butler farm, where she'd gone the evening before to see Lancy Butler, spoiled son of a widowed mother, and each fears that Maureen has run off with the feckless Lancy. And since everyone in the area knows—knowledge essential to local acceptance of the official version of events—that Lancy has been spoiled to the point of uselessness by a stereotypically possessive Irish mother, there is apparently good reason for the McDowds to have opposed the relationship as much as Mrs. Butler has. And so they set off to the Butler farm four miles away.

What they find in the Butler farmyard is revealed serially. Mrs. McDowd sees Maureen's dead body by the pump, her bicycle and two dead rabbits nearby. Mr. McDowd discovers the dead Mrs. Butler in a doorway several yards off, her face blown away. Then, near Maureen's body but behind two barrels, Mrs. McDowd finds Lancy's body with the Butler shotgun nearby. Neither now nor later are specific distances given—only "another part of the yard" or "a yard or so away" (twice) or "nor far from it"—so that more exact knowledge of the physical relationships of the bodies and thus possible fuller knowledge of the course of events is withheld. We learn eventually that Lancy and Maureen had often taken the shotgun and, with Lancy peddling Maureen's bicycle—Lancy having none of his own—and Maureen riding sidesaddle on the rear carrier, holding, we might reasonably infer, as does the Sunday supplement account, the shotgun, gone off to shoot rabbits; so that when they returned to the farmyard from the evening's expedition it was entirely probable that Maureen carried both the rabbits found near her and the shotgun.

"O'Kelly of the garda arrived at a swift conclusion," Trevor tells us (p. 42). Knowing, as do the people in the area, of Mrs. Butler's possessiveness of her son, her determination that no one should take her from him, and her reputed oddness and rages, O'Kelly concludes that Mrs. Butler had shot Maureen; that Lancy had then wrenched the gun from her and by accident or design had discharged it and killed his mother; that Lancy, never a strong man and unable to face what has happened, killed himself. These conclusions, "borne out by the details of the yard, satisfied O'Kelly. . ." (p. 43); Drimaghleen folk arrived at the same conclusion, and the matter is settled. It will not do.

In 1985, even in remote rural Ireland, a case of this magnitude would surely result in certain standard procedures. However, there are no autopsies; there is no ballistics test; there is no clarification of distances; there is no reenactment of events; there is no information on the proximity and trajectory of the three shots; there are no data on what an examination of the wounds might reveal; there is no revelation to us—or, as far as we know, to O'Kelly—about the possibility of Lancy having shot himself—where?—with the shotgun. There is no consideration of fingerprints or their location on the gun, though later we learn that those of all three victims are there, blurred and in several different locations, this discovery seeming to be the sole concession to normal procedures in such cases. This discovery is also natural enough since Maureen carried the gun, Lancy used it to shoot rabbits, and, since it was the Butler family gun, Mrs. Butler would have had occasion to handle it even apart from O'Kelly's deduction that she handled it to shoot Maureen. Even setting aside the absence of forensic ballistics, chemistry, medicine, and psychiatry, there are problems with the official story.

This version holds that Mrs. Butler shot Maureen. If so, how did the gun come into her possession on this occasion? Presumably from Lancy, who, in this account, shot his mother, whether by accident or design, when he was wrestling it from her after she'd shot Maureen. But why would Lancy have taken the gun from Maureen, who would have been holding it after the rabbit hunt, and walk—how far?—to his mother with it and allow her to take it and shoot Maureen—how far away? Even if, for some unknown reason, he did let her take it, then take it back and shoot her, why would he walk back to near where Maureen lies dead and shoot himself there? None of these questions is asked by Trevor, and, so far as we know, by O'Kelly either. And none is answered by Trevor.

And so the case is closed, and after mention of the events in the media, quiet again descends on Drimaghleen. For the McDowds, there are letters of sympathy, neighbors call in briefly, and Father Sallins places himself on call. But heartbroken, inconsolable, haunted, the McDowds retreat into their customary silence and isolation. May passes into October, when strangers come into the farmyard in a red car.

Trevor's words are right for this intrusion—the car "edged its way"; it is like "some cautious animal"; it has a "slow creeping movement"—because the McDowds do not welcome outsiders and are not only reticent but belligerent and threatening. Doubtless, they would have reacted this way with any strangers but these and their mission are charged with provocation. Jeremiah Tyler, from Dublin, and Hetty Fortune, from England, are photographer and Sunday supplement writer, respectively, and they have come to reopen the case. Trevor's details for them are the right ones to elicit the McDowds' distrust and belligerence. Tyler, seedy and unkempt, "was florid-faced, untidily dressed in dark corduroy trousers and a gabardine jacket. His hair was long and black, and grew coarsely down the sides of his face in two brushlike panels. He had a city voice . . ." (p. 46). Hetty is somber-faced, wears sunglasses and matching blue shirt and trousers, smokes, speaks with an English accent, and strikes Mrs. McDowd as insincere, an acute appraisal.

Having spent time at the Butler place, they say, and in the area talking with a number of people, they declare repeatedly that the truth of the case has not been established, that they want to talk with the McDowds to help them settle it and have it published together with color pictures. Characteristically, the McDowds resent and resist—until Hetty mentions a payment in excess of £3,000, when the McDowds, realizing what could be done with the sum to ease their lives, capitulate and agree to talk.

There follows Hetty Fortune's version of events in the Sunday supplement, together with "fashionably faded pictures," interspersed with information supplied by Trevor about the pictures and something of the conduct of the interview and then with the reactions of the McDowds when Father Sallins brings them the newspaper.

This version of events, placed by Hetty Fortune in the context of Ireland's sensational Kerry babies mystery and the Flynn case,[6] suggests that the mystery of this case is typical of what occurs all over Ireland in "small, tucked away farms like the Butlers' and the McDowds' " (p. 49), where "These simple folk . . . of Europe's most western island form limited rural communities that all too often turn in on themselves" (p. 55). Maureen is pictured as "helpful," "special," gentle, sweet-natured, considered by her parents a perfect daughter, a near saint—nothing that we have ever learned of her and somewhat different from the "bitch" her father had called her before the discovery of her body; indeed, "The Saint of Drimaghleen . . . never missed mass in all her twenty-five years" (p. 49). But, the account adds, she was "young, impetuous, bitterly deprived of the man she loved" (p. 52) and ripe for any action to keep Lancy. Additionally, the newspaper quotes a letter purportedly written by Maureen to Lancy a week before the shootings and found behind a drawer in a table of the Butlers sold at auction, in which she admits that the relationship may be at an end because of the objections of all parents. Deduced from this by Hetty Fortune is Mrs. Butler's knowledge that the affair would soon be over so there would be no reason for her to kill

Maureen. If Mrs. Butler did not kill Maureen because she did not need to, who did and what really happened?

In the revised scenario, Mrs. Butler, rather than acting in jealous rage and shooting Maureen, is instead shot by a Maureen determined not to lose her man. Maureen then shoots Lancy and then herself. This will not do, either. Setting aside, as before, the whole question of forensics and a complete investigation, and setting aside much, if not most, of the revelation of Maureen's saintly character as serving some purpose other than the truth, there are as many flaws in this version as in the original.

Chastising Superintendent O'Kelly on the issue of fingerprints on the gun, Hetty Fortune concludes that Maureen's are there because she carried the gun on returning from hunting rabbits, a reasonable conclusion but one that undercuts her further view that the prints are part of the evidence that Maureen shot Mrs. Butler. There is the question of Maureen's letter to Lancy. Was there in fact such a letter? If so, was it proven—and how and to whom—to be Maureen's? Who, exactly, discovered it and turned it over to Hetty Fortune? Hetty Fortune deduces from this letter that Mrs. Butler knew that the affair was over and thus had no need to kill Maureen, but there is no evidence that Mrs. Butler knew of the purported letter, one hidden away at that. "It is known," writes Hetty Fortune as part of her scenario, "that Maureen McDowd wept shortly before her death" (p. 52), but we do not in fact know this any more than we know the things claimed to be in the victims' minds. Is the state of Maureen's wound consonant with what is expected in self-inflicted wounds? We do not know. Finally, if Maureen shot Mrs. Butler, then Lancy, and finally herself, how did the gun come to be beside Lancy's body? Did she shoot herself and then toss it there?

On the basis of what we know, this version of events will not wash any more than O'Kelly's and we must ask why Hetty Fortune told it at all. Part of the answer is simply to boost her paper's circulation through the sensationalism of the case—like the Kerry babies and Flynn case. Part seems to be simply to indict O'Kelly and the rural Irish in a particularly invidious fashion. The people are reputed in the article—there is no evidence that this is so—to believe, along with the older McDowds, in Maureen's "unblemished virtue." Thus believing, Hetty Fortune writes, they swept O'Kelly into a similar belief publicly stated, a part, in fact, of a conspiracy of silence to protect against revelation that their saint was only a plaster saint: "Had he publicly arrived at any other conclusion Superintendent O'Kelly might never safely have set foot in the neighborhood of Drimaghleen again, or the village of Kilmona, or the town of Mountcroe. The Irish do not easily forgive the purloining of their latter-day saints" (p. 53).

The story moves to its conclusion amid the spoils purchased with the £3,000, electric stove, carpets, radio, television. Mr. McDowd remains silent. Father Sallins fears that more than household goods have been purchased—more magazine articles, more strangers, perhaps a film, Maureen's nature argued over in books, "the mystery that had been created becoming a legend" (p. 55). And Mrs. McDowd shrills scream after scream.

Having wondered why Superintendent O'Kelly and Hetty Fortune, whose jobs are ostensibly to report accurately "the news from Ireland," arrive at flawed versions, in some ways transparently so, we must also ask why Trevor has withheld the truth not only from his characters but from us. Similarly, we might well ask why the truth about the child with Christ's stigmata is reserved not only from the casual curiosity of the Pulvertafts but from Anna Maria Heddoe, who, up to a point, seeks it assiduously, and from readers.

In the several other stories briefly noted, the truth behind secrets is either known to readers almost from the outset or is eventually plainly displayed or can be divined with some certainty. If Trevor in these other stories has wandered at will in and out of the minds of his characters and has assumed the omniscience that explains and clarifies, why has he not done so with these two? Some obvious answers suggest themselves. For example, Trevor is under no obligation to be consistent in his techniques. Similarly, he is not required to have the same purposes in every story. Again, he as well as we would soon weary of all matters plainly put. Taking this a step further, readers have an obligation to remain alert and to join Trevor in his pursuit of what is elusive in human experience.

This point opens up what may be one reasonably satisfactory reason for Trevor's strategies in these two stories and at least the tentative conclusion that these strategies have helped create the two most interesting of this whole set of stories and some of the best of his work.

Generous in granting interviews, in at least three of them Trevor has marked out his consistent fictional concerns. In a 1983 interview for the *Guardian,* Hugh Hebert reports two relevant Trevor observations. First he says, "I think you have to know a tremendous amount about your characters that you never put down on paper. I love cutting things, it's the short story writer in me, and I love taking chances with readers." And then, "I've never been interested in politics. What I'm interested in is what happens to people."[7] A later 1983 interview conducted by Amanda Smith and appearing in *Publishers Weekly* finds Trevor using his novel *Fools of*

Fortune to make his point: "I don't really have any heroes or heroines. I don't seem to go in for them. I think I am interested in people who are not necessarily the victims of other people, but simply the victims of circumstance, as they are in *Fools of Fortune*. I'm very interested in the sadness of fate, the things that just happen to people."[8] Finally, in a 1985 interview with Sean Dunne in the *Sunday Tribune*, Trevor says, "I don't like to think too much about where my stories are set—I think they're about people."[9]

There we have some of it: "What I'm interested in is what happens to people"—"I think I am interested in people. . . ."—"I think [my stories are] about people." Secrets, in ways suggested early in this essay, work very well as springs of motivation and action in several ways, and many of these are illustrated in all the stories discussed. But in "News" and "Events" Trevor has complicated matters because, as he says, he knows more than he says, because he likes to cut things, because, finally, he loves to take "chances with readers."

For the writer who is more interested in people than in, say, plot, and who likes to take chances by "cutting things," chancing that readers will involve themselves, stories in which secrets are revealed give us one level for probing and pondering. Stories in which secrets remain unrevealed by an omniscient narrator and/or by characters and/or lack of evidence force us to some deeper level of thought and, if the chance has succeeded, some profounder sense of human personality and conduct. Perhaps we might say that by mystery—in the case of "Events" quite literally a murder mystery—Trevor wishes to illustrate by technique the enigma of human personality that is at the heart of the stories' substance. For instance, why does Superintendent O'Kelly not reveal all that might be revealed? Or, for example, why would Fogarty the butler in "News" not tell all that he might and why does Anna Maria Heddoe abort her search for the truth? And so the questions multiply and we touch more deeply than if we were not required to ask because we have been told. Beneath the ordinarily unadorned and plain style of Trevor's stories there are often human enigmas that might give up revelation to those who take Trevor's dare.

The persistence of secrets—of several kinds and at different levels of interpretation—in Trevor's Irish stories leads inevitably to the question: Does Trevor mean that there is something in the Irish personality that is more predisposed to secrecy than in that of other peoples or something in Irish circumstances that create this predisposition?

One possible answer is that Trevor does not find the Irish any more inclined to secrecy than any other people. The closest that he comes to an outright suggestion that there is such an inclination is in "Events," as

we have seen, when he tells us of Mr. McDowd that "Part of his countryman's wiliness was that he preferred out-siders not to know, or deduce
what was occurring in his mind"; but the same wiliness might be attributed
to the Slavic peasant, for example. And Trevor has made some effort to
claim universality for at least some of his Irish stories. For example, in an
"Author's Note" to The Distant Past and Other Stories, Trevor's own se-
lection of his Irish stories, he says of one of them, "Miss Smith," that it
"might perhaps have come out of anywhere, but in fact is set in a town
in Munster. . . ."[10] Similarly, in the 1985 Sunday Tribune interview, he
observes, "Even 'The Ballroom of Romance,' and this might sound
strange"—as indeed it does to those who think of "Ballroom" as a quin-
tessentially Irish story of isolation, deprivation, and loneliness—"I don't
think of as a particularly Irish story—the film [of the story] seems to have
gone down just as well in places like Israel and Norway. It has a universality." And there are traits of jealousy and possessiveness, for example,
everywhere, and Ireland has no corner on stultifying provincial towns or
the yen for more land.

On the other hand, to begin with, the particular circumstances of some
of the stories place them ineluctably in Ireland. Some facts of the Great
Hunger may be similar to those of other famines, but some of the facts
of Ireland's and its consequences are intractably Irish, some analysts even
having argued that they have marked the contemporary Irish character.
Similarly, for instance, one might argue that it is typical strictly of the
Irish-English relationship that a Hetty Fortune would invidiously attack
the rural Irish; or that Protestants in Ireland occupy a position utterly
unique; or that Ireland's geography and the history of land ownership are
sufficiently singular to have created exceptional attitudes toward ownership.

Furthermore, despite what might appear as Trevor's at least implicit
wish for a kind of universality to his characters, and even without an
extensive analysis of the Irish personality in search of a penchant for
secrecy, we can draw briefly on a handful of commonly held views of the
Irish and their uses or nonuses of language to suggest that "secrecy" in its
many forms is engrained in the Irish nature.

For example, we can draw on the very fact of the physical isolation of
many Irish communities, families, and individuals as a means of explain-
ing—as Hetty Fortune does—a kind of tribal reticence that does not
readily yield up its secrets even to other Irish. Carried a step further, it
is a commonplace that the Irish as a whole, as a people so long dominated
by the British, have been driven to a conspiratorial mode of life in dealing
not only with the British but with one another. Thus, in both "News"

and "Events," for instance, to cite only the Irish authority figures, Fogarty the butler and Superintendent O'Kelly do not tell all that they might to either the other Irish or to the British outsiders.

Taking an antithetical but complementary tack, we can observe that rather than being characterized by reticence, the Irish are more often and more traditionally marked by their loquacity, and loquacity not merely as small talk and chatter, though it is often enough that, too, but as a wondrous if sometimes manipulative way with words, a trait that often manifests itself in talk as performance. And with talk as performance—in addition to the truism for all peoples that merely the existence of verbal fluency has never been a guarantee of its veracity—Irish loquacity, in some of its flights of fancy often takes the form of indirectness, obfuscation, obscurity, ambiguity, innuendo, exaggeration and/or understatement—to say nothing of outright lies—all with the same practical effect of secrecy more strictly conceived.

In a fascinating 1982 essay, "Irish Families," in the collection, *Ethnicity and Family Therapy*, a compendium of studies designed to assist therapists in dealing with family problems by introducing the therapists to the characteristics of different ethnic families, Monica McGoldrick writes:

> The paradox of the general articulateness of the Irish and their inability to express inner feelings can be puzzling for a therapist who may have difficulty figuring out what is going on in an Irish family. . . . Family members may be so out of touch with their feelings that their inexpressiveness in therapy is not a sign of resistance, as it would be for other cultural groups, but rather a reflection of their blocking off inner emotions, even from themselves. Thus, although the Irish have a marvelous ability to tell stories, when it comes to their own emotions, they may have no words. The Irish often fear being pinned down and may use their language and manner to avoid it. The affinity of the Irish for verbal innuendo, ambiguity, and metaphor have [sic] led the English to coin the phrase "talking Irish" to describe the Irish style of both communicating and not communicating at the same time. Some have suggested that, in the extreme, this style of communication is responsible for the high rate of schizophrenia found among the Irish. . . .[12]

It would probably be unwise for a literary study to pursue too far—to say nothing of uncritically accepting—the clinical implications and conclusions of these observations, at least for Trevor's stories, but there is no escaping that a study such as McGoldrick's helps us to understand how and why, perhaps even without his full awareness but simply as something taken as a given, Trevor has infused so many of his characters and situations with the kinds of secrecy we have found. At bottom then, it seems reasonable to conclude that in the Irish circumstances and characters he has chosen to explore, Trevor has found an unusually rich and natural matrix from which to develop his understated—and sometimes unstated—dramas of character.

Notes

1. William Trevor, *The News from Ireland and Other Stories* (New York: Viking Penguin, 1986); "The News from Ireland," 9–46; "The Property of Colette Nervi," 85–106; "Bodily Secrets," 147–72; "Virgins," 173–204; "Music," 226–49; "Two More Gallants," 250–61; "The Wedding in the Garden," 262–85.

2. William Trevor, "The Third Party," *New Yorker*, 14 April 1986, 35–44.

3. William Trevor, "Kathleen's Field," *New Yorker*, 12 May 1986, 36–45.

4. William Trevor, "Events at Drimaghleen," *Grand Street* (Winter 1987): 39–56. Further references to this story appear in parentheses in the text. With a cutoff date of January 1987, I have not included in this essay two additional Irish stories by Trevor: "Frau Messinger," *New Yorker*, 2 March 1987, and "Family Sins," *New Yorker*, 6 July 1987.

5. John Dunne, "Good and Averagely Good," *Books Ireland* (September 1986):157.

6. Setting aside its vast and labyrinthine developments, the Kerry Babies Case, simply put, was—and remains—searing and sensational melodrama. Starting in April 1984, it concerned the death of two male infants. One, the illegitimate child of Joanne Hayes, died shortly after birth, was placed in a plastic bag, then deposited in a well on the family farm. A second baby, unidentified, was stabbed twenty-eight times and left on a Kerry beach, where it was found the following day, a plastic bag nearby. I am grateful to Dolores MacKenna of Dublin for the following information on the Flynn case: "In August 1985 the body of Father Molloy was found in the bedroom of Mr. and Mrs. Flynn of Clara, Co. Offaly. Fr. Molloy had that day been a guest at the wedding of the Flynns' daughter in the house. The police, who were called to the house after midnight, found that Fr. Molloy had been beaten to death. Richard Flynn claimed that a row had developed about who would fetch drinks, that he had struck Fr. Molloy and that the priest had fallen and hit his head. Flynn was charged with manslaughter but was found not guilty. Journalists, however, pursued the case and discovered that the priest's body had been moved before the police had been called. They also discovered that Fr. Molloy and Mrs. Flynn had been involved in extensive business

operations, from which he wanted to withdraw. Fr. Molloy's family is still pursuing the case." (4 July 1987)

7. Hugh Hebert, "Love Among the Ruins of War," *Guardian*, 23 April 1983, 10.

8. Amanda Smith, *"PW* Interviews William Trevor," *Publishers Weekly*, 28 October 1983, 80.

9. Sean Dunne, "The Old Boy," *Sunday Tribune*, 2 June 1985, 17.

10. William Trevor, "Author's Note," *The Distant Past and Other Stories* (Swords, Co. Dublin: Poolbeg Press, 1979), 5.

11. Dunne, "The Old Boy," 17.

12. Monica McGoldrick, "Irish Families," *Ethnicity and Family Therapy*, ed. Monica McGoldrick, John K. Pearce, and Joseph Giordano (New York: The Guilford Press, 1982), 315–16.

The Silence of God: Priest as Martyr in Brian Moore's Fiction

John W. Mahon

A martyr, a saint, is always made by the design of God. . . . A martyrdom is never the design of man; for the true martyr is he who has become the instrument of God, who has lost his will in the will of God, not lost it but found it, for he has found freedom in submission to God.[1]

From the beginning of his career, Brian Moore has demonstrated an interest in the silence of God, the fact that God may listen but that He rarely speaks as He does, for example, in the biblical stories of the burning bush and the Transfiguration. The protagonist of *The Lonely Passion of Judith Hearne* (1955) despairs partly because God does not speak. "Why do You torture me, alone and silent behind Your little door?"[2] she asks, before attacking the tabernacle. Thirty-two years later, in *The Color of Blood* (1987), Moore's protagonist, Cardinal Stephen Bem, also experiences the silence of God. But while Judith Hearne interprets the silence as denial, Bem finds in it the environment for his prayer. In three of his books, Moore has created priest-protagonists who encounter the silence of God as they seek to serve Him; striving to do God's will, each becomes a martyr in the terms of the epigraph at the beginning of this essay.

In *Catholics* (1972) there are actually two priests at the center of the action, but James Kinsella, the young American troubleshooter, represents Moore's vision of the Church in the 1990s, an already dated vision because the Church will in fact not have changed as much as Moore supposed. The story of Tomas O'Malley's personal struggle, mingled with religious politics, will endure. Some years later, in two novels in succession, Moore again uses priests as protagonists: Paul Laforgue, the Jesuit missionary in *Black Robe* (1985), and Stephen Bem, the Cardinal in *The Color of Blood* (1987).

O'Malley, the abbot of a monastery in the west of Ireland, can be viewed as a sketch for Moore's later priest-heroes, possessing as he does the authority of Cardinal Bem and the doubts of Paul Laforgue, doubts that also reflect the ordeal of Moore's first protagonist, Judith Hearne. Just as Cardinal Bem must contend with an atheistic state on one side and a revolutionary Catholic element on the other, so Abbot O'Malley is caught between the demands of the Church in the 1990s (Rome now participates in the "World Ecumen Council" and is about to launch an *apertura* to the Buddhists) and the faith of ordinary Catholics, drawn to remote Kerry by the Latin mass and private confessions that his monks celebrate. For his part, Paul Laforgue must deal with the clash of strange cultures as he tries to convert American Indians to Christianity, struggling all the while with his doubts both about his ability and about the whole enterprise. Similarly, O'Malley struggles with his loss of faith even as he tries to sustain it among his brothers, and Bem is assailed by doubts about his role as a leader and by his haunting sense of the silence of God. All three of these priests possess a strong sense of mission, and each ultimately succeeds, although not as he might have originally expected. The environments they operate in are exotic in time or space, at least in terms of Brian Moore's usual practice: in *Catholics*, Ireland some years from now; in *Black Robe*, seventeenth-century Canada; in *The Color of Blood*, an eastern European country. These settings become metaphors for the serious challenges facing priests in any environment.

Dealing with a young American priest sent to bring him into line, O'Malley stoutly defends the Latin mass for pastoral reasons. He asks Kinsella, who styles himself "James Kinsella, Catholic priest" rather than "Father Kinsella," if he knows Francis Janson's *An Unbeliever's Faith*: "He believes there can be a future for Christianity, provided it gets rid of God." When Abbot O'Malley asks Kinsella what the mass means to him, Kinsella answers that it is "a symbolic act. I do not believe that the bread and wine on the altar is changed into the body and blood of Christ, except in a purely symbolic manner. Therefore, I do not, in the old sense, think of God as actually being present, there in the tabernacle."[3] This position stands in striking contrast to that of one of the most outspoken monks, Father Matthew, who voices the traditional belief that "the Mass is the daily miracle of the Catholic Faith. The Mass, in which bread and wine are changed by the priest into the body and blood of Jesus Christ" (84).

When Kinsella claims that the mass as symbol is "the standard belief in this day and age," Abbot O'Malley responds, "Or lack of belief. I think that I was born before my time. A man doesn't have to have such a big

dose of faith anymore, does he?" (71) How convenient the faith of James
Kinsella would be for the tormented Judith Hearne beating her fists on
the tabernacle door, or for Tomas O'Malley himself, who can no longer
pray without entering a dark night of the soul. He sits in the abbey church
convinced that the tabernacle contains only a ciborium with "twelve round
wafers of unleavened bread . . . in this building which is said to be the
house of God" (81).

After Kinsella has accomplished his mission and departed with Abbot
O'Malley's letter of submission to Rome, O'Malley makes the ultimate
sacrifice. Trying to calm the rebellious monks,

> he saw in these faces that he was failing, that he was losing them, that
> he must do something he had never done, give something he had never
> given in these, his years as their Abbot. What had kept him in fear
> since Lourdes, must now be faced. What he feared most to do must be
> done. And if, in doing it, I enter null and never return, amen. My time
> has come. (106)

Earlier, staring at the tabernacle, O'Malley has tried to pray: " 'Our Father
Who Art in Heaven,' but there is no Father in heaven, His name is not
hallowed by these words, His kingdom will not come to he who sits and
stares at the tabernacle" (82).[4] Now, kneeling in the center aisle of the
church to lead the monks in prayer, " 'Our Father, Who art in Heaven,'
he said. His trembling increased. He entered null. He would never come
back. In null" (107). Raymond Porter's analysis suggests that this conclusion can be read in two ways:

> Moore ends his book with O'Malley's act of faith, which sends him into
> null. But at the other side of null, as St. John of the Cross has written
> and as I contend Moore suggests, one encounters God, "God will come"
> (107). Moore's ending, then, is an affirmation of faith in the face of
> doubt. O'Malley's act of prayer gives the monks faith: "Relieved, their
> voices echoed his" (107); and his act moves him toward God.[5]

Sub specie aeternitatis, O'Malley can be viewed as a martyr. In human
terms, he may never return from the void. Such an ambiguous conclusion
is characteristic of Moore's work. Thus, Judith Hearne experiences complete despair but in the end she prays, "I do not believe, O Lord, help
my unbelief" (222). The action that opens her Lonely Passion is repeated,

as she asks the nun in the nursing home to set up her personal props, the pictures of her aunt and of the Sacred Heart, reminders of family and faith: "She closed her eyes. Funny about those two. When they're with me, watching over me, a new place becomes home" (223). O'Malley, too, has a personal prop, a "horrid oil" (in Kinsella's view), a "Victorian painting of a ship sailing in a storm-tossed sea, under heavens rent by the Virgin Mary, prayerful, in blue and white robes, imploring her Heavenly Son for the vessel's safety" (41). Whether or not O'Malley's personal struggle will be resolved remains unclear; what is clear is that he accomplishes God's will, his primary mission: by sacrificing his own peace of mind, he restores some peace to the troubled monks committed to his care.

If, like the saint for whom he is named, Tomas O'Malley is a doubter, Paul Laforgue, the Jesuit missionary of *Black Robe,* similarly becomes his name, as he struggles to save the souls of the Savages (the French term for native Americans) in colonial Quebec. Laforgue undertakes a long and perilous journey into the dark heart of the Indian lands in 1635. His journey is reminiscent of Marlow's in *Heart of Darkness,* but it is even more suggestive of the fearful pilgrimage to Japan undertaken by the Portuguese Jesuit Rodrigues in 1637 in Shusaku Endo's *Silence.* In all three stories a clash between cultures dominates; the horror in Moore and Endo is that there are no villains, yet innocent people suffer and die anyway. Endo's Japanese and Moore's Savages dread losing their way of life if they submit to the "water-sorcery" practiced by the Jesuits. In a kind of perverse tribute to the revolutionary nature of Christianity and to the power of the Western culture Christianity usually comes clothed in, people as different as the Japanese and the native Americans shared an instinctive and strong resistance to Jesuit missionary efforts.

Moore is particularly effective in depicting the wide gulf that separates the Savages and their way of life from the French. Immediately apparent to the French are the Indians' scatological language, carefree sexuality, lazy life-style, disgusting eating habits, and slovenly personal hygiene. Less obvious are the traits described by the young Frenchman Daniel: "The Savages are truer Christians than we will ever be. They have no ambitions. They think we are mean and foolish because we love possessions more than they do. They live for each other, they share everything, they do not become angry with each other, they forgive each other things which we French would never forgive." Daniel describes the Indian belief in a world of the dead: "They believe that at night the dead see. They move about, animals and men, in the forests of night. The souls of men hunt the souls of animals, moving through forests made up of the souls of trees which have died."[6] The Indians believe in the power of dreams and in the power of nature to communicate with them. In a later discussion, an Algonkian warrior about to die makes clear that the two cultures are virtually mirror images of each other. For the Indians, this life is to be treasured because it is so much better than what follows: "It is because you Normans are deaf and blind that you think this world is a world of darkness and the world of the dead is a world of light. We who can hear the forest and the river's warnings, we who speak with the animals and the fish and respect their bones, we know that is not the truth" (184–85).

To the Indians, the French are hairy and greedy, and the Blackrobes avoid sex in order to increase their power as sorcerers. Also, say the Indians, "In each of the Blackrobe habitations there is a special room. In that room, there is a small box placed on a high ledge. Inside the box there are pieces of a corpse which they brought from France. They say this corpse is the body of their god. They have secret ceremonies in which they eat little pieces . . ." (169–70). When the Indians board the French ships and are served wine and dry biscuit, they return to tell their people that the French "were devils who lived in a floating wooden island and drank blood and ate dry bones" (58).

The confrontation between cultures appears primarily in the experiences of Laforgue and, to a lesser extent, in those of Daniel and Annuka. Daniel, a young layman likely to be accepted as a Jesuit novice after he assists Laforgue on this mission, really makes the journey in order to accompany Annuka, the Algonkian girl with whom he is already sexually involved. Daniel realizes that, despite his efforts to live like the Indians, he will never really be accepted. Annuka, meanwhile, is torn between loyalty to her tribe and family and her growing love for Daniel. Ultimately she will accept baptism and marry Daniel.

By the time an entire Huron village seeks baptism from Laforgue, at the end of the novel, the Jesuit has travelled further spiritually than physically, overwhelmed by the contrasts between his culture and that of the Indians. At the start, he eagerly embraces the dangerous assignment and recalls dreams of heroic witness; when he visits his mother in Rouen, she prays for him at the site of Joan of Arc's martyrdom and tells him that " 'God has chosen you, just as He chose the Maid.' . . . Surely it was foolish to compare him with a saint like Joan of Arc, but still it was true that ever since the Order had granted his petition to be sent to New France he had dreamed of the glory of martyrdom in that faraway land" (33).

Remembering the two years of training at the residence in Quebec City, the missionary realizes that he is now journeying toward a place where martyrdom is "more than just a pious hope. This is my hour. This is my beginning" (34). But God has chosen a different fate for him, and the story of his struggle against doubt and despair matches the poignancy of Judith Hearne's. Nevertheless, Laforgue never betrays his Jesuit vow of disponibility—he goes where he is sent and completes his mission.

Brian Moore has described himself as an agnostic,[7] but in these novels about men of faith, he shows remarkable insight into the demands and the rewards of the spiritual life. In a note prefaced to *Black Robe*, he describes the influence of Graham Greene's essay on Francis Parkman's *The Jesuits in North America*, but his portrayal of priests owes more to a novel like *The Diary of a Country Priest* than it does to *The Power and the Glory*. In O'Malley and Bem, Moore presents older men, seasoned in their vocations; O'Malley has despaired, but *Catholics* is so brief that we do not learn the background in any detail. Bem could be an older Laforgue, who not only *says* that he trusts in God but *believes* what he says. Laforgue is an apprentice in the spiritual journey, still to be tested, while O'Malley and Bem have already been tested. *Black Robe* traces the process of Laforgue's spiritual maturation, in a testing that alternates between despair and exaltation, as the priest moves even closer to complete acceptance of God's will for him and recognition that he is merely God's instrument. Moving steadily toward his goal, he gradually recognizes his limitations and sinfulness; we see what Laforgue cannot see, that his exhaustion and despair dispose him to serve God more effectively.

Early in the journey, Laforgue has difficulty reading his breviary because it "seemed strange in this place, and the Latin sentences jumbled in his head" (35). Yet he manages in prayer to thank God for this mission and when, next morning, he sees an eagle in flight, he takes this as a sign that God is "not hidden. . . . In the beauty of this wild place, his heart sang a Te Deum of happiness" (44). He experiences this joy while suffering from a serious ear infection and fever.

After this reaffirmation, he witnesses a sexual encounter between Daniel and Annuka, masturbates and, shamed, flagellates himself, convinced that he has lost all moral authority over his younger companion. Meanwhile, he begins to doubt that the Indians can ever be converted, in this country "far from the sun of God's warmth. Even I, who now beseech His aid, can only think of eating my fill, then brutishly huddling among other warm bodies" (99). He develops a deeper awareness of his own sinfulness. Yet when he finally escapes the infection and fever, he thanks God for restoring his health and experiences the kind of exaltation he has known occasionally in prayer in France: "It was as though Paul Laforgue no longer existed . . . but instead a body and mind made for Jesus did Jesus' will. . . . Everything that he did, everything that he suffered, he did and suffered as a Jesuit, for the greater glory of God. God had tested him and would test him further. . . . God is with me. God honors me with this task" (120–21).

He is indeed tested further, made to undergo hideous torture as a captive of the Iroquois, again made to feel inadequate when he tries to baptize Annuka's dying mother and realizes that he is too late: "Tears came to his eyes as he saw her glazed pupils gaze past him at those heavens now forever denied her" (154–55). He demonstrates great courage in the face of torture, while he and Daniel chant the "Ave Maria" as their "war song." The real testing follows his escape from the Iroquois. He has lost almost all hope of reaching the Huron village that is his goal: "He who all his life had put his trust in God now paddled silent, . . . his mind empty of prayer. At night he lay down like an animal and slept without thought of his nightly devotions. It was as though in these last days of degradation, pain and horror, his mind had become numb to moral judgments" (182).

But he presses on to the Huron country, only to discover a village wracked by disease and villagers convinced that the Jesuit "sorcerers" are responsible. They have already killed one Jesuit; now they plan to torture Laforgue and Father Jerome to death, and only an eclipse of the sun saves the priests. When Father Jerome thanks God for this miracle, Laforgue feels "no sense of miracle" (223). Instead, he asks himself, "Is this the martyrdom, the glorious end I once desired with all my heart and all my soul? Why have I ceased to pray? . . . The Savages will not come to kill me. God did not choose me to be a martyr. He knows I am unworthy of that fate" (224–25). Again, we see what Laforgue cannot see, that his ordeal has disillusioned him but made him a more effective instrument of God's will.

Father Jerome is anxious to take advantage of the Indians' fear and sickness and baptize them all immediately, but Laforgue argues that they should be instructed first. Still, deferring to his superior's wishes, he prepares for mass baptisms. At this point, Jerome is slaughtered by a terrified Indian and, left alone, Laforgue faces the emptiness of his heart and prays for belief to return. When the village chief says the people are ready for baptism and Laforgue hesitates, the chief asks,

"Are you our enemy?"
"No."

"Do you love us?"
"Yes."
"Then baptize us." (245)

Moments earlier, he had knelt before the tabernacle and an image of
the Virgin; he "looked at the empty eyes of the statuette as though, in
them, some hint might be given him of that mystery which is the silence
of God. But the statuette was wooden, carved by men. The hosts in the
tabernacle were bread, dubbed the body of Christ in a ritual strange as
any performed by these Savages. . . . a wooden box and a painted statuette could not restore his faith. Yet somehow he must try" (242). Confronted by the chief's demand, he wonders, "What *was* God's will? He
looked at the tabernacle. He felt the silence. *Do you love us? Yes*" (245).
Baptizing the villagers, he questions whether indeed he is doing God's
will, whether his act is "true baptism or mockery. . . . a prayer came to
him, a true prayer at last. *Spare them. Spare them, O Lord. Do you love us?*
Yes" (246).

Black Robe ends with these words, with a man torn by doubt but buoyed
by a new hope in "a true prayer at last." The question and answer repeated
three times in the closing paragraphs of the novel reverberates with meaning. When Laforgue agrees that he loves the Indians (what else, after all,
is Christianity about?), God's assumed response affirms His love for them
all. The repetition of the question and answer recalls a passage in the
final chapter of St. John's Gospel, when Jesus asks Peter three times,
"Lovest thou me?" When Peter responds, "Yea, Lord; thou knowest that
I love thee," Jesus says, "Feed my lambs. Feed my sheep" (21: 15–19).
This exchange follows Peter's sin of denial and sense of failure; it restores
the close bond between him and the Lord. Paul Laforgue, too, has sinned
and felt failure. God ratifies his work and supersedes the failures. In the
Gospel, Jesus concludes the exchange by referring to the martyrdom Peter
will eventually suffer; Laforgue's experience confirms that martyrdom takes
many forms, but central always is the martyr's conformity to God's will,
a conformity Laforgue earnestly seeks in all his actions.

But questions remain to haunt the reader. Laforgue's objection to Father
Jerome's enthusiasm for mass baptisms is valid, yet valid also is Father
Jerome's concern that the villagers be baptized so that they will go to
heaven if the disease strikes them. As usual in Brian Moore's fiction, there
are no easy answers, no clearcut conclusions. Paul Laforgue doubts the
efficacy of his actions, but through Moore's presentation we sense that,
sub specie aeternitatis, his mission has been successful.

In his next and most recent novel, *The Color of Blood*, Moore dispenses
with detailed interior monologues and focuses on a fast-moving plot, the
closest he has come to writing a thriller. Although Moore takes some
trouble to make clear that Cardinal Stephen Bem is not Polish, the dif-
ficulties he faces closely resemble those of the Cardinal-Archbishop of
Warsaw. Unlike O'Malley and Laforgue, Bem is confident of God's action
in his life but, like them, he experiences God as silence. At the beginning
of the novel, as he tries to "withdraw into that silence where God waited
and judged,"[8] an unknown assailant attempts to assassinate him. He is
thus forcefully reminded that his red Cardinal's robes represent the blood
Christ shed for His people. His baptismal name, of course, is that of the
first Christian martyr. Shortly after the assassination attempt, Bem prays
in his room, before "a lithograph of the bruised Christ-face found on the
Turin shroud," and his words here suggest a confidence in God that never
leaves him during the extraordinary three days which follow: "I am Your
servant, created by You. All that I have I have through You and from
You. Nothing is my own. I must do everything for You and only for You"
(18).

Not a Jesuit, Bem has nevertheless been trained by them and his best
friend and confessor is a Jesuit; so he too has been formed to disponibilité.
He journeys many miles in the service of his mission, to save both his
Church and his country. The Cardinal is caught between the "Power"
and its "Raincoats," as the state and its security police are known, and
right-wingers in his own Church who object to the Concordat he has
signed with the government, demanding instead a national movement of
resistance aimed at toppling the communist state. The Catholic extremists
plan to use the forthcoming celebrations at Rywald to ignite a popular
uprising. Two hundred years before at Rywald, the September Martyrs,
110 men and women, died for their faith. Bem shares the concern of
Prime Minister Urban, his Jesuit-trained schoolmate, that such internal
strife will force "our larger neighbor" to respond with repressive measures.

In this climate, just a few days before Rywald, someone attempts to
assassinate the cardinal. Bem is then kidnapped by the extremists, escapes
his captors, is caught again, escapes again, manages to warn a union leader
that he opposes any uprising inspired by the Rywald celebrations, is arrested, negotiates with the Prime Minister for freedom to stop the revo-
lutionaries, and finally reaches Rywald in time to deliver a homily against
political violence. As he maneuvers through these incredible developments, various thoughts cross his mind. For example, after he first escapes
his kidnappers, he is picked up by the local police but fortuitously released:
"Into his mind like a half-forgotten incantation came the words: *Pro nomine*

Jesu contumelias pati. To suffer in Jesus' name. That is now my fate and I must give thanks for it. My task is to serve you. For that task I must be free" (62). He is a realist; he knows that he possesses more power than the "Power" itself "not because the people love God, but because they fear their leaders. God's kingdom cannot be of this world. That is why I walk these streets as a fugitive" (64).

Moving incognito, without Roman collar or episcopal ring, he experiences the lives of his people and gains new insight into their hardships. Blessing the family of the union leader, "he closed his eyes seeking, once again, to enter that place of silence where God waited, watched and judged. O Lord, we ask Your blessing. Grant us peace" (119–20). When he is arrested and recognized, he remembers Saint Paul's words about the inscrutability of God's ways and he recalls, "To suffer contumely in Jesus' name, wasn't that what I once wished for?" (125). The story moves swiftly to a startling conclusion as Bem prays, "From now on, I must draw the danger toward me. As always, I am Your servant. Do with me what You will" (145).

Escorted and protected by the Raincoats, Cardinal Bem reaches Rywald but, as he vests for the procession and the Mass celebrating the martyrs, the kidnappers again threaten him. At last, with the prime minister in attendance at the shrine, he delivers the homily he hopes will move his people in the right direction, away from the inflammatory rhetoric preached by his fellow prelate Krasnoy. After days of journeying in every possible conveyance and risking his life on several occasions, he accomplishes his mission; he warns his people that "there must be no demonstration of the national will, no demonstration of any kind" (180). Moments later, as he distributes Communion,

> the next communicant did not open her mouth. She stared up at him
> . . . [He recognizes the driver of the car from which the assassin shot
> at him four nights earlier.] Then he saw the revolver that she had taken
> from her handbag and in that moment knew: This is God's will. Yet
> . . . he felt a moment's hesitation. It was as though he stood on the
> edge of a dark crevasse, unable to see the other side. The silence of
> God: would it change at the moment of his death? He held up the Host
> as though to give it to her. He saw her finger tighten on the trigger.
> And heard that terrible noise. (182)

Yet again, Brian Moore leaves us with an open-ended conclusion. Has Stephen Bem, true to his namesake, suffered a martyr's death at the instigation of Catholic extremists? Or has a Raincoat hidden behind the altar observed the girl and shot her before she can fire at Bem? The concluding words of the novel, quoted above, certainly argue for Bem's martyrdom, but not definitively. Even if Bem is martyred, will his impassioned plea for peace be heeded? Will his arduous struggle be vindicated? Or will the crowds now listen to the extremist Archbishop Krasnoy?

Encountering the silence of God, each of Moore's priests loses his will in the will of God. It is possible to trace a progression in these three: O'Malley has lost his faith and fears he will never regain it; Laforgue doubts his faith but then hears God; Bem trusts in God and embraces the silence. As His very different instruments, they accomplish God's design and thus succeed in their missions. Although only Stephen Bem surrenders (most likely) his physical life in the service of God, all three earn the accolade of martyrdom.

Notes

1. Thomas Beckett's sermon on Christmas morning, in the "Interlude" of *Murder in the Cathedral,* T. S. Eliot, *The Complete Poems and Plays, 1909–1950* (New York: Harcourt, 1962), 199.

2. *The Lonely Passion of Judith Hearne* (New York: Dell Publishing Co., 1964), 209.

3. *Catholics* (New York: Holt, Rinehart, 1973), 70. Subsequent references appear in parentheses in the text.

4. One is reminded of the waiter in Ernest Hemingway's 1933 story, "A Clean, Well-Lighted Place," who prays, "Our nada who art in nada, nada be thy name thy kingdom nada thy will be nada in nada as it is in nada." (*"The Snows of Kilimanjaro" and Other Stories* [New York: Scribner's, 1970], 32.)

5. "Mystery, Miracle, and Faith in Brian Moore's *Catholics,*" *Éire-Ireland* (Autumn 1975):87.

6. *Black Robe* (New York: Dutton, 1985), 101–2. Subsequent references appear in parentheses in the text.

7. "I'm a person who doesn't know. It's not intelligent to be convinced that there's no such thing as a force, as God. It is intelligent to think about it, to wonder about it." Quoted in Michael J. Farrell, "The Lonely Passion of Brian Moore," *National Catholic Reporter,* 13 September 1985, 17.

8. *The Color of Blood* (New York: Dutton, 1987), 2. Subsequent references appear in parentheses in the text.

Sons and Fathers in John McGahern's Short Stories

Eileen Kennedy

John McGahern is surely one of the best living Irish writers of fiction. In his four novels, *The Barracks* (1963), *The Dark* (1965), *The Leavetaking* (1974), and *The Pornographer* (1979), he shows himself a master of an economical, spare, and resonating prose style. Critics have examined the thrust and techniques of his novels, but his collections of short stories, except for reviews at the time of publication, have not received much scrutiny. Highly praised, the stories are rarely explicated—perhaps because they place heavy demands on the reader and the effect is felt more in the reverberations than in the narrative itself. Each detail in the stories is heavily freighted; dialogue—clipped, even elliptical—subtly advances the movement, and the climax is reached almost imperceptibly.

Of the twenty-three narratives in the author's first two volumes of stories, *Nightlines* (1973) and *Getting Through* (1980), fifteen are set in rural Ireland, that countryside of farms and small towns west of the Shannon where the author grew up. Of these fifteen, ten center on the son–father relationship. In McGahern's landscape persons use others to insulate themselves against poverty, loneliness, and abandonment—and nowhere is this to be seen more clearly than in the author's portrayal of the son–father relationship.

The misshaping begins in childhood, McGahern seems to say. Take "Coming into his Kingdom," for example. Here a motherless boy listens to hints about sex in his schoolmates' jeers, and he bribes his older sister for more details. Think of the bull and cow they have seen, she tells him. The new knowledge scares the boy but fills him with desire. He thinks of his father's sexual fumblings with him, and he remembers how when his mother was alive he wanted "to creep into her bed and touch every

65

part of her body with his lips and the tips of his fingers" (*Nightlines*, 28).
A terrible sense of aloneness fills him. He senses dimly that his desire for
his mother and his father's furtive acts are somehow wrong—to be censored
by the "Our Father" he breaks into. As the title "Coming into his Kingdom" ironically suggests, the knowledge of sex is a terrifying, isolating,
and yet pleasurable experience that collides with the moral values taught
in school. In "Christmas," a less successful story (perhaps too manipulative, too consciously artistic), a troubled boy, a ward of the state, lives
with the Morans but secretly wishes for a real home with a rich neighbor,
Mrs. Grey. When she gives him an expensive model airplane for Christmas, he burns it, and kicking the smoldering toy, he has a bitter sense of
new life, one that grows "out of the ashes, out of the stupidity of human
wishes" (*Nightlines*, 36). All of his past experiences have shown him the
folly of hope. Why should he think his life could be better? In "Strandhill,
The Sea," the adolescent narrator, bored with the competitive talk at the
guest house on a rainy day, and ashamed that his schoolteacher father is
bested in conversation by his peers, escapes to the drugstore where he
steals three comic books. Their heroes transport him among the "performing gods," which he desires to become.

"Bomb Box" takes its title from the bit of war surplus a father bought
to hold his savings and will. In this story, which is almost a parody of the
Resurrection, the hypochondriac sergeant determines he is mortally ill.
His first step is to throw all the responsibilities of keeping the motherless
family together on his fifteen-year-old son. The boy is terrified by the
overwhelming duties thrust on him so casually; but the father cunningly
reinforces his commands by couching them in language that echoes Christ's
injunctions to his apostles. For the boy, then, terror at his new responsibilities is compounded by guilt feelings should he fail to fulfill them; and
his turbulent emotions are encapsulated in one symbol—the key to the
bomb box, the strong-box he was to open only if his father died. When
the hospital finds nothing wrong with the imaginary invalid, he rises from
his sick bed to resume his nagging and bullying. The boy, incapable of
mentioning the key to his father, but eager to rid himself of it, anxiously
and defiantly throws it as far away as he can toward the river. It fails to
hit the water; and the story suggests that though temporary release from
the father is possible, successful escape is not. In "Korea," another boy,
slightly older, listens to his father, the last in his townland to make his
living by fishing, urge him to emigrate to the United States. While in
the lavatory, the boy overhears the real reason: his father, speaking of a
neighbor's son who emigrated, said the father got a little money when the

son was drafted into the army, and when he was killed, the father got $10,000. Because the ban on fishing will make the father's livelihood nonexistent, he is calculating another way to survive, and in his fear and greed he is willing to risk his son being killed. With this new knowledge, the boy decides against going to America, and he says in words echoing ironically his father's, "It'll be my own funeral" (*Nightlines*, 69).

"The Stoat" tells of a young medical student, vacationing with his widowed father at Strandhill, who comes upon a rabbit, slick with blood, its jugular vein cut by a long grey stoat. The student, holding the rabbit's body "trembling in a rigidity of terror" (*Getting Through*, 59), kills the rabbit with one stroke and takes it with him. He joins his father, a pedantic schoolteacher who wishes to remarry for companionship, a desire the son shares so that he will not be shackled by his father's need for companionship. His father receives numerous replies to his ad for a possible mate, women he labels "wrecks and battleaxes" (*Getting Through*, 63). Finally, the father meets the nervous Miss McCabe, well into her forties and excitable. At the opening of the story, the father and son are in a cottage at Strandhill, Miss McCabe is staying at the local hotel, and the two are engaged in a chaste courtship, pragmatic on the father's side, pathetic on hers. If all goes well on this holiday, they will become engaged before school opens. Wanting to encourage the marriage, the son suggests he cook the rabbit for dinner and invite Miss McCabe to join them. At dinner Miss McCabe, anxious to please, lets them know that she has savings the son would be welcome to for his postgraduate work. "Soiled by meal and rabbit and whole evening," the son realizes he, too, has been conspiring to snare the willing Miss McCabe (*Getting Through*, 67). But the next day when they learn that Miss McCabe has suffered a severe heart attack in the salt baths, the news makes the father break the proposed engagement; he bolts for home and wants his son to come with him. The son, however, sees now another chance for freedom: he will stay with his uncle, a doctor. As for Miss McCabe: she is the rabbit for whom the stoat, death, had marked for his prey. In the selfishness of the father and son, only the son seems more sympathetic because he has some insight into Miss McCabe's pathetic condition and his part in the complicity. And yet, according to his law of survival, he, too, must abandon her to death.

In all six stories the father, or surrogate father, is rejected, in one way or another, by the son; the father in "Coming into his Kingdom" is pictured as so frustrated sexually that he uses his son to fulfill his erotic needs; the surrogate father in "Christmas" is a heavy drinker who covets the tip his ward may get; the father in "Bomb Box" is a self-pitying bully; the school-

teacher father in "Strandhill, The Sea" is timid and ineffectual, so cowed
by his fellow boarders that his son escapes into fantasy through klepto-
mania. Only in "Korea," where the father will chance his son dying so
that his old age will be financially secure, is there some forgiveness on
the son's part. The son, feeling his "youth had ended," watches closely
his father fishing, "as if I too had to prepare myself to murder" (*Nightlines*,
69). The suggestion here is the Freudian one: that the son, to establish
his own self, must psychically murder his father, just as his father to survive
would risk his death. The insight into his father's motive—and the realization of his own potential deed—brings some sense of understanding
of the father by the son. And in "The Stoat" the medical student, though
breaking free of his callous father, realizes how selfish he, too, can be.
As McGahern's protagonists reach early manhood, they become aware
not only of their fathers' failures but also of their own potential cold-
heartedness.

Only in one story, "Faith, Hope, and Charity" does the father seem to
be a finer person than the son, but that relationship is used to highlight
the differences between two kinds of civilization, two contrasting ways of
looking at life. Joe Cunningham is an illegal construction worker in England who slaves all year long to make a big splash the month he spends
at home in Ireland. Greedy, stupid, and careless, full of hatred for England, he is killed on a construction site when a trench caves in. In Ireland the schoolteacher James Sharkey drives to the Cunningham farm
where the family are working in the hayfields. They receive the news
quietly, the father saying he will have to go to London to bring the body
home, "to do the best by him [Joe] the few days more he'll be with us"
(*Getting Through*, 54). In a move he cannot afford, the father flies to
London, brings the coffin back with him, and two days later his son is
buried. The leading villagers—the priest, the postman, and the teacher—
gather for a meeting. Whether it was a wise thing or not to fly the body
home is not the question. The question is how to pay for the funeral costs
so that the old father will not have to go to England to work. The trio
decide the village will raise the money through a dance, where the musicians will be Faith, Hope, and Charity, three old bachelor brothers who
will play for a few crates of stout. On a clear night in September when
the harvest moon shines on the fields, the dance is held, with the old
coming to put in an appearance and the young to enjoy the merriment.
The debt is paid: the father will not have to go to England.

The story gains its resonance from the quiet contrasts, which creep on
the reader unaware, between the two civilizations, one agricultural, the

other industrial. The son curses and digs in the trenches where no machine can go; the family, rooted in the land, rake in the hay together. In England the son, full of hatred for the country, feels alienated; in Ireland a tacit sense of community binds the villagers together. At the news of the death the cursing foreman on the construction site orders the men back to work immediately; out in the hayfield the family join together to say the "De Profundis." But "Faith, Hope, and Charity" is no sentimental picture by Millet. McGahern undercuts any sentimentality inherent in the situation by using, as a character here, a recurring figure in his stories, the disappointed bachelor teacher, James Sharkey, who wonders if the young country lovers at the dance are as happy as the postman thinks. And the three old musicians, whose nickname embodies the three theological virtues, appear more comic than saintly. Through subtle modulation the narrative uses the son–father relationship to underscore the contrasts between Ireland and England and to lay bare the meaning of the easily uttered triad, Faith, Hope, and Charity.

It is in three stories—"Wheels," "Gold Watch," and "Sierra Leone"—that McGahern probes most deeply the son–father relationship, but no one, so far as I know, has pointed out that although the stories were published separately, they all concern the same son and father and the final resolution of their painful bond. In point of fact, the stories, if put together, could be a novella.

The plot of "Wheels," the opening story in *Nightlines*, is deceptively simple. A young man pays an overnight visit to his old father who lives on a farm with Rose, the son's stepmother, and the farmer's patient and hard-working wife. The father refuses to acknowledge his son's presence, even eating his meal silently while Rose and the son watch him. Finally the son forces the issue, and the old man spits out his venom. Against his father's wishes, the son, years earlier had left the farm for his freedom in the city. Then the father, iron-willed in his determination that the son care for him, had asked the son to find him a home in the city. He would, the son said, but he would not live with his father there. Playing on the son's sense of guilt, the old farmer now weeps and claims: "The one important thing I ever asked you you couldn't even be bothered" (*Nightlines*, 14). The parent-child relationship, the son sees, is like the turn of the wheel:

> Fathers become children to their sons who repay the care they got when
> they were young, and on the edge of dying the fathers become young

again, but the luck of a death and a second marriage had released [him]
from the last breaking of the ritual wheel. (*Nightlines*, 15).

The story is also Rose's: in old age she is bound to her husband in a
mixture of hatred and caring, waiting on him, putting up with his violent
moods and anger, and knowing, the reader senses, that he prefers the son
to her. Married too late to have children of her own, she finds that any
dreams she may have had are useless. Now her life is reduced to serving
an old man who regrets his second marriage: if he did not have Rose, his
son would have to care for him. In this picture of bitter wedlock, Rose
emerges as the tacit peacemaker between father and son, the woman
without choice or hope who is unembittered by life. The story ends with
the son returning to the city and recalling childhood memories, ". . . all
the vivid sections of the wheel we watched so slowly turn, impatient for
the rich whole that never came but that all the preparations promised"
(*Nightlines*, 17). Not only is the son–father relationship a turning of the
wheel but also all of life's happy experiences are sections of the wheel. It
is foolish, however, the narrator realizes, to think those sections portend
fulfillment.

Although "Gold Watch" (which appears in *Nightlines* and is reprinted
again in *High Ground*) can stand independently of "Wheels," it continues
that relentless tug-of-war between the two men. In "Gold Watch," the
forty-year-old narrator is a successful lawyer enjoying wedded life with his
wife, probably in her mid-thirties. His father's only comment on his son's
wife is, "She looks well on her way to forty" (*Getting Through*, 126). That
statement, repeated to her, makes her determined not to go with him
when, out of duty, habit, and a forlorn hope that things will be better
with his father, he returns to the farm to help with the annual hay cutting.
When he arrives, Rose and his father tell him that the cutting has already
been done—an unforeseen and unwanted break in the rhythm of his life—
but he stays with them. During his visit he learns that his father's gold
watch—a gift from *his* father that at various milestones in his life the
narrator had hoped would be passed on to him—is broken and impossible
to fix. " 'I might as well have it,' " (*Getting Through*, 132) says the son,
laying claim to the keepsake, and he promises his father a new watch.
Soon afterward his wife, in a surprise gift that is a portent of their new
life, presents him with the gold watch—fixed.

At his next visit to the farm he presents his father with a new gold
watch—"dustproof, shockproof, waterproof" (*Getting Through*, 136). The
father is churlish about the gift, but the next morning he is flaunting it,

seemingly wanting the son to think he is forgiven. Then, in a secret gesture, the father attempts to break the watch, a repudiation of the son's claim to manhood, a rejection of the son's attempt to forge some bond between them. The watch is unbreakable. That evening the son sees the barrel of water in which his father had been preparing a lethal spray to use on the potatoes. Into that barrel of pure poison the father had put a fishing line on the end of which hangs the new watch. When the son finds it, the casing of the watch has already been eaten away by the poison, the ticking would soon stop. The son knows now the folly of his hope for reconciliation with his father. Self-will and hatred have so corroded the old man's heart that even as death grows nearer only those violent emotions keep him alive.

The final story in *Getting Through,* and the third story in this relationship, is "Sierra Leone." Here the narrator, probably in his late twenties, meets Geraldine, a beautiful black-haired woman about his age, who is always seen with Jerry McCredy, a married middle-aged Dublin politician with a reputation for womanizing. The narrator drifts into an affair with Geraldine just as she, an orphaned girl out of a convent school, had drifted into her affair with the ageing profligate. Feeling guilty in his pleasures with another man's mistress, the narrator will make no emotional commitment to her, although she wants him to and seems to be in love with him. Partly out of dependency and partly out of the lure of glamour, the rootless Geraldine, who has always maintained her own rooms, decides to follow Jerry to Sierra Leone where he has been appointed to a high government post and where he will set her up in style. The narrator sees the end of his affair with her as just another part of life. Linked to this plot—and in strong counterpoint—is another one: the narrator is called home to the farm where his father and stepmother Rose live. Although Rose has tried to make her husband's final years peaceful, the old man delights in spiting her. The father has summoned his son home to tell him of a new law likely to be enacted: the widow gets so much of a man's property after he is dead, whether he likes it or not. If Rose inherits the farm, she will leave it to her relatives and already, the father claims, they are stealing from him. To subvert this possibility, the father wants now to transfer the property to his son so that the disinherited Rose will be totally dependent on him. Even though he knows Rose is not concerned about her inheritance, the son refuses to go along with his father's malicious plan, so degrading to the faithful wife. Just as the elderly Rose has devoted her life to caring for a mean-spirited man, so the youthful Geraldine, rejected by the narrator, commits herself to a rapacious politician. Both women, McGahern seems to say, with only limited powers of choosing, are victimized by men. In the final turn of "Sierra Leone" Rose unexpectedly dies, and the two men, the father and son, are left alone on the farm together, "that is," the son says, "until things settle a bit, and we can find our feet again, and think" (*Getting Through*, 172). In this unforeseen and ironic turn of the wheel, the son may have to take care of the father, even live with him. What the son has been trying to escape for so many years, he must now accept. In these, the three most powerful stories treating the son–father relationship, there is no reconciliation and no peace, only a dazed acceptance of the inevitable.

In his latest collection of stories, *High Ground* (1985), McGahern returns twice to the theme that fascinates him, with "Oldfashioned" and the title story of the book, "High Ground." "Oldfashioned" chronicles the changes since 1945 wrought on the rural landscape and on the lives of the country people. These changes are reflected in the character of Johnny, the adolescent son of Police Sergeant Moran (who seems a combination of the sergeant in McGahern's novel, *The Barracks* and the father in the author's second work, *The Dark*). When Johnny is offered the opportunity by Colonel Sinclair, a member of the fading Ascendency, to become a British officer, his father, furious, will have none of it and orders his son to stop gardening for the Sinclairs. As the son laconically puts it, "The years his father was most proud of were the years of the War of Independence when he was the commander of a small company of men on the run" (*High Ground*, 45). The Sergeant thrives on a sense of injured merit, and his son should not rise higher than he. The son, scholarly, quiet, and self-possessed, has learned to outwit his father by guile and assumed indifference. Through scholarships, Johnny leaves his rural surroundings and eventually becomes a documentary filmmaker of the darker side of Irish life. His work is celebrated and controversial. But despite his fame and success, his attempts to get on with his father are vain. In their rarer and rarer meetings, the father cuts him down mercilessly. When Johnny protests, the father asks him what will he do about it.

"I just won't see you."

"I don't think that will kill me." (*High Ground*, 55)

The rupture between the two is complete. As the son realizes the futility of trying to communicate with his father, the reader realizes that the father's final words seal their separation. Human contact is useless when the father is so ungiving that he refuses to acknowledge the human bond.

"High Ground," ostensibly a study in conflicting loyalties, scrutinizes the son–father relationship at a profound level and may even be an allegory of contemporary Ireland. Perhaps this is the reason the collection takes its title from it.

"High Ground" tells of the inexperienced narrator, young Moran, who must make a decision regarding the Master, his surrogate father—a choice that will affect the education of the entire rural community. One after another, the young man's illusions are destroyed as this returning star pupil must choose: for the good of the children should he accept the principalship of the local school offered by the dishonest, despised, and successful politician? To take the post would be to oust the Master, the man he dared hope he would become, once his "clear star," now a courtly, shabby alcoholic who every evening shamelessly feeds the illusions of his former students. Drinking after closing hours in Charlie's Bar, the Master with the other regulars play a nightly game. Prodded by them, the old Master reminds his ageing students how bright they were, how successful they could have been: "Ye had the brains. There are people in this part of the country digging ditches who could have been engineers or doctors. But instead they had stayed and passed on their brains to their children. (The Master's adult sons are far from clever, though none of his listeners point out this fact.) "If you had to pick one thing, Master, what would you put these brains down to?" (*High Ground*, 102) ask his fantasy-fed drinkers, eager to have the nightly "life-lie" repeated to them. The Master speaks with authority:

> "Well, the people with the brains mostly stayed here. They had to. They had no choice. They didn't go to the cities. So the brains were passed on to the next generation. Then there's the trees. There's the water. And we're very high up here. We're practically at the source of the Shannon. If I had to pick on one thing more than another, I'd put it down to that. I'd attribute it to the high ground." (*High Ground*, 102–3)

The story does not reveal Moran's final choice, but a hint is given when the narrator remembering how he had idolized the Master realizes, "It seemed horrible now that I might come to this" (*High Ground*, 99). Rather than supplant the Master, the surrogate father, the star student may go away, but the story reverberates with a deeper subtext. If the brightest seem to emigrate, how do those who remain cope with their near-poverty? And how responsible are they for their rationalizations, their dwelling on past glories, their escape into alcoholism? The surrogate father may appear benign but his failing nurtures the failings of his former students.

Fathers are seen only through their sons' eyes in McGahern's stories, and the author has no stories, so far as I can determine, in which sons are seen through the fathers' eyes—although a weak argument could be made for "Faith, Hope and Charity." In the stories where the narrator is still in early adolescence, the son rejects or repudiates the father. In the stories where the son is an adult, he tries to keep the frail ties from completely breaking. But if the son has some insight into or understanding of the father, the father, in these relentless mirrors, has none. In old age fathers are stamped with obdurate bitterness; sons sometimes can accept, with near-fatalism, the loss of hope of reconciliation. But in McGahern's world, sons do *not* become like their fathers: too long a sacrifice has not made a stone of their hearts. The final resolution may be sad, even grim, but it is not despairing.

Works Cited

McGahern, John. *Getting Through*. New York: Harper, 1980.
———. *High Ground*. London: Faber, 1985; New York: Viking, 1987.
———. *Nightlines*. London: Granada, 1973.

Notes from the Land of Loss: Thomas Kinsella's Latest Work, 1980–1987

Daniel T. O'Hara

Thomas Kinsella has devoted most of his energies over the last decade to two major scholarly projects: An *Duanaire: Poems of the Dispossessed, 1600–1690* (Dolmen: 1981) and *The New Oxford Book of Irish Verse* (1986). These two volumes, together with his other translation and editorial achievement, *The Tain* (1969), span the dual tradition of Irish poetry, as Kinsella understands it, from the beginnings to the present. (He is currently working on a book in which he will lay out that understanding at greater length than prefaces and introductions permit.) In the last three years, he has also published the final four volumes of poetry for his Peppercanister Press; his *Songs of the Psyche* (1985), *Her Vertical Smile* (1985), *Out of Ireland* (1987), and *St. Catharine's Clock* (1987). Like his earlier collections for Wake Forest, *Poems, 1956–1973* and *Peppercanister Poems, 1972–1978*, each set of two volumes represent Kinsella's work in, respectively, the short lyric and the long poem made out of suites of lyrics. (*Songs of the Psyche* and *Out of Ireland* collect individual poems, and *Her Vertical Smile* and *St. Catharine's Clock* are single poems in their own right.)

The recurrent theme of all the poems, and it also hangs over the translations, selections, and introductions in the scholarly editions, is put best by Kinsella himself in reflecting on John Scotus's pedagogical fate in "The Land of Loss" from *Out of Ireland:*

> Nothing certain of this world,
> Iohannes teaches,
> except for certain impediments
> we might carry with ourselves:

our legs bound, for our failure
to walk in the Divine Law;
our hands hindered, for their hesitation
in virtuous deeds;

and it grows dark and we stumble
in gathering ignorance
in a land of loss
and unfulfillable desire.

He himself was driven out of France
and half way home
for heresy.

He taught at the Abbey at Malmesbury
and died there
at his students' hands

They stabbed him
with their pens
because he made them think.

(16)

Like a contemporary version of a medieval emblem poem, "The Land of Loss" has the effect of aphoristic wisdom, even if, unlike some of its ancient models, it achieves that effect by conceptual rigor, rhetorical purity, and imagistic economy. Traditional religious sentiment is deployed to express a modern's perennial sense of abandonment and betrayal.

Kinsella's poetry is really like no other being written today in the English language. It scorns all obvious musical effects, even as it aspires to the condition of a more difficult music. And, as the line about the "unfulfillable" nature of human desire makes clear, it does not court a self-conscious stance of innocent optimism before those things none of us cannot not know, such as the inevitability of loss and death. This poetry is a poetry of meditative exactitude and self-examination concerning the sources—personal, historical, political, and "metaphysical"—of those unforgetable experiences that make the self what it must be. (Out of Ireland, for instance, is subtitled "a metaphysical love sequence.") The pattern of identifications and detachments that constitute the affective life of the imagination is the subject matter of Kinsella's latest, as of his earliest, work.

St. Catharine's Clock is my choice for the finest recent example of Kinsella's characteristic achievement. It is a poem whose theme is indicated by its epigraph: ". . . chosen and lifted up against the light / for the Fisherman's thumb / and the bowel-piercing hook." In other words, what follows in the volume are to be significant experiences selected for examination because of their consummate pang. The first section of the poem enlarges this theme, and indicates how the entire poem is formally organized:

> The whole terrace
> slammed shut.
> I inhaled the granite lamplight,
> divining the energies of the prowler.
>
> A window opposite, close up.
> In a corner, a half stooped image
> focused on the intimacy
> of the flesh of the left arm.
>
> The fingers of the right hand are set
> in a scribal act on the skin:
> a gloss, simple and swift as thought,
> is planted there.
>
> The point uplifted,
> wet with understanding,
> he leans his head a moment
> against the glass.
>
> I see.
>
> Thomas Street at the first hour.
> The clock
> on the squat front of Saint Catharine's
> settled a gilded point
> up soundless into place.
>
> (7–8)

Alert as a prowler, the speaker becomes a voyeur of his own pain as he observes the self-inflicted, self-tormenting pleasure of being an addict of

Faustian knowledge. As the terms used to describe the injection make clear, we can see the emblematic significance of the experience for the poet. We sense, as well, the organizing presence of the passing of time, itself like a painful injection of experiental loss but formal order, settling "a gilded point / up soundless into place." (The cover design depicts the black hands of a clock telling the third hour from which falls into empty space a single blood-red drop.)

The rest of St. Catharine's Clock alternates between personal memories of childhood and the cultural memory of Ireland's troubled history, as enshrined in paintings and illustrations, often made by English rather than Irish artists, thereby doubling the sense of pain and loss with the implicit knowledge of such alienating representation. The final section speaks directly and allegorically about what the poet has learned about his own and his country's fatal identity:

> 1740
>
> About the third hour.
>
> Ahead, at the other end
> of the darkened market-place
>
> a figure crossed over
>
> out of Francis Street
> reading the ground, all dressed up
> in black, like a madwoman.

Ireland as an old mad woman and the Irish poet as her self-sacrificing son emerges from the process of "reading the ground" of Thomas Kinsella's self, via this Swiftian figure.

The long middle section of the poem (13–19) details the personal family history of the poet in ways that freshens territory familiar from earlier volumes, especially *Notes From the Land of the Dead* (1973). In an un-published response to some questions I put to him, Kinsella selects as his most typical achievement the "establishment of 'character' via eye of actual infancy, youth operating on first significant experiences of thing, event, person, relationship. . . ." And here the reader encounters once again the young boy first tasting desire and loss in the events of family

life, especially as they cluster around the figure of his grandmother, the
personal model for the final figure previously cited. In addition, however,
this section also discloses one source of a form of comic judgment uniquely
Kinsella's own:

> Sometimes some of the aunts
> wouldn't talk for weeks,
> in a bad temper after passing remarks.
>
> They chewed their teeth
> and passed each other by
> with their glasses and stiff faces.
>
> But some of them would keep muttering
> together in the middle room.
> And then someone one day suddenly
>
> would laugh up out of her throat
> and all the put-on pain and the high snout
> would go out of their stares.
>
> (15)

This vignette is crucial for any comprehensive understanding of Kinsella's
poetry, which is far from being simply the dour and stoical recitation of
the vicissitudes of existence. Humor plays an increasingly important part
in the career, so much so that *Her Vertical Smile* (a title that is as bawdy
as anything in Chaucer's "The Miller's Tale") concludes with a self-parodic
coda literally revealing all concerning the would-be Faustian composer-
poet of epic works:

> Nine are the enabling clements
>   in the higher crafts
> and the greatest of these is Luck.
>
> I lift my
>   baton and my
> trousers fall.
>
> (25)

This capacity for comic (self-) judgment helps to compose that difficult
music I mentioned earlier, which Kinsella himself realizes has been seen

as typically Irish. One of the notes appended to the poems in *Out of Ireland* comes from Giraldus Cambrensis's description of the Irish people's art of polyphony, and it applies equally as well to Kinsella's own representative effect: "They glide so subtly from one mode to another, and the grace notes so freely sport with such abandon and bewitching charm around the steady tone of the heavier sound, that the perfection of their art seems to lie in their concealing it" (26). So, too, comedy in the latest poems freely sports "around the steady tone of the heavier sound," which is the still sad music that humanity makes in the passage of time:

> On the right,
> up in the slatted turret,
> a tooth on the big measuring wheel
>
> re-engaged,
> protestant,
> inch by inch.
>
> (24)

Thus concludes the main portion of *St. Catharine's Clock* on the central theme of Kinsella's career—how, as in the more extreme experiences of sexual love, human beings acquire the taste of time—which another recent poem, "Model School, Inchicore" from *Songs of the Pscyhe,* sums up in terms of the bitter origins of the poet's art:

> I sat by myself in the shed
> and watched the draught
> blowing papers
> around the wheels of bicycles.
>
> Will God judge
>   out most secret thoughts and actions?
> God will judge
>   our most secret thoughts and actions
> and every idle word that man shall speak
> he shall render an account of it
> on the Day of Judgment.

The taste
of ink off
the nib shrank your
mouth.

(12–13)

Kinsella writes poems that read like excerpts from the bleakest of gnostic mythologies about living in an essentially demonic world. And yet, their final effect is never merely fatalistic. Instead, there is always another opening of possibility for the creation that arises out of love:

God is good but
he had to start
somewhere out of the ache
of I am

and lean Himself
over the mothering pit
in faith
thinking

a mouth
to My kiss
in opening

let there be
remote
("A New Beginning," *Songs
of the Psyche*, 39)

However remote it appears, what we get equally from life and Kinsella's poetry is another "let there be."

The Price of Stone: New Directions in Richard Murphy's Poetry

James D. Brophy

When Richard Murphy was teaching at Bard College in 1973, he told me that while writing the poems of *High Island* he had thought that "they might turn out to be a lyric sequence equivalent to a long poem." "But that," he remarked with disappointment, "did not happen." Why so, he did not say, and unfortunately I did not pursue what now seems an important point in the light of his new collection, *The Price of Stone.*[1]

A few years earlier Murphy had written *The Battle of Aughrim* (1968), a traditional kind of long poem divided into clearly organizing parts designated "Now," "Before," "During," and "After." *High Island,* however, was twenty-seven apparently autonomous poems, each with its own title. Since Murphy had thought that this group could have turned out to be the equivalent of a long poem, he obviously recognizes at least two types of extended poem: the more or less conventional (like his *Battle of Aughrim*) and what, in the light of his own remarks, I might somewhat tentatively call the "collective" or "sequential" long poem where the organizing parameters are subtle and, perhaps, as one gathers from Murphy's comment on *High Island,* so elusive as to be almost serendipitous.

The Price of Stone is an important development in Murphy's career. In appearing to be the fulfillment of his earlier desire for a "lyric sequence or the equivalent of a long poem," it has a new formal complexity. And in placing emphasis on the imperatives of human love rather than those of belonging to a place and community, it is distinctly different from his previous work's central concerns of *pietas* and Ireland.[2]

82

I

The Price of Stone principally consists of fifty sonnets (part 2). Although each sonnet is individually titled, the group assumes the character of a sonnet sequence or the equivalent of a long poem (with the title "The Price of Stone"). What is more formally ambiguous in this edition are the preceding twenty-one poems that are presented as part 1. Although these twenty-one poems are individually titled and are separated from the fifty sonnets, they have such a special relationship to them that I believe they are an integral part of the sonnet sequence of part 2 and function as a prefiguring of those poems that have the eponymous title of the British edition. These two parts of *The Price of Stone* have such a number of remarkable parallels and connections that it is my conclusion that they are meant to suggest in Murphy's own phrase, "the equivalent of a long poem": *The Price of Stone* consisting of "Part 1" and "Part 2: The Price of Stone."

The first poem of part 1, "Moonshine," immediately strikes me as being incongruously flippant and cynical about love. It concludes:

> Alone I love
> To think of us together:
> Together I think
> I'd love to be alone.

This does not sound like a poet who to my knowledge has never published a flippant or cynical line. And indeed, "Moonshine" signals and ushers in a new Richard Murphy—not, I hasten to add, one that is flippant or cynical. What "Moonshine" does brilliantly is to trap us into a rejection of love, a rejection we find more and more incongruous as we read the subsequent poems. "Care," the next one, is a litany of loving services to an infant goat that documents the force of love. The fact that the animal dies in spite of this outpouring of love—ironically, *because* of the protective care—underlines the perilous and fragile nature of love rather than undercuts its necessity. Subsequent poems ("Trouvaille," "Mary Ure," "Shelter," and "Niches") all stress the importance of loving personal relationships, so that before we proceed very far into part 1 we are forced to reinterpret "Moonshine" and realize that Murphy is being wittily satiric with a title that must be read as "unreality" or "nonsense." To dismiss love, to want to be alone rather than together, is made to be seen as folly. "Moonshine," of course, can also be defined as "folly," the significance of which will be seen in the parallel opening of part 2 ("The Price of Stone") with the poem, "Folly."

"Swallows," the seventh poem of part 1, continues to expand on the imperatives of love in describing a woman hurrying to a tryst with her lover:

> She wades through wet rushes,
> Long autumn grass,
> Over rusty barbed wire
> And stone walls that collapse.

And here is introduced the theme that will be further developed in these poems of part 1 and especially stressed later in "The Price of Stone": the inadequacy and treachery of what stone or a structure of stone symbolizes—man's effort to establish dominion over his world. The woman hurrying to her assignation in "Swallows" leaves behind "stone walls that collapse" to find fulfillment in "a shed with a tin roof."

It is "Stone Mania," however, the next poem of this section, that most clearly suggests that part 1 is closely related to the following section, "The Price of Stone." And the direct statement of the title confirms the role of clarifying introduction that this section plays in relation to the more allusive and complex sonnet sequence. No poem of the twenty-one poems that stand as part 1 is at all ambiguous about describing the inadequacies of trusting in the values of stone for fulfillment in life. "The Price of Stone" will be more complex, in that about one third of the sonnets demonstrate that stone may play a part in the nurturing of human love, although the total picture of the sonnet sequence is one of rejection of that choice. Murphy first works out a bold outline of his main thesis in the introductory twenty-one poems (part 1) and then reworks the idea with more sophisticated care and subtlety in part 2, "The Price of Stone."

"Stone Mania" unequivocally establishes the folly of the speaker's "passion for building in granite" as a "mad obsession," which ironically keeps him away from the friends whom he is building his rooms to entertain. In a syntactically witty conclusion Murphy states that they die

> before we can say

> I'd love you to see and enjoy the house whose construction
> has kept us entirely apart.

It is clear that the real tragedy is that one's friends die before one can say "I'd love you," and that the rest of the sentence is ironic window dressing. This key poem literally demonstrates the "mania" for hurrying past "love" to seek the putative pleasures of "house."

Adumbrating comments on "mania" and "obsession" are obvious in the poems "Husbandry," "Arsonist," and "Elixir." "Husbandry" notes the "peculiar hunger" that possesses sheep in grazing on headlands to lean over the edge to reach a tuft of grass. This perilous pursuit above the "raging sea" that makes Murphy dizzy to watch suggests in context that it is not man alone who is prone to foolish acquisition. The punning "husbandry" suggests that one (shepherd as well as husband) who cares for seeks to remove this danger:

> If I were their shepherd.
> I'd put them to fatten in a small safe paddock

"Arsonist" describes the owner who is so "possessed" by his house and so burdened with debt that all he can think of is how he can burn it down. The act is not attempted, and the obsession with "his tongued and grooved floors" is so absolute that we suspect that it never will be, that he will be locked in his perverse stasis forever. "Elixir" is about the alchemy of "turning a stone house into seven figures," old granite walls to "bars of gold," "his home into a foreign room," all of which turned "his heart to zero." The theme here is the misuse of stone: that a "home" is desirable, but speculating on real estate to make a "killing" indeed kills the heart. This note prefigures the kind of greater complexity we will see more of in "The Price of Stone" where the perverse obsession with stone and its symbolic dominion tends to displace the benign, and ultimately the poet's choice is to transcend the risks of material possession for the realm of personal love. Each stanza of "Elixir" begins with "turning," emphasizing the endless anxiety and restlessness of a perverse mania. Alternatively, "A Nest in a Wall" presents the peaceful haven of personal love that loosens "the stonework of [the] heart." In that life

> Although we have no home in the time that's come,
> Coming together we live in our own time,

and the conclusion sets forth the priorities of all of the collection in the injunction:

Make your nest of moss like a wren in my skull.

Although I have said above that part 1 is more direct and accessible than its succeeding part, I do not wish to give the impression that it is lacking in subtleties and indirections. It is less complex than "The Price of Stone," but it has its interesting dimensions of irony. "Altar," for example, describes a large boulder that has blocked his "way to get behind the house." The poet asks, "Was it a mass-rock . . . better left undisturbed?" and without answering proceeds to bury "the bald obtruder." Acknowledging the use of stone by religion and perhaps the religion of stone conveys further meaning to what becomes a symbolic burial.

As a final demonstration of the parallel work of part 1 with "The Price of Stone" I adduce the concluding poem of the first part, "Visiting Hour." Here the opening line is "How can I comfort you? What can I say" probably directed to the Tony White who has been the subject of two previous poems in this section, in one of which ("Tony White") the poet praises Tony for seeing that "Nothing but unpossessive love could cure" the "disease" that afflicted his friends: the "increase" of "incomes, houses, families." In "Visiting Hour" White is dying in a hospital bed with only the comfort that his "poetry will stay unblurred." And although there is irony in the observation that his words cannot renew his life, there is the traditional consolation in the thought that while life is short, art is long. Importantly for the function of this poem in the collection, the theme of the insubstantial nature of possessions is paramount and compelling. As we shall see below, the ultimate poem of the total collection, "Natural Son," similarly has its setting in a hospital, and while, significantly, the scene is of birth rather than death, there is the same emphasis on acknowledging something that transcends the realms of material possessions. Why Murphy does not underline the priceless nature of human love in "Visiting Hour" as he does in "Natural Son" is not easy to say, but I have a suggestion. He has in a number of poems throughout part 1 (as we have seen above) stated the overriding value of personal love demonstrating rather obviously the parallel and introductory nature of part 1 to part 2. To mirror "Natural Son" in "Visiting Hour" would seem mechanical and obvious. As this part of the long poem stands, there is the sense of incompleteness, a sense that although the lesson of love has been stated, it has not been fully accepted or understood. It is after all not an easy lesson to learn, and one of the achievements of *The Price of Stone*, as it works through the twenty-one poems of part 1 and the fifty sonnets of part 2, is conveying the sense of process in learning to be loving. There is indeed more to be said and understood in part 2.

II

"Folly," the arresting opening poem of "The Price of Stone" (part 2 of *The Price of Stone*), introduces us to Murphy's technique of creating a persona for each of the structures that speak from and describe the past. It ironically confronts us at the outset with the absurdity of the "Lord's pride" that constructed the folly to establish dominion over the landscape. The opening lines:

> I rise from a circle standing on a square
> And cock my dunce's cap at the firmament

and the final lines:

> My four doors bricked up against vandals, still
> Tumescent, scrawled with muck, I crest the hill

set forth unambiguously Murphy's attitude toward the love of land and building that will be further satirized in "The Price of Stone" and that has previously been satirized in part 1 for having replaced or prevented personal love. "Folly" is an emblematic beginning not only with the above connections but also, I believe, with allusion to Wallace Stevens's "Anecdote of the Jar" where a similar statement of dominion ("It made the slovenly wilderness / Surround that hill") symbolizes a benign power of art very different from the risible vainglory ("I crest the hill") of Murphy's folly. Murphy's sequential long poem does not go on to develop Stevens's theme, but I believe that he employs ironic allusion to it to reinforce the rejection of this malevolent position of "lord's pride." More obviously, in satirizing the dominion symbolized by stone there is also operative here not only some implicit political satire (the "Folly" being of colonial,

Anglo-Irish origin), but also an effective parallel with Shelley's "Ozymandias."

The opening lines of "Folly" ("I rise from a circle standing on a square / And cock my dunce's cap at the firmament") are especially relevant as we read through the opening poems of this fifty-sonnet sequence. "Lead Mine Chimney," the second poem, opening with "Pointlessly standing up," recalls taking "the heart from oakwoods to smelt ore" and "all that foul stress" and "fury" of its furnace, and leaves us in an aura of "a sooty chill of hollowness." The lead mine persona characterizes all this as speaking "of cut stone symmetry" and as utterance "in granite style, with not a word to say." "Portico" next gives us a dark, shadowy picture of some ominous seaside structure where "ghosts questing blood" haunt "a deviate church" on "a bay of mud." The hymns that inhabit this nightmarish vision are "hog-snorts, squealing bottle-glass / Screwed underfoot." Murphy's design begins to manifest itself as revelation of the questionable past, duncelike in ignorance, and this is confirmed by the progression of the first seven sonnets, each a voice of a structure from Murphy's past adding its own particular part to the whole structure of his life.

All but three of the fifty sonnets are voices of structures: "Queen of the Castle" projects, perhaps, the voice of a nanny, "Planter Stock" that of a tree, and, importantly in conclusion, "Natural Son" the voice of the poet. The technique is unusual and very effective: the emphasis on speaking structures becomes slightly and purposefully oppressive; the diversions in "Queen" and "Planter" suggest that a change may be forthcoming. The concluding voice of the poet indeed brings that relief and accomplishment that confirms the poet's theme: it is indeed joyful to leave behind the cold world of stone and its voices for the welcome of a "birth-cry."

The "dunce's cap" of "ignorance" conferred by Murphy on his opening structure and the continuing unbroken emphasis in the first seven poems on witnesses of various degrees of error and folly suggests that the poet is creating a modern *Dunciad*. Like Pope, Murphy names "Folly" at the outset of his work: Murphy in the title of the first sonnet of "The Price of Stone" and Pope in "Close to those walls where Folly holds her throne" (1: 29). Moreover, the theme of the debased games in Pope's Book 2 is echoed in "Gym," where Murphy trenchantly satirizes men

> Ingled in clutches masked by sauna steam,
> ....
> In tableaux mixed with musak, cocaine, jism.

This is a vicious environment recalling the participants in Pope's games

> List'ning delighted to the jest unclean
> Of link-boys vile, and watermen obscene
> (2: 99–100)

> . . . .
> As oil'd with magic juices for the course.
> (2: 104)

Murphy's poem, of course, is not a parody of Pope's *Dunciad;* it is a thoroughly modern poem (in the sense of being individual and innovative) incorporating several apposite allusions to Pope. We do not have whole poems of heroic couplets, but we do have one couplet concluding each of the fifty sonnets. Since Murphy has never published an English sonnet prior to this collection, I suggest that he may have chosen this particular form with its final couplet to contribute another subtle echo of the form of *The Dunciad* as well as for its affinity to the sequence or "equivalent of the long poem."

More importantly, there is a parallel between this sequential long poem of Murphy's and Pope's roll of dunc“: Pope, for all the ridicule he lavishes on his characters is never deceived about their power. He does not underestimate their status nor suggest that his satire will rid the world of their folly; it is important to remember that the dunces conquer in the end as "universal darkness covers all." Murphy's dunces, of course, do not triumph, but we are not deceived as to their power. The poem dramatizes a long and difficult struggle against them.

Similarly, I suggest, Murphy—especially in "The Price of Stone"—has taken special care to demonstrate the formidable task of withstanding the allure of all that stone symbolizes: acquisition, power, status, permanence, and the ethos thereof. It has taken him the good part of a lifetime to understand this; hence, the long poem of many parts to convey the sense of this long process. Of the fifty sonnets of part 2, two-thirds of them unambiguously portray deprecatory dimensions of stone's realm. But one-third of them present a benign voice that is puzzling until one realizes that Murphy is deliberately demonstrating the complex and seductive nature of the appeal of possession. It indeed does seem attractive and benign and nurturing at times. But the danger, of course, is that once we are seduced we are diverted from what Murphy comes to emphasize in the poem as the more important concern of life, personal love.

"Ice Rink," the seventh poem of "The Price of Stone," introduces Murphy's technique of including voices that represent benign elements of his past. The opening line, "Reflections of a spotlit mirror-ball," together with the expectations set up by the title and the context of this poem, leads us to expect something garish and unpleasant. But surprisingly this is not the case. The memory is that of "pure fun" where "initiates feel exalted" and "their figure-carving feet" have wittily chased the rink "with puckish onslaught." The recollection is one that honors beginnings ("small fry" and "initiates") and forgiveness:

> Midnight, my crushed face melts in a dead heat:
> Old scores ironed out, tomorrow a clean sheet.

The poem introduces the alternative choice that will finally emerge in the final poem, "Natural Son," where the ultimate new beginning, an infant's birth, is the symbol of all that is the desirable opposite of lifeless, static stone. "Ice Rink," curiously contrasting to the previous poems of "The Price of Stone," presents no imposing dimension of stone, as in the immediately preceding "Knockbrack" where "dark granite cropped up an ancient head / To check your feet, your line of living dead." The stone that is present in "Ice Rink" is "slate" over which the ice is frozen, not at all an imposing or monumental position. Here the stone plays a supporting role enabling the human skaters to be their own living monuments. The exaltation here is of the human not the edifice.

This important contribution of "Ice Rink" significantly contrasts with "The Gym," the fifth poem in the sequence, which opens with "Vice-regal walls [that] dominate the back street." One expects (at least at first reading, before becoming aware of Murphy's use of irony and surprise) that this edifice might be so imposing because it is indeed one that suggests healthful and vigorous life. But this is not the case. The gym encloses a most antipathetic world of male society that "immune from women" is a "heartless mime." This is realm of ultra isolation, "past all immunity," full of macho facade of "cock and bull." Here life is only a half-life, the vice-regal walls are not just the gym's, but the perverse world of spurious male dominion.

"Ice Rink" suggests at least one more dimension of its importance in its insistence on human renewal. Its approbation of a melting that erases old scores and gives a clean sheet for tomorrow and a witty tolerance of human error as

> starlets glide
> To cut more ice with convoluted skill
> Practising tricks that lure them to backslide

strongly suggests to me the attitude and tone of Auden's "In Praise of Limestone." Auden in his paean of human love celebrates the yielding, accommodating quality of limestone as the perfect landscape for love and specifically rejects the recalcitrant world of "granite wastes." Auden's descriptive comment on stone's symbolic relevance to humanity may add resonance to "The Price of Stone": his conclusion, that granite is incompatible with love, is also Murphy's.

When I divide Murphy's sonnet voices into two main types, benign and malign, I should add that, as expected, there are variations of degree in each type. For example, while I would place both "Gym" and "Connemara Quay" in the malign category there is a considerable difference between them. The gym, as described above, is a thoroughly nasty environment that offers my reading no redeeming quality. Murphy's quay, however, is a different matter.

"Connemara Quay" opens with "I should have done this," a line that alludes to failure—perhaps not necessarily of great culpitude—but still of some degree of failure to achieve what the quay was designed to do, "to end the poor land's hunger." The stone pier was supposed to have provided more food, to be a "godsend," to have brought together ("married") the "green earth" and the "grey sea." "Fine wooden craft" were "attached by strings of warps to my stone head" but they were "overcome by torpor." The desired result did not happen:

> Keels took root in a silt of seabed
> Ribbed frames rotted in a frayed hemp dream.

The quay's voice is sad with only a hint of what went wrong: the fault according to the omniscient speaker is that

> Men stood me up here, promising that I'd be
> Their godsend: ocean would provide more food.

The fault seems to have been too much confidence placed in something outside and beyond the men themselves. The voice remarks that "The green earth should have married the grey sea." But of course it did not work out that way. The quay is in a sense another figurative folly, standing as a reminder of the impossible task of dominion: marrying earth and sea, and finding ultimate harmony in such a union. The dream, the attempt is, of course, understandable and forgivable, but it teaches a lesson of humility nonetheless.

The poem ends with the quay's voice directly challenging the poet:

> You played in these hulks half a century ago.
> What did you think you might do? Now you know.

There is no harsh indictment here implying that the boy of fifty years ago should have known differently. The sense of this poem and the long sequence of which it is part is that understanding of life comes only after a long process of often painful experience. The poet thought no differently from others *then*, but there is certainly in context *now* the implication that he has learned from experience. Not only, as the poem more or less directly states, that men must look to themselves and not to stone's power for salvation, but also in the context of the whole sequence that whatever choice we make for our life it must be a personal commitment of love. Love is not mentioned in "Connemara Quay," and its absence is instructive. What the poet now knows that he did not previously is that it belongs, and, as he dramatically presents in "Natural Son," it should be paramount.

There is considerable pathos in the revelation of the quay's voice, and it is clear that Murphy is aligning much of his past life and poetry with those unfulfilled hopes of happiness described in the poem. The voice is benign to the extent that it understands its own failure, and thus the poem stands in definite contrast to others like "Gym" that arouse unalloyed contempt. "The Price of Stone" is not a simple work; it demands much of its readers. In conclusion, I wish to discuss two of these demands.

The first is the hermetic nature of many of the scenes recalled by various voices. Previously I noted that I thought "Queen of the Castle" was a nanny, but there are other possibilities. "Portico" in its ominous tone seems to be deliberately vague in giving details of its location and relevance to the poet, whereas a piece like "Nelson's Pillar" is rigorously specific and clear. And what is one to make of the confused chronology of the parts? "Natural Son" is undoubtedly last in time as well as in form, but "Birth Place," the scene of the author's birth, stands fifteenth! I suggest that this confusion is intended as part of the total comprehension of the poem. The theme of *The Price of Stone* is the discovery after a long process of learning that a past life has been largely spent pursuing inadequate and ultimately unsatisfying goals. The poet knows at last what he did not know before. It is really not surprising, therefore, that a recollection of this confused and ignorant past would be reinforced structurally by the fragmentary and oblique.

A second and more difficult demand is of accepting the abrupt change— or what appears initially to be an abrupt change—that comes when one turns the last page to encounter "Natural Son." Suddenly, after a long collection of forty-nine sonnets (preceded by the introductory part 1) dealing with various associations with stone, we are confronted with a radically new and different world of personal love. It is a difficult leap to make, but I believe that Murphy has given us various artistic justifications for this sudden move. First, the move is supposed to have the shock of surprise. The opening line of "Natural Son" speaks of the snipping of the umbilical cord, and this last poem is also to be a new birth breaking with the past as definitively as the cutting of the cord. It is the nature of an epiphany to take us by surprise; therein lies its power to instruct or reform. Second, upon consideration, one realizes that we have been rather carefully prepared for this decision by the rest of the long and complex poem. For example, the previous poems (including part 1) have built up such a negative view of stone that we should be ready—and indeed most willing— to accept an alternate view, however sudden. When we look back over this extended poem, not only do we find a number of reasons to reject the aggrandizement of stone in and over lives, but we have also been directed in many poems, both specifically and obliquely, to the preferable ethos of love. Those directions were more obvious in the twenty-one poems of part 1, but they exist also in the eponymous part 2.

"Suntrap" (of "The Price of Stone") is a memory of home, recalling a time when "learning and love made peace" and "heart and mind were shuttled into place." Here was a "walled demesne" (presumably of stone) that was benign in its nurturing of love, because it sponsored "Rewards beyond my laurels, birches, oaks," that is, its stone presence did not spiritually confine or oppress. There, "A peeled light, dipped in tallow, carried light / From the dark ages, kissing you good night." "Newgrange" describes a megalithic tomb's dark emptiness, "waiting for dawn inside my skull to streak," and "fixed on rebirth." "Canterbury Cathedral" recalls a beneficent part of his youth to which the poet returns to retrieve the love that he gave the cathedral then for tuning his ear to poetry and training his voice. The curfew sounded him asleep with its all's well then, and indeed all is well where there is love. When we look closely we discover that we have been variously prepared for the final acceptance of love, although, as the poem dramatically demonstrates, that climax can still be surprisingly, perhaps painfully sudden, as birth often is. Embodying the long gestation of a disordered past for the birth of a new vision, it is most appropriate that *The Price of Stone* is extended, complex and ultimately surprising.

Notes

1. *The Price of Stone* (London: Faber and Faber, 1985). *The Price of Stone and Earlier Poems* (Winston-Salem: Wake Forest University Press, 1985). The British edition consists of two parts: part 1 and part 2: "The Price of Stone." The American edition, after three parts of the earlier poems, lists part 4 as "Care" and part 5 as "The Price of Stone." [The poem "Care" is included in part 4 of the American edition and part 1 of the British.] Throughout my essay I refer to the arrangement of the British edition.

2. For a discussion of Murphy as a poet of *pietas* see my essay in *Contemporary Irish Writing* (Boston: Twayne Publishers, 1983), 49–64.

The Vital Bond of Distance:
Irish Poetry on the Road

John Engle

In the best Irish poetry of the last quarter century, the motif of the journey appears with striking, disproportionate frequency. There is little new in the emblematic use of distance and motion: read Homer, Dante, Cervantes, Wordsworth, Tennyson. What merits attention in the poetic landscape of Ireland today is the sheer density of its recurrence—the journey appears not only frequently but tellingly, in works authoritatively staking out the broken heartland of Irish poetry. Derek Mahon, John Montague, Richard Murphy, Thomas Kinsella, Seamus Heaney—each has made of travel constructs for thought and feeling central to his oeuvre. From Murphy's voyages through Montague's land crossing in *The Dead Kingdom,* from *Sweeney Astray* through "Nightwalker" through Mahon's fire king striking "out over the fields . . . not knowing a word of the language," Irish poetry has discovered in movement an expressive subject and apt metaphor. Such is its importance that a trustworthy map of Irish verse drawn today must chart the journey in its varied incarnations: sea voyage, lonely quest, aimless trek, the long, purposeful drive, the pilgrimage.

As figure, the journey responds equally to the demands of our century and the particular needs of the Irish mind and heart. In fact, as Kinsella has suggested, the two predicaments resemble each other (we are all impoverished heirs to "a gapped, discontinuous, polyglot tradition")[1], and in the best Irish poetry today one settles upon the other like an evocative double exposure. "Writing out of a people to a people" (as Yeats wrote of Davis), Mahon, Murphy, et al. address equally the flaccid spirit of our age and world, that which is uncircumscribable by any boundaries but those created or accepted by the individual himself. Together, these concerns churn in what Seamus Deane has aptly identified as *the* preoccupation of Irish literature, the urge to hold the nation close or force it away, "to create identity on its terms or to dictate identity on the poet's own."[2] Here, inevitably, Joyce strides into view (as he enters the work of at least four of the poets named above).[3] Unlike Yeats, artificer of an essentially private Anglo-Irish tradition, it is Joyce who simultaneously revives the Irish tradition and admits the modern world,"[4] and Joyce who, not co-incidentally, made a virtue of mobility in his life and art. The Baroque enthusiasm may be Stephen's but the credo is his creator's: "I go to encounter for the millionth time the reality of experience and to forge in the smithy of my soul the uncreated conscience of my race." So too is his choice of the verb "go."

For the journey as metaphor is compelling and multitudinous of implication. "The white arms of roads" and the "black arms of tall ships" promise Stephen "close embraces," yet they simultaneously sign the message "We are alone." Emerson insists that "everything good is on the highway," for travel can be the most romantic of enterprises, an open field for the play of instinct and individual freedom, or an occasion for connection, a fertile merging of complementary or contrary possibilities. But it may equally represent the individual lost in a Forsterian nightmare where nothing connects: the first quality of the romantic soul, "organic dynamism,"[5] become an ugly restiveness, Whitman's tramper of the open road, Morand's *homme pressé* in the crowded *vide*. Such possibilities multiply in the case of the modern Irish writer qua Irish writer, and here one thinks not only of the writers at hand but of Brian Moore and his fictional wanderers, Austin Clarke of "The Straying Student," the promising Eiléan Ní Chuilleanáin drawn, in *The Second Voyage*, to Odysseus; even Yeats for whom the metaphor of sailing drove forward one of the greatest poems in the language. Ireland is an island of frontiers and divisions where the question of staying in place or shuttling between "states" is posed by the simplest of daily adventures, like studying a street sign or buying contraceptives. The journey offers evident thematic possibility in divided political states still unsure whether they are dragging themselves together or farther apart; in a culture fractured by memory, religion, language; in a populace to a large degree still teleguided by a Manichaean Catholicism or a Protestantism marching into the future behind the drums of 1691. Movement may suggest a flying by of these nets or, as easily, a redemptive attempt to bridge the gaps they restrict and clog.

The poetry of Richard Murphy, for one, charts voyages between poles of opposition. Murphy as poet knows where he wants to sail, but throughout the voyage he will shimmy up the mast to cast glances back to port and ahead to his destination, and measure the distance, and muse about the cost of the whole enterprise. The result is a straining toward wholeness countered (almost unwillingly) by honest attention that sunders, then heals through its patient admission of complexity. Murphy's position as a truly Anglo-Irish poet is well-known, as is his intention to come livingly into contact with the Irish half of a bifurcated self. In his work the personal and collective seem at times to blur indistinguishably, and we do not need Donne to see that the remarkable number of emblematic islands dotting his work figure more than the workings of Murphy's personal fate. "What I really wanted to get clear were my origins and where we came from and who we were and what our past was,"[6] he writes simply, significantly gliding from first person singular into plural. Though certain readers have discerned a "programmatic" air in the poetry,[7] I find that this widening of focus occurs without fuss, naturally. In the end an inventory of Murphy's freight reveals questions of personal and cultural inheritance, the dichotomy between "English mind and Irish feeling,"[8] broader questions about the nature of language and the spiritual price exacted by "civilization."

Murphy's anthology piece is rightly "Sailing to an Island," for it tells much about how he thinks and feels and the way his poems mean. Describing a romantic voyage to the island of Clare, storm-transformed into more authentic contact with the islanders of Inishbofin, the poem remains soberly descriptive while almost immediately courting symbolic reading:

> The boom above my knees lifts, and the boat
> Drops, and the surge departs, departs, my cheek
> Kissed and rejected, kissed, as the gaff sways
> A tangent, cuts the infinite sky to red
> Maps, and the mast draws eight and eight across
> Measureless blue, the boatmen sing or sleep.[9]

Contrasts emerge naturally here—between something "infinite" or "measureless" and a measuring, mapping consciousness, between the nervously conscious poet and the sailors lost naturally to sleep or song. Alternately kissed and rejected by the spray, by the boatmen's world, the speaker hears as well his own poetic rhythms lose their will before those of nature. Wind lifts line 1 out of its iambic norm, while a wave drops the boat free of an easy anapest. Lines push off trochaically, disquietingly, then tack back hesitatingly to iambs. This is the rhythm of doubt.

Doubt—or, more exactly, gentle humility allowed to chasten a will that seems otherwise to consider unity its due—gives Murphy's poetry much of its charm. He is not afraid to deflate himself, as he does in purpling the language to describe a tourist-mythic isle of Clare or over-excitedly recognizing in high seas "the ribald face of a mad mistress." Handed ashore at Inishbofin, the speaker finds at least his real destination, a native Ireland far from postcard color-heightening but still "mysterious and imaginative" in its "home-built" pride and courtesy. Honesty makes for two reactions to the locals. "Tonight we stay," he says, "drinking with people / Happy in the monotony of boats." With its abstraction rooted in a perfect simplicity of diction, this is a convincing expression of felt understanding just next door to kinship. Yet the poet is not completely in tune with the local music. As he drinks the room surges like the first stanza's sea, and he slips outside only to trip among nettles. The man who would contact the native Irish ancestry within himself then cracks twigs in an elder tree chosen, clearly, for its legendary identification with the art of healing and for the pun. We are left with an individual come at best to a temporary, troubled peace with his past—someone entering a crowded room knowing he belongs, but not sure he'll be accepted and too well-bred anyway to push in.

Murphy's islands suggest both the hooped wholeness of secure collective identity and a countercurrent of individual estrangment. "Sailing" between such alternatives, Murphy evidences ease in the presence of unwieldly, resistant oppositions. His use of the emblematic journey, in fact, may say just that, for physical mobility always admits the presence or two realities, the here and the there, if not as well an expansive third, the in-between. As in "Stormpetrel," an acute, observed allegory of the poet at work. Bullied by the elements yet "jooking" lightly above it all, the bird is crow's itinerant cousin, a bandity "waif" or "gypsy." Singer of a song "older than fossils, / Ephemeral as thrift," able to "hatch an egg in a hermit's skull," he passes nights secure, then bobs off again on the wind, his element. The love nest by night, storm-buffeted homelessness by day: life, modern life, Irish life, breaks down into such patterns. Despite a persistent urge to haul his selves into harmony, Murphy resists the temptation to wave the wand of poetry and fuse the contrarieties he encounters. His song contains the permanent and ephemeral as, in an easy formulation, his blood runs practical Saxon and mystical Celt. In a salty, textured rendering of ritual sex and violence among the "Seals on High Island," Murphy recognizes the demarcation lines hacked across experience. "I must re-member," he muses, "How far their feelings are from mine marooned. / If there are tears at this holy ceremony / Theirs are caused by brine and mine by breeze."

Murphy wants to swim such passages; he is drawn toward instinct, emotion, blood-knowledge, the "ancestrial bias" of the "truly Irish"[10] he ached to be as a child. Yet the poet Murphy deliberately rejects any sort of glandular abandon. In poems like "Coppersmith" and "Trouvaille," he portrays language as limited before magical Lawrentian imperatives, yet his own calm pleasure in and cautious precision with language, as well as the distance he maintains between self and subject, belie such sentiments, uphold "the manners of a lost empire." Murphy longs for wordless union while his poetry reflects knowledge he can't shake, that others' "feelings are from mine marooned." Against a backdrop of island and accidents, though, optimism sings in the rigging. "Forget about the disaster," he imagines a descendant of the Cleggan drowned calling out, "We're mounting nets today!" Romantic hope and respect for the old salt of tradition send him to sea in a craft bearing ancestral memories long as spillets and the isolated modern imagination yearning for connection he knows will prove difficult: "Old men my instructors, and with all new gear / May I handle her well down tomorrow's sea-road."

This is the "cargo of the individual spirit and wider responsibilities" catalogued by Edna Longley in a fine 1975 essay.[11] Among other things, she convincingly argues that Murphy's poetry resembles that of John Montague in its sense of "individual or Romantic separateness," a self-consciousness about Irish and poetic identity, and frequent reliance upon "myths and metaphors of lonely questing." The key to such resemblance, I would argue, is at least partly biographical for, despite their evident differences as poets and individuals, both have passed identity-confounding lives: Murphy the scion of a Church of Ireland bishop, born in Galway, brought up in colonial Ceylon, back to the West after Oxford; Montague the Catholic from Brooklyn, shipped far from his parents to be raised in County Tyrone, then off in adulthood to America, Paris, now Cork. It would surprise if these men did not question themselves about individual and tribal identity and if the journey, so familiar and significant in each life, did not figure in the way they map experience.

In both poets movement intimates the presence of contending alternatives. Where they differ is in the attitude taken toward the journey between antinomies. Murphy would press on, informed by hopeful assurance like Carlyle's, that his road connects to all the roads in the world. After sailing to an island, Inishbofin offers him nettles and a cobwebbed moon but also a bed; why not finally a home? While Murphy is too honest to force reconciliation where for the moment there is none to be had, his poetry is propelled by goodhearted perseverance and the faith that unity and integration can occur, even in a country where the past is always "happening again"; and so Murphy rises at times to strange, sympathetic understandings, like that for the Cromwellian planter in *The Battle of Aughrim* loyal to "hard work / Deepening the soil for seed." Montague is at least as large of heart but his imagination, at once more self-consciously modern and more wounded at its old Northern Catholic core, finds disjuncture the natural state of things. Survey his work and you discover a mind constitutionally committed to understanding in terms of indecision and contradiction. The enigmatic conclusion of *The Great Cloak* speaks to this awareness of a world in which the point of rest is almost accidental and certainly temporary. At last come to loving security after storms of guilt and deception, the speaker refuses the easy reassurance of "a sheltering home." His fate linked to one with the "Edenlike" name, he knows that no home deed comes without an eviction clause. As great contending tides surge, the volume ends warily, "openly": "on the edge is best."[12]

Despite the persuasiveness of much of Longley's argument, this is not really a creative imagination "seeking on various levels for structures in which to lodge"[13] itself, as one could characterize Murphy. Montague emphasizes the journey rather than the destination—culminating vision less than meaning or unity showing themselves amid, as part of, life's divisive flux. Riding out tempests of Ulster memory and politics and the choppy waters of modern love, "we balance and slide," he writes in *Tides*, upon the "periodic rhythms of the open sea / . . . hoping for pattern." The value of balancing and sliding "on the edge" is something like an intended irresolution finds expression in the frequent journeys traced across Montague's work. Like Murphy he has a geographical imagination, one seizing naturally upon physical features and distance for symbolic terms. This is evident in the volume titles alone: *Forms of Exile, Poisoned Lands, The Rough Field, Tides, The Dead Kingdom.* Or look at the way Montague has characterized himself in campaigning actively for a new look at the Irish poetic identity. What he calls the "global regionalist" knows the root truths of the parish but also that "over the hill is an airport with planes departing for Paris."[14] "This," he says, "is a richly ambiguous position."[15]

From his earliest work Montague has been attracted to images of fixity, mobility, and their ambiguous collision. In "Like Dolmens round my Childhood, the Old People," for example, reverence for "that dark permanence of ancient forms" is tempered by spat bile: "Ancient Ireland, indeed! I was reared by her bedside, / The rune and the chant, evil eye and averted head. . . ."[16] The "mould of death" into which old Maggie

Owens is cast connotes the preserving power of poetry, myth, and memory, but it is also physical decay and the rigor mortis of provincial restraint. Another early piece, "Midland Village," sees the past with a similar double vision. A donkey's "rusty commentary" may "taunt an exile in some industrial town / . . . with an image of unchanging life," but we discover what has made the animal squeal: the gelding knife, tormenting too "the respectable one who stays / With too much stillness." Montague, who did not stay, seems to tip his hand in titling the volume *Poisoned Lands*. The book's 1977 reissue, though, leads off with this complicating epigraph: "Some who travel light / May feel deprived / Of all the love that weighs / On other people's lives." "Exile" and "stillness"—the trick is to admit the truth and the lie in each.

Neither rooted man nor rootless wanderer, Montague spends his time en route between these extremes. *The Rough Field* and *The Dead Kingdom*, long sequences of public and private history (and, with *The Great Cloak*, Montague's finest achievements), take place literally on the road. "*Catching a bus at Victoria Station,*" begins the first, while the latter is structured around a long, tense drive and set in motion like the figurative salmon drawn "*Northwards,* annually, / a journeying back. . . ." In both works travel functions as a central dramatic and thematic force. Like the poetic sequence—which too moves temporally, "topographically," Montague's chosen form in recent years—the journey allows the participating narrator multiple perspectives on past and present, public and private, to enact themes of growth, memory, and individual vs. communal identity. Moving through a physical and emotional landscape, Montague seeks what he calls in an early poem "a way and a motion / That stills disturbance."[17] Drawing into simultaneous focus the complexities of a bittersweet youth and a province trapped in ceaseless cycles of self-laceration, the poem is finally about freedom: "One explores an inheritance," Montague writes, "to free oneself and others."[18] At one extreme squats tradition calcified to the "unchanging life" of "ancient Ireland." Soothing in its solidity, it can petrify to dead stone. At the other scurries the dispersion of modern life (with exile its eternal Irish cognate). Contemporary mobility enriches the self through access to Berkeley and Boulez, but it also forces the New Omagh Road through Tyrone and isolates man in his "self-drive car." For Montague the center must hold *and* release. True freedom partakes of both extremes, motion that stills disturbance.

In *The Rough Field* progression through the landscape, actual or imagined, almost invariably develops key concerns. "The Road's End," for example, recalls the poet's reflective walk past the "half-way mark / Between two cottages," where he assists at the pained passing of a slower, more rural Ulster. Later he sees the trying linguistic, cultural crossing from English to Irish as "the longest journey / I have ever gone." Such images exist in the context of a continued metaphorical exploitation of physical space and its traversal: poet and father figured in the myth of Odysseus, the bad marriage of "by-passed" and "dying," parochial closure in the old woman to whom a foreigner is someone from the next parish, tipsy pals "marching through memory magnified," the Loss and Gain of the Omagh Road, "seismic waves / zigzagging through / a faulty world." Montague's ability to focus simultaneously upon intimate and communal relations makes of this final image a central symbol in a reading of both histories. At once the fissures cleaving North from South, Catholic from Protestant, East from West Berlin, and the culpability, actual or imagined, that brought such divisions into being and furthers them, "the fault" ran as well across the creased forehead of the speaker's exiled father. And, hopeless love and acid disillusion before Ireland, life itself, "the same fault ran through / us both," only the son had poetry. Internal contradictions *are* Montague's understanding of the impossible North. The same poet who writes "A New Siege" expressly as a distanced "historical meditation" finds little strange about including within it "one of the most personal passages I had ever written."[19] Truth is the fault abstracted to the conceit of invisible "lines of history / lines of power" knotted in timeless opposition, and it is also a lonely boy of four arriving at Lough Foyle and someday himself to write

> Lines of leaving
> lines of returning
>
> . . . .
> this sad sea city
> my landing place
> the loneliness of
> Lir's white daughter's
> ice crusted wings
> forever spread
> at the harbour mouth.

In their essential complementarity, leaving and returning form one of the many "circles" in Montague's poetry. *The Rough Field* concludes with another: "with all my circling a failure to return / to what is already going, /

Going / GONE. . . ." Here one is tempted to insist upon "failure" when, in fact, the sequence is much more about the action of circling, success in finding the right way to move and distance to keep. On one hand recurrent circle imagery mimics the endlessly repetitive nature of the Irish problem ("Once again, it happens"). As importantly, it figures Montague's faith in the multisided wholeness of truth (he once spoke on "The Unpartitioned Intellect"[20]), and it enacts both the centrifugal and centripetal forces in Irish culture, those to be held in rough equilibrium if any truth is to be found at all. The image appears frequently: in the standing circle of stones from "Like Dolmens," the bright cartwheel propping open "The Road's End," Fortune's Wheel taunting the O Neills, in the world of *A Slow Dance* "turning in wet / and silence, a / damp mill wheel" or its profane counterpart, an upended Army lorry, "wheels slowly turning." Circularity governs as well Montague's fine recent volume, *The Dead Kingdom.* The opening lines of the sequence, with their evocation of the salmon's pull to the source, establish the themes of origin, completion, and cyclic altertance. The poet's mother dead, he heads north to bury her and, perhaps, the hatchet of childhood abandonment, before returning to the new woman in his life. More circling, always moving, never there and always there, this time between the poles of life and death, youth and age, absence and presence, and, of course, North and South: "And have you no part in the other world?" asks Kafka's Burgomeister in the epigraph to the first of five sections: " 'I am forever,' replied the hunter, 'on the great stair that leads up to it. . . . I clamber about, sometimes up, sometimes down . . . always in motion!' "

Despite the credolike placement of the epigraph, this valued spiritual mobility is considerably harder won than in *The Rough Field.* Where Montague manages a kind of intimate distance in the earlier sequence, here he is before such explosively personal material that it must be defused before any more disinterested examination can take place. Contact with the past occurs almost immediately as the changing landscape sends him, again geographically, down "minor roads of memory." On the road, as Hazlitt knew, "I plunge into my past being" until "long-forgotten things . . . burst on my eager sight, and I begin to feel, think, and be myself again."[21] In Montague's case, retrieval of self means going down the longest road of all, back to a Freudian womb or at least the "primal hurt" of abandonment, when he was sent away at four to be raised by a far-off Irish aunt: "All roads wind backwards to it."

Montague arrives at understanding via "rites duly performed" that allow the generous imagination to find hope even in the North's "ultimate

coldness." Summary renders schematic a process that in fact occurs grace-
fully over time, in a slow accretion of imagery (often of cold and light)
and the gradual, touching rehearsal of biographical detail. Thumbing
bruises dully as the miles fall past, Montague leads us past sentimentality
to his home truth, that in every truth, even that of absence, inheres a
counter truth. A found locket bearing the picture of a young boy, a hint
of love cradled in remembered ends of dialogue, instinct pulling toward
a new home and love, and the speaker is able to find in "this final death,
a freedom; a light battling through cloud." For Montague the road to
illumination means first border crossing into the North, "that shadowy
territory / where motives fail." With the lightest, surest touch yet in his
poetry, he integrates the reach of culture and place with the little world
of intimate relations: the evil of our harsh hearts (and the recompensatory
glint of warmth) in each realm mirroring that of the other. In "Border
Lake," a sonnet almost precisely at the volume's halfway point, he offers
a chilly, luminous image of the North as political and emotional landscape,
and of joined souls who have found how to move just above the threatening, mirroring waste:

> The farther North you travel, the colder it gets.
> Take that border county of which no one speaks.
> Look at the straggly length of its capital town:
> the bleakness after a fair, cattle beaten home.
> The only beauty nearby is a small glacial lake
> sheltering between drumlin mounds of mountains.
> In winter it is completely frozen over, reeds
> bayonet sharp, under a low, comfortless sky.
> Near the middle there is a sluggish channel
> where a stray current tugs to free itself.
> The solitary pair of swans who haunt the lake
> have found it out, and come zigzagging,
> holding their breasts aloof from the jagged
> edges of large pale mirrors of ice.

Montague imagines that the children of Lir and the Wild Geese can
learn both to keep their distance and head home. For Derek Mahon home
has remained a fact to be dodged if the self is to be discovered or created:
"I am man self-made, self-made man, / No small talk now for those who
ran / In and out of my dirty childhood. / We have grown up as best we
could."[22] With such lines Montague's friend and fellow Ulsterman traces

a curve beyond Murphy's urge toward integration and Montague's own dual ease in and out of cultural harness. Protestant and awakened from the "historical nightmare," Mahon has sought to put distance between himself and Ulster, literally in almost continuous exile, figuratively in images of escape and the "start from scratch." In fact, in his terms, leavetaking is perhaps the essential quality of life. "I have already come to the verge of / Departure," says "An Unborn Child." In *Night-Crossing*, the title itself significant, Mahon places this poem between "Gipsies" ("We are all gipsies now") and "Canadian Pacific" with its train-borne tracking shot on wild geese, their "great wings sighing with a nameless hunger."

Since his first poems in 1962, Mahon has hungered for values to sustain the willingly estranged self. Throughout he offers images of inviolable inner space correlated, frequently, to terms of physical distance: that of MacNeice, Van Gogh, Villon, Marilyn Monroe, De Quincey, his "head removed," off "dark roads taken at random," the grandfather who in his senile magic "escapes us all." Against this honored privacy, a making it new down one's own road, crouches in ambush Belfast and its reminder "not to forget." The decision to forget, gone without a history, comes naturally but not painlessly to Mahon's mobile imagination. Obsessed with the question "of lost futures, / The lives we might have led," he frets even about possibilities left in this "desperate city": "if I lived long enough in this house," "if I'd stayed behind / And lived it bomb by bomb. . . ." Yet, while guilt at times balls up these conditionals into "musts" and "shoulds" ("my mind must learn to know its place"), home rarely elicits more than casual interest. Scarred more than any of his contemporaries by the "fire-loving / People" of his homeland, he is concerned less with raking through ashes—Ulster comes in for remarkably little direct attack in Mahon's work—than with acts of healing.

The rehabilitation he has in mind must begin with the distanced self; and, in his dealings with the question of individual consciousness and autonomy, Mahon is a lively blend of romantic and contemporary ironist or even nihilist. Drawn instinctively to images of freedom in movement, he celebrates the individual at last "through with history": in the best-known passage in his work, the man who starts off after errands "and vanishes / Where the lane turns," or

Who drops at night
From a moving train

And strikes out over the fields
Where fireflies glow
Not knowing a word of the language.

Here and in "The Apotheosis of Tins" and "The Snow Party," Mahon
imagines such escape from the barbarous cycle as the first step toward a
Yeatsian "cold dream / Of a place out of time." Yet, he knows, man self-
made may also be a "lost traveller" or the remembered self in "Day Trip
to Donegal," "alone far out at sea / Without skill or reassurance . . .
Cursing my failure to take due / Forthought for this."

Between such positions Mahon hesitates, but he is finally willing to
choose—it is better to be a "prisoner of infinite choice" than a prisoner
tout court: "The pros outweigh the cons that glow / From Beckett's bleak
reductio / And who would trade self-knowledge for / A prelapsarian metaphor . . . ?" The Beckett to whom Mahon turns is not the poet of
despair most recognize but Robbe-Grillet's brilliant "source of energy":
"This waiting for death, this growing physical deprivation . . . all this
gradual decay of the present [which] constitutes in spite of everything a
kind of future."[23] Demolition back down to "hard boards / And darkness,"
the self primally alone, is Mahon's necessary first step to regeneration.
Such a realization is in the truest sense of the adverb a radically political
position—a chopping back to the simplest truths of being, before civilization and its "insolent ontology." For this denuded *liberté*, again the
figurative journey: "Now all we have / / Is the flinty chink of Orion . . .
To light us through . . . Before we go plunging into the dark forever."
Hurtling through the night demands scrupulous honesty and the existential
courage to believe in nothing: the radical ignorance Mahon cultivates,
something like the simple "immanence" of the object qua object. "We
travelled on," he remembers in *The Hunt by Night*, "to doubt and speculation, / our birthright and proper portion."

Preparation of the self is groundwork, for a resilient if thin streak of
utopianism animates Mahon: "The ideal future / Shines out of our better
nature. . . ." In "The Sea in Winter," a long verse letter sent from
Ireland to Greece and one of the finest epistolary poems of recent years,
Mahon addresses the value of art and a spindly dream of completion. In
a voice at once crafted and "human," blunting couplets with enjambment
and the near rhyme, speaking iambic tetrameter far from the metronome,
he achieves a "truly civil presence"[24] that brings alive the presence of
community. Elsewhere, in poems closing down to the reality of self alone,
this combination of verbal elegance and warmth intimates at best another

lost future; here, turning back up from his *reductio,* Mahon permits himself to see "colours we scarcely dare to dream": One day "the rainbow ends, / The wine goes round among the friends, / The lost are found, the parted lovers / Lie at peace beneath the covers."

Meanwhile, in the "given life" that continues, the speaker persists: "I who know nothing go to teach / While a new day crawls up the beach." Ending the poem (and his collected *Poems 1962–1978*) on this note of modest limitation, Mahon argues implicitly that a social role (in this case represented by the poet's teaching post) can be fulfilled by the "I" willing to "know nothing" and start again daily. This is the emblematic "narrow road to the deep / North." As elsewhere in Mahon's work, "The Sea in Winter" works by such images of mobility and distance. The epigraph—Rimbaud's "*Nous ne sommes pas au monde; la vraie vie est absente*"—echoes wickedly in a letter sent from gray Ireland to ultramarine Greece. Much of the poem is about "the curious sense / Of working on the circumference," the odd pleasure in "staring out / Of windows, preferably from a height." Finally, near the end of the poem, Mahon heaps together an almost embarrassing profusion of such images: "make it new, / 'Forsake the grey skies for the blue,' " "leap / Before we look," the ideal future "dimly visible from afar," the transfiguring "road to Damascus." In going to trite expression and imagery, Mahon seems to be insisting simultaneously upon the universality of truth in the journey and, by ironic displacement, the absolute need to make it new. The stanza that follows, in fact, enacts this meaning without sentimentality or irony:

> In Botticelli's strangely neglected
> Drawings for *The Divine Comedy*
> Beatrice and the rest proceed
> Through a luminous geometry—
> Diagrams of that paradise
> Each has a vision of.

Here, in the presence of individual vision transcending public neglect, we are invited to see life as a solitary journey starting in a dark wood. The way to luminous pattern passes by—*mi retrovai*—the recovery of self.

The theme of self menaced by what Mahon calls the "loaded world" marks as well the recent work of another Northerner, Seamus Heaney. Since perhaps 1976 with the publication of *North* (and some seven years into the latest round of the troubles), Heaney has looked up from the echoing darkness of personal and racial past to question obliquely and directly the societal role, if any, of the creative imagination. Exploring this theme and, in particular, a contested personal decision to pull up stakes in the North, Heaney has turned with almost predictable frequency to terms of erratic or spontaneous motion. "How often these Ulstermen journey forth!" exclaimed a critic in a recent review.[25] How otherwise to keep head and spirit high where the gravitational pull of custom and culture is so strong? Even at a distance, in Malibu (where Heaney was visiting another Ulster emigré, Brian Moore), footsteps billowed with sand only recall the "suck of puddled, wintry ground": "Why would it not come home to me?"[26]

The lines of Heaney's early poetry resemble those of kites, "strict and invisible" in their range of middle space, communicating the tug of home to the free blown soul. "Gravities" he even names the beauties and fears that fostered him in country Ulster, an imaginative center that held: the punning "gravid ease" of a warmly treasured churning day or troubling advancements in learning effected by rotting berries or frogs like "mud grenades." So much has been made of Heaney's avowal to take his pen and "dig with it" because the metaphor is apt. Through at least the first part of *North* he remains a poet of the bog and its damp magic of preservation. From volume to volume vivid, tactile childhood memory sharpens to the extraction of mythic potential in unearthed objects like neglected Irish place names or the quick tar of the Grauballe Man. This is not an instinct lending itself to representation by sudden acts of liberating movement; it is that of the dowser methodically "circling the terrain," man fundamentally at one with place.

The pressure of contemporary event pushed this equation out of plumb. From the beginning the Northern situation shadows Heaney's poetry if only via the surrogate of barnyard violence or nature imagined in martial metaphors. Later, with the reignition of the North in 1969, political realities begin to penetrate the private world more directly, in meditations upon primordial victims recovered from the bog or the pitting of consonant against vowel. By *North* the pressure is such that Heaney begins to define his position explicitly as an artist relative to the violence. He enters a poem like "Punishment" to explore through empathy with an executed "little adultress" ambivalence in the hesitant Catholic dumb before vengeance, torn between outrage and the "tribal, intimate revenge." The second part of the volume recollects in tranquility first awareness of the situation and, at last, in the lovely quiet of "Exposure," a decision to leave the North altogether for a loaned house in Wicklow. Under the lost promise of a comet, the speaker walks, "weighing / My responsible *tristia*" against the demands of the inner life, the modesty of private illumination against the risk of missing "the once-in-a-lifetime portent, / The comet's pulsing rose."

Field Work (1979), which follows, is a curious, unachieved book, perhaps because, in temporary residence in Wicklow and a stretch teaching in California, Heaney did not have fully to come to terms with questions raised in "Exposure." They are there, still questions, in three poems about murdered friends ("my tentative art / His turned back watches"), in "this strange loneliness I've brought us to," and in the perilous choice "not to love the life we're shown." In general, though, Heaney seems, if not to be biding time, to be checking his vision by the sure daylight of love, friendship, and the quotidian life of family. In the 1980s, in *Sweeney Astray* and *Station Island*, Heaney is back on the track, instinctively sensing his way down a path one feels he was not yet ready to follow in the years after *North*. With time and the commitment to permanent residence in Dublin (split with Harvard), the question asks itself if the kite strings first traced in "Gravities" still hold or if the "strain" of "the strumming, rooted, long-tailed pull of grief" is to be borne alone. At least part of the answer comes in Heaney's version of the tale of mad Sweeney. Even without their rhyming names and Heaney's coaxing introduction to "the constraints of religious, political, and domestic obligation," birdlike Sweeney clearly lives the disjointed alienation of the modern poet. Like "The Master" in "Sweeney Redivivus," his addendum to the sequence, "he dwelt in himself. . . ."

Station Island treats the theme of chosen distance directly, and it brims with images of motion and marginality. The title resonates: the pilgrimage, first of all, with its notions of purposeful journeying and private vs. communal devotion, but also station as outpost, suggesting a faraway center of hostilities, and the evident play on "island." The provocatively titled "Away from it All" quotes Milocz "*stretched between contemplation / of a motionless point / and the command to participate / actively in history.*" These are the options, a forked up lobster "the colour of sunk munitions" the individual stretched between them:

> And I still cannot clear my head
> of lives in their element
> on the cobbled floor of that tank
> and the hampered one, out of water,
> fortified and bewildered.

Out of his element, bewildered, the poet remains nevertheless "fortified,"
free inside like far-off Chekhov on Sakhalin "to try for the right tone—
not tract, not thesis— / And walk away from floggings." The path away,
the path back, Hansel, Orpheus, Lot—in poems like "The Underground,"
"Changes," "Unwinding," and "On the Road" (which turns the solitary
journey into all journeys), Heaney praises freedom from history's unfair
chains upon the self but implies that this be tempered by the accompanying
right to look "backward through area that forwarded / understanding of
all I would undertake."

Birds figure in a good number of the poems, most, naturally, in the
new Sweeney sequence. From the snipe-heavy soul in "A Kite for Michael
and Christopher" through Noah's dove, the bird represents spirit no longer
"mired in attachment." Of course, Joyce with his birds and nets roosts
here, the genius of the place, almost certainly the Master Sweeney clam-
bers up to visit. "A rook in an unroofed tower" far from Thoor Ballylee,
he sends the suppliant down feeling flimsy, ears resounding with (in lines
echoing Stephen's solid joining of abstract and animal in the *Portrait* diary)
"the purpose and venture / in a wingflap above." Joyce is spiritually there
throughout *Station Island,* behind "A Bat on the Road" or in exile's sweet
religious magic "On the Road," and it is a face-to-face with the master
that concludes the long title sequence. A kind of updated medieval vision
constructed of twelve sections and imagined meetings with, among others,
a self-exiled priest, Kavanagh, and William Carleton, the poem has been
criticized as a set-up with "Heaney giving advice to Heaney" and the
unfortunate result of inspiration forced "across the frame of its form."[27]
This is a critic clearly unhappy with anyone but Heaney the miniaturist,
creator of the perfect little talisman. To be sure, "Station Island" is a
rangier tent than usual and one demanding different fictions for support,
but it is a clever, hardy structure and it forcefully stakes out necessary
artistic ground.

"Station Island" is the most recent in a series of fine poems seeming to
bid Heaney's farewell to one emotional or artistic position while anticipating its evolution into another—works like "Personal Helicon," setting
off the broadening echo patterns of *Door into the Dark;* that volume's
"Bogland" and its bottomless "wet centre"; the regretful musing of "Exposure." When Joyce enters the scene, he is, can only be, Heaney advising
Heaney, but he is also precisely imagined and felt, and worth the listen.
Scolding that "Your obligation / is not discharged by any common rite,"
his voice "eddying with the vowels of all rivers" settles the question that
has pained Heaney: Trade the nest for the "alien comfort" of air, "take

off from here. . . . Let go, let fly, forget. / You've listened long enough.
Now strike your note." Fortified now, bewildered, a life in its element:
"It was as if I had stepped free into space / alone with nothing that I had
not known / already." The poem concludes with Joyce's tart, appropriate
dismissal of the net of language ("a waste of time for somebody your age")
and his continued evocative linking of free movement and the creative
faculty unbound. " 'Keep at a tangent,' " he says, " 'it's time to swim

> out on your own and fill the element
> with signatures on your own frequency,
> echo soundings, searches, probes, allurements,
>
> elver-gleams in the dark of the whole sea".
> The shower broke in a cloudburst, the tarmac
> fumed and sizzled. As he moved off quickly
>
> the downpour loosed its screens round his straight walk.

The final image enwraps silence, exile, cunning. Joyce moves off at a
measured pace made his by the ashplant-stiff determination of the closing
cadence: "round," "straight," "walk," hard integrity and isolation.

For Heaney, Joyce represents the preservation through distance of the
creative self's sanctity and, more largely, the enforcement of a liveable
relationship between the one and the many. In varied forms, this is still
the central issue in Irish poetry and the force most consistently impelling
its extraordinary reliance upon the journey as myth and metaphor. Certainly in the work of Thomas Kinsella such matter and manner run together, but they do so in a direction peculiar to his intense introspection.
The only contemporary Irish poet to have taken Jung as poetic subject,
Kinsella has—to the point of near obsession—sent his personae on rum-
inative evening walks and shocked, bony drops into memory and the
subconscious. His narrators tour nighttime landscapes searching the many
in the one. Such sojourns evidence little concern for the individual defining his place in the daylit world of social relations. Instead they boil
down the "common plight" and the "individual plight" to find in the
residue of both the same essence. "Where is everybody?" Kinsella demands
in *A Technical Supplement*. "Look / in the mirror, at that face."[28]

Not surprisingly, Kinsella's question recalls *Finnegans Wake* ("Here comes
everybody").[29] Kinsella too has sought Joyce's benediction, and he has
written at length about Joyce's simultaneous address of Irish and modern

reality. Again, there is little to choose between the two for, Irishman, modern man, or "doubly cursed,"[30] we all inherit a "gapped, discontinuous" nontradition. In a world that has heaved itself past Hiroshima and Auschwitz, where "the most sensitive individuals have long since been shaken loose into disorder . . . every writer has to make the imaginative grasp at identity himself."[31] Unlike Mahon, though—and perhaps because he was not born with the burden of Northern blood—Kinsella feels no pressing, particular need to sweep the Irish decks clean before starting. If he can find material "in his inheritance to suit him," fine; but even if he can, as indeed Kinsella and the creator of Leopold Bloom do, he knows anyway that art means an eventual return to a kind of cultural scratch, "what a man in his life shares more with all men than he does with any class of men . . . eating, sleeping, loving, fighting, dying."[32]

Though Kinsella frequently assumes the matter of Ireland as freight, his poetry is finally about these basics—or, further back, their bases in "nightmare-bearing tissue" and cellular memory. The logic of Kinsella's gaze inward thus finds public horror "inner catastrophe," history but "massed human wills." "It is out of ourselves and our wills that the chaos comes," he writes, "and out of ourselves that some order must be constructed."[33] The construction of order—or, more precisely (particularly in the later work), its gentler fostering or encouragement—is Kinsella's high theme, and the archetypal journey his way there. As one critic has written, Kinsella's achievement lies less in his recognition of physical and moral decay than in "his resistance to this skepticism."[34] Against a backdrop of isolation, wearing process, and sagging opposition to evil, Kinsella looks unflinchingly inward, bound to the hope of enduring towards understanding or even glimpsing an undefined, growing order near the frustrating core of things. The motif of active questing seems a kind of personal corrective to the widespread "numbness and dullness" Kinsella characterizes in "The Divided Mind," the lassitude of loss into which the contemporary spirit has been jarred. It is his way of imaging man's position, navigating alone among the grotesqueries of history and the indignities of physical decay, and his record "nonetheless" of attempts to return with understanding and value.

Journeys—literal, imagined, potential—wind through nearly every one of the volumes and individual poems that have made Kinsella's reputation these thirty years. Among them "Nightwalker" marks a turning point, a slight change of focus that changes everything or, more exactly, it seems, Kinsella's overt recognition and embrace of what he had in fact been writing about all along. In the decade and five slim volumes before 1968, he established the concerns that rule his mind and work, what he called in the intensities of the prose introduction to *Wormwood* the "common plight," "individual plight," and the search for "maturity and peace. . . . through ordeal after ordeal." From this period the three works that drew the most attention to Kinsella and which most clearly enact these preoccupations each place a narrator in movement, or at the point of movement, through a symbolic landscape. "Baggot Street Deserta" set the pattern with its mobile nocturnal consciousness restively clarifying and synthesizing. Bowed by the weight of a dispiriting present and past, he still endures to feel his pulse, its tight

> Beat tapping out endless calls
> Into the dark, as the alien
> Garrison in my own blood
> Keeps constant contact with the main
> Mystery, not to be understood.

"Downstream" and "A Country Walk" later place the poet literally in this dark where, paddling time's river by dusk or striding a riverbank, they aggressively "thrust ahead" to "confront" and decode the physical environment and its message of permanence, mutability, and the disappointments of history. The poems at last illustrate Kinsella's emerging belief in the possibility of recompensatory vision, what he calls in *Wormwood* "a wider scope, a more penetrating harmony" briefly held before return to the fatiguing route and the next ordeal. In "A Country Walk" this is the current's brief kiss in "troubled union," an image testifying to the capacity to endure towards order amid the destructive current of the national past; in "Downstream" we witness the extremities between which man runs his course stunned momentarily into harmony, "the slow, downstreaming dead" of the temporal water "blended / One" with the perfect constellations above.

Like the trembling gossamers binding friends and family in "Cover Her Face" or the crystals and intermittent flames of the later "Phoenix Park," such images engender themselves within the gaps in shattered human experience, the chasms into which Kinsella sends his voyagers.[35] According to Kinsella, these fissures traverse both the individual and common life ("gaps in ourselves," "a gapped . . . tradition"), and it is in the failure of "Downstream" and "A Country Walk" to do similarly double duty that they break promises made in "Baggot Street." For the most part, these celebrated poems are written from *outside* their subjects. We do follow an internal topography of observation and reflection, but Ireland's extinguished heroism and the moral acid of the "European pit" remain realities essentially foreign to the speaker—the effect is that of a condemnation of the Holocaust heaping guilt on a few monstrous individuals while ignoring what we all have in common with them: the poet's heart does not finally beat in contact with the main mystery. This is perhaps why the conclusions of the poems seem off. Imitations of consciousness in the Romantic tradition of "Tintern Abbey," the poet courting a changing natural scene until it half-creates thoughts too deep for tears, "A Country Walk" and "Downstream" end with the slightest rehearsed, mechanical tidiness; water responds a trifle too conveniently in the former, as does the swan in the latter, a ringer and *avis-ex-machina* too magically fusing water and sky.

Next to these, the concluding "vision" of "Nightwalker" is a disquieting experience, but one better aligned with the inertial progression of Kinsella's thought. The central image is the moon's "fat skull," a "mask of grey dismay" that assumes dark luminence as it reflects the ample human evil meditated upon by the speaker during his evening peregrination. Over time we see as well that it mirrors the narrator's "brain in the dark." When at last, in the companionship of the perverse, he hails the "Hatcher of peoples! / Incline from your darkness into mine," he unleashes an hallucinatory, expressionistic flight across cislunar space that distills violence, and "it has a human taste." This is not reassurance, but it is understanding—the darkness he would search, send endless calls into, seen as what it is, human, yours, mine, ours. With "Nightwalker" Kinsella alters the direction of his "arrow piercing the void." The moon voyage becomes a voyage into self, the journey out a journey in. This is what Kinsella identified as a goal in "Wormwood" but never fully achieved in the earlier work: "penetrating our context to know ourselves."

For Kinsella the point is that the reverse is also true, and his work in the last twenty years has headed resolutely inward and backward, and from will that gropes for structure towards ease with "things not right nor reasonable." The presence of Jung is everywhere felt in the long quest poems and sequences that have continued to comprise Kinsella's best work—one thinks first of "One" and "Notes from the Land of the Dead" (thematically and syntactically rooted in another poem of travel and ordeal, "Phoenix Park"), but also of such a poem as "Tao and Unfitness at Inistiogue on the River Nore," clearly a sequel to "Downstream" and corrective to its autocratic authorial will. In complex works meriting far more discussion than is possible here, cast and props are assembled, archetypal mother, child, wise old man, shadow, the journey into the dark after the dragon, rebirth as the reintegrated self. The Jungian apparatus sets up big questions: no less than these, how and from where the individual comes into being, and his role in a process encompassing primordial first causes, growth, and "oblivion, our natural condition."

In "Notes" and then "One," "ourselves" and "our context" interpenetrate in a nearly suffocating underworld of retrieved childhood memory and a mythodramatically condensed Voyage of the First Kindred from the earliest reaches of collective Irish memory. En route images from both realms recur (the wall or dolmen, the pit) or evolve into new forms (the drop as river or flood, bird of prey as angel) to place the poet's highly individualized memories and experience in the context of race and the passage of endless generations. Here at the crux of particular and general, where birth is death, death birth, we are invited to see a flickering, Heraclitean order, "darkness, fire, darkness, threaded on each other." Alone with paradox, fortified by what Lawrence called "the glimpse of chaos" as "a vision, a window to the sun,"[36] the returned quest hero can find even in "nightnothing" a kind of sufficiency and comfort. Quiet "survivor" (in at least two senses), he "ungulfs a Good Night, smiling."

The journey in Kinsella's poetry ends always in some measure of achievement and growth. In "One" it is the nostalgic speaker's presence at the epiphanic, representative moment of individuation, when his grandfather's old workblock splits open, "countless little nails / squirming and dropping out of it." Dactyls tumbling, discrete being frees itself, though, the coda notes, it carries always its chained ball, the "dark urge." Here, on a route laid out in "Notes," occurs a collision, between the poet speeding backward towards potentiality in "the dark beyond our first father," and our first father Bith from the *Lebor Gabala* laboring forwards towards completion—shadowed barber-shop mirrors: "my father looked in from the dark, / my face black-mirrored beside his."

In Kinsella the use of such traditional and personally generated myth, both roughly Jungian in character, seems to rise from a craving for something like spiritual presence reaching backward, forward, beyond the sterile world of objects and flesh that decays (the landscape of the drear earlier poetry). He shares with Jung the goal of integration of personality, a state brought about by a process involving, in part, "*archetypes of transformation* . . . typical situations, places, ways, animals, plants" that symbolize and encourage the interfusion of conscious and unconscious until "a decided change of consciousness is brought about."[37] One is tempted to extend the analysis and here consider the images rewarding Kinsella's voyagers, descendents of water's ordered disorder in "A Country Walk": the mutating crystals in the ordeal cup of "Phoenix Park," monsters coiling and uncoiling in our quotidian substance near the end of "Notes." The illumination achieved may, in fully Jungian terms, bring us "back to ourselves as an actual, living something, poised between two world-pictures and their darkly discerned potencies," where the self, now including the whole personality, transcends the Ego. Beyond it, the unified self can push forward to gain "kinship with beasts and gods, with crystals and with stars"—with the world, the disconnection from which in much of the earlier poetry is a prime article of Kinsella's non-faith.

Reading Kinsella, we are in the presence of a chaotic loneliness straining towards order and community. Because such qualities do not reside for him in what Beckett called "the nullity of extracircumferential phenomena," they must be sought inward through "a contraction of the spirit, a descent."[38] Breaking through the bottom of isolation, the "shell of solitude," he comes at last upon the self in the whole, the whole in the self, upon "whole matter in itself." For all that seems to set Kinsella apart from his contemporaries—the fathomless interiority, poetic fragmentation, the strained extremity of voice—this preoccupation and its expression in the archetypal quest place him recognizably in the Irish poetic landscape. Questions about the individual and the mass arise almost invariably in the work of recent Irish poets, then seem to lodge themselves naturally in structures provided by the figurative journey. Positively, negatively, travelling taps "the mystery of 'any place' "—says Updike in *Rabbit, Run*, this mystery is the necessary prelude to the first question of the separate, questing individual, "Why am I me?"[39] Simply put, travel means a leaving behind or a going towards, and it draws into meaningful opposition the solitary act of journeying and the powerful attractions of community. The theme of individual vision peering out from the thicket of society, blood, and tradition centers itself in the great literary journeys of the century—in Harry Angstrom's own, in those of Bellow's *Augie March*, Styron's *Set This House on Fire*, Walker Percy, Lawrence, Lowry, Kerouac, Ellison. The route to *Catcher in the Rye* or Sartre's *Les Chemins de la Liberté* extends that earlier taken by Odysseus, Cúchulainn, Childe Harold, Huck. "The road," Cervantes said, "is better than the inn."

On the road Irish poetry has contributed sizeably to what Calvin Bedient identifies as a new sub-genre, "the modern poem of travel."[40] Whether Larkin's "The Whitsun Weddings," Graham's "The Nightfishing," or Kinsella's "Downstream," these are reflective poems that "face a solitary modern consciousness towards place and time yet do not, as it were, sit still, are not even ostensibly at rest, but move through the world, constantly stimulated to new observations, reactions, associations." In their fluttering, flickering inconstancy, such poems act out modern instability and loneliness, even as their relentless forward drive testifies to the will searching for, *still believing in,* order and wholeness: Gunn's "condemned" walker "contained in my coat" cousining Wordsworth's wayfarer "from stage to stage / Advancing." Informed by "our hypersensitivity to the moment," they increase our "sense of exposure to existence," but do not, as Bedient contends, "say that life is only here and now." To the contrary, awakened to reflection and association by a changing landscape, the solitary consciousness feels more strongly than before the layered depth of existence, history, and place adding their weight to the moment's burden. History and place weigh more in Ireland than elsewhere.

In the poem of travel, Irish poets are seeking ways to move under a double load, the psychological and philosophical luggage borne by the modern writer and thinker, and the heavy pack of "Irishness" with its strange gear. In their lives, this has expressed itself most frequently as a kind of semi-exile, what Kavanagh called "the simplicity of going away and the simplicity of return"[41] forged by more than dual residence and airplane tickets into a trenchant complexity. Contradiction, it seems, rules their steps as it rules Mahon's centuries, "two steps forward, one step back." Following the dual promise of distance and proximity, Montague circles, bearing pure and rust-tinged water in balanced buckets. Kinsella finds the meaning of home in a "ritual of departure" and the main mystery in his own veins. Murphy has his islands, Heaney's Sweeney his new roost and power of flight. Mahon's disaffection is a form of affection—distance as a proof of hurt as a proof of love. If one image can begin to mirror the complexities broached by the Irish poem of distance and movement, it is Mahon's enigmatic figure in two neighboring works from the collected poems, "The Window" and "The Sea in Winter." The terms are window and wind. Though invisible, the first is solid, caulked into place, protective, the glass through which we draw the world into focus. Wind, viewed from up close, is invisible too, but a nothing. Afar, though, sighted at large in the world, it takes on substance, becomes both that against which one mounts windows and the very principle of freedom and life inspiriting "the shivering grass, / The creamy seas and turbulent skies." In Mahon's vision, as orthographically, the wind is transparently of the window, and not of it. "Distance," he says, "is the vital bond / Between the window and the wind."

Notes

1. Thomas Kinsella, "The Irish Writer," in Sean Lucy, ed., *Davis, Mangan, Ferguson? Tradition and the Irish Writer: Writings by W. B. Yeats and Thomas Kinsella* (Dublin: Dolman Press, 1970), 66.

2. Seamus Deane, "Irish Poetry and Irish Nationalism," in Douglas Dunn, ed., *Two Decades of Irish Writing: A Critical Survey* (Chesire: Carcanet Press, 1975), 17.

3. Joyce appears physically and is addressed in the title poems of Kinsella's *Nightwalker* and Heaney's *Station Island;* he is otherwise present in Montague's "Portrait of the Artist as a Model Farmer" (*Poisoned Lands*) and Mahon's "The Joycentenary Ode" (*The Hunt by Night*). For perceptive critical commentary on Joyce's influence upon Irish poetry, see Robert F. Garratt, *Modern Irish Poetry: Tradition and Continuity from Yeats to Heaney* (Berkeley and Los Angeles: University of California Press, 1986).

4. Kinsella, "The Irish Writer," 65.

5. Morse Peckham, "Toward a Theory of Romanticism," *PMLA* 66 (1951):5–23.

6. Quoted in Maurice Harmon, *Irish Poetry After Yeats: Seven Poets* (Dublin: Wolfhound Press, 1979), 21.

7. I think of Edna Longley, "Searching the Darkness: Richard Murphy, Thomas Kinsella, John Montague and James Simmons," in Dunn, *Two Decades of Irish Writing,* and, to a lesser extent, Seamus Heaney, "The Poetry of Richard Murphy," in Maurice Harmon, ed., *Richard Murphy: Poet of Two Traditions* (Dublin: Wolfhound Press, 1978).

8. Quoted in Seamus Deane, "The Appetites of Gravity: Contemporary Irish Poetry," *Sewanee Review,* 84, no. 2 (Winter 1976): 207.

9. Quotations from Murphy's work are drawn from the following volumes: *Sailing to an Island* (London: Faber and Faber, 1963); *The Battle of Aughrim* (London: Faber and Faber, 1986, *High Island (London: Faber and Faber, 1974); and Selected Poems* (London: Faber and Faber, 1979). In order to minimize the number of notes, I have chosen not to footnote individual quotations from Murphy's poetry and those of the other poets covered in this essay. In most cases, the source is indicated in the text; when this is not so or when the quotation is particularly difficult to locate, I have noted the entry.

10. Richard Murphy, "The Pleasure Ground," *Listener* 70, no. 1794 (15 August 1963): 237.

11. Longley, "Searching the Darkness," 123.

12. Quotations are drawn from the following volumes of Montague's poetry: *Forms of Exile* (Dublin: Dolmen Press, 1958); *Poisoned Lands* (Dublin: Dolmen Press, 1977; new edition of 1961 volume); *Tides* (Chicago: Swallow Press, 1971);

The Rough Field (Dublin: Dolmen Press, 1974; 2nd edition); *A Slow Dance* (Winston-Salem: Wake Forest University Press, 1975); *The Great Cloak* (Winston-Salem: Wake Forest University Press, 1978); *The Dead Kingdom* (Dublin: Dolmen Press, 1984).

13. Longley, "Searching the Darkness," 123.

14. John Montague, "Global Regionalism," interview by Adrian Frazier, *Literary Review* 22, no. 2 (Winter 1979): 174.

15. John Montague, "In the Irish Grain," introduction to John Montague, ed., *The Faber Book of Irish Verse* (London: Faber and Faber, 1974), 37.

16. Critics have correctly noted the syntactic and emotional resemblance of these lines to those of Louis MacNeice in "Autumn Journal," Part 16: "Scholars and saints my eye, the land of ambush, / Purblind manifestoes, never-ending complaints. . . ." Not uncoincidentally, perhaps, "Autumn Journal" is another Irish poem of travel. Shortly after the passage above, the expatriate MacNeice reflects ambivalently upon Ireland and distance from it: "I thought I was well / Out of it, educated and domiciled in England, / Though yet her name keeps ringing like a bell / In an underwater belfrey" (*Collected Poems* [London: Faber and Faber, 1979], 132).

17. Montague, "Song of the Lonely Bachelor" (1952), *Poisoned Lands*, 47.

18. Montague, cover note, *The Rough Field*.

19. John Montague, "The Impact of International Modern Poetry on Irish Writing," in Sean Lucy, ed., *Irish Poets in English* (Cork: Mercier Press, 1973), 157.

20. Lecture delivered in Caen, France, 26 February 1982.

21. William Hazlitt, "On Going a Journey," in M. H. Abrams, et al, eds. *The Norton Anthology of English Literature*, vol. 2 (New York: W. W. Norton & Co. 1979), 468.

22. Quotations are drawn from the following volumes of Mahon's poetry: *Night-Crossing* (London: Oxford University Press, 1968); *Poems: 1962–1978* (Oxford University Press, 1979); *The Hunt by Night* (Winston-Salem: Wake Forest University Press, 1982).

23. Alain Robbe-Grillet, "Samuel Beckett, or 'Presence' in the Theatre" in Martin Esslin, ed., *Samuel Beckett: A Collection of Critical Essays* (Englewood Cliffs: Prentice-Hall, Inc., 1965), 115.

24. Eamon Grennan, " 'To the Point of Speech' ": The Poetry of Derek Mahon," in James D. Brophy and Raymond J. Porter, eds., *Contemporary Irish Writing* (Boston: Iona College Press, 1983), 30.

25. Adrian Frazier, "Pilgrim Haunts: Montague's *The Dead Kingdom* and Heaney's *Station Island*," *Éire-Ireland* 22, no. 4 (Winter 1985): 143.

26. Quotations are drawn from the following volumes of Heaney's poetry: *Death of a Naturalist* (London: Faber and Faber, 1966); *Door into the Dark* (London,

Faber and Faber, 1969); *North* (New York: Oxford University Press, 1976); *Field Work* (London: Faber and Faber, 1979); *Sweeney Astray: A Version from the Irish* (New York: Farrar Straus Giroux, 1984); *Station Island* (London: Faber and Faber, 1984).

27. Frazier, "Pilgrim Haunts," 137.

28. Quotations are drawn from the following volumes of Kinsella's poetry: *Poems: 1956–1973* (Winston-Salem: Wake Forest University Press, 1979), *Peppercanister Poems: 1972–1978* (Winston-Salem: Wake Forest University Press, 1979).

29. For helpful commentary on the "HCE" motif, see Brian John, "Imaginative Bedrock: Kinsella's *One* and the *Lebor Gabala Érenn,*" *Éire-Ireland* 20, no. 1 (Spring 1985): 111–12.

30. Calvin Bedient, *Eight Contemporary Poets* (London: Oxford University Press, 1974), 119.

31. Thomas Kinsella, "The Divided Mind," in Sean Lucy, ed., *Irish Poems in English.*

32. Kinsella, "The Irish Writer," 65–66.

33. Thomas Kinsella, "Poetry and Man," *Directions* (Summer 1968), quoted in Maurice Harmon, "By Memory Inspired: Themes and Forces in Recent Irish Writing," *Éire-Ireland* 8, no. 2 (1973); 7.

34. Bedient, *Eight Contemporary Poets*, 119.

35. For an intelligent discussion of such fissures and the bonding "daimonic" force in Kinsella's work, see Daniel O'Hara, review of *Song of the Night* and *The Messenger, Éire-Ireland* 14, no. 1 (Spring 1979): 131–35.

36. D. H. Lawrence, "Chaos in Poetry," rep. in *Selected Literary Criticism* (London: William Heinemann, 1955), 90.

37. C. G. Jung, from *Essays on a Science of Mythology* and, later in the paragraph, *Two Essays on Analytical Psychology*, quoted in Lillian Feder, *Ancient Myth in Modern Poetry* (Princeton: Princeton University Press, 1971), 54–55. I am indebted to Feder's discussion of Jung in the chapter entitled "Freud and Jung on Myth."

38. Samuel Beckett, *Proust and Three Dialogues with Georges Duthuit* (London: Faber and Faber, 1970), 48.

39. John Updike, *Rabbit, Run* (New York: Penguin, 1964), 229.

40. Bedient, *Eight Contemporary Poets*, 129.

41. Patrick Kavanagh, *Collected Pruse* (London: MacGibbon and Lee, 1967), 20.

Next to Nothing: Uses of the Otherworld in Modern Irish Literature

Dillon Johnston

I

In his novel of 1952, *The Sun Dances at Easter*, Austin Clarke inserts a framed tale of two lovers, a Christian novice and a woman from the other world, in which two views of the supernatural are opposed. Eithne, the otherworldly heroine is torn between a Christian afterlife, a "glory of being" toward which "the human race [is] moving through the wretchedness and misery of time," and a timeless but coterminous otherworld in which "substance is finer. . . . closer to will than mind and body in this world," a world "bright with an eternal summer."[1] According to Myles Dillon, Eithne's ambivalence was present in an early-medieval legend inscribed in the fifteenth-century *Book of Fermoy*,[2] from which Clarke must indirectly have borrowed the tale.

Proinsias MacCana has argued that, in the historically Christian society of Ireland, concern for a pagan otherworld, "together with the ambiguities and relativities of time and space which were implicit," was "one of the underlying continuities from primitive to modern Irish society."[3] Tracking such "underlying continuities" into the written literature of our century, from Yeats and Joyce to current writers, can establish in general terms the traditionalism of modern Irish literature. More specific reflection on the fiction of John McGahern and the poetry of Paul Muldoon can reveal that this ancient topic of the otherworld can also embody the most contemporary anxieties of postmodern literature.

Before considering how recent writers employ the otherworld, we should reflect on its use by storytellers. If asked why they included the otherworld in their tales, storytellers might have responded, formerly, "because it's

there" or, more recently, "because it continues to fascinate listeners."
Seamus O'Duilearga recalls a modern seanchaí's reception at a wake that
must follow a timeless pattern: "He would always be given a good seat
near the fire, and soon would be asked to tell a tale. He would tell one,
five, ten, till light and day came next morning."[4] We need only visualize
ourselves in front of a stupefying televised narrative, snoring and drool-
webbed, to appreciate how strongly such tales attracted their listeners.
Beyond the release from tedious and confining farm routines, the otherworld offered, according to various scholars, these attractions: an explanation for seemingly inexplicable events, for in the underworld every event
has its traceable cause;[5] a field for erotic fantasies, for desire, and therefore
for the unconscious;[6] a location for those who had disappeared, or suffered
untimely deaths;[7] a comforting primer for death;[8] and a paradigm for rites
of passage.[9]

Traditionally, the otherworld was portrayed in *echtrae*—narratives of a
hero's adventures in the underworld—or in *immra,* which recounted a
heroic voyage to a series of otherworld islands. Although timeless in their
setting, these subgenres usually distinguish themselves from fairy tales in
which nonheroic countrypeople are the protagonists. All stories of the
otherworld conventionally feature a relativity of time; two-way traffic
between this and the otherworld; metamorphoses and contortions; rituals
and taboos; dualisms and polarities; and stereotyped otherworldly figures.[10]
Alwyn and Brinsley Rees emphasize the paradoxical qualities of time and
space in the otherworld:

> The limits of such a world cannot be "defined" in terms of distance or
> direction. Situated far beyond the horizon, it is the goal of the most
> perilous journey in the world; present unseen all round us, it can break
> in upon us "in the twinkling of an eye." . . . Defying definition in
> space, the Other World also transcends mundane time. Characteristi-
> cally, this is expressed in the stories in two opposite ways. On the one
> hand, a very short time in the Other World corresponds with a very
> long time in this world. . . . On the other hand, a long time in the
> Other World sometimes transpires to have been but an instant in this
> world.[11]

This relativity of time appears especially in the entrances and exits from
the otherworld, as in this tale recorded in this century in the Blue Stack
Mountains of Donegal. In this case the boundary of the otherworld is a
stream:

The man went out, put the pail under the flow and stood while it was filling. When he looked down the sea was rising up towards him and on it the prettiest little boat he had ever seen. There was a little old red-haired man sitting in the stern of the boat: he was dressed in speckled clothes and juggling with three little yellow balls. The boat came in to the man's very feet, and began to beat against his shins. In a rush of rage he lifted his foot and made a kick at it. No sooner had he done so than he was taken into the boat which went off to sea. . . .[12]

After extensive adventures in an island world, the boat returns him to his bucket and chores:

When he looked about him, the pail was just exactly as he left. He caught hold of it and brought it into the house. The maid was standing in the middle of the floor with the measure of meal, just as she had been when he left. "Isn't it long you have been out!" she said.[13]

II

Characters in modern Irish writing may not be shanghaied so directly into the otherworld as was the protagonist of this Blue Stack's tale. Although Yeats in *The Wandering of Oisin* and Clarke in his romances have adapted ancient otherworldly tales, most modern references to the otherworld are couched in psychological or naturalistic phrasing. As with "The Dead" when Joyce's hero "approached that region where dwell the vast hosts of the dead," critics tend to explain such voyaging as a drift into dream or a dive into metaphor. Often modern writers merely reflect those "ambiguities and relativities of time and space" that, MacCana has reminded us, are "never absent from Irish narrative."[14] Through settings, scenes, or emblems, writers may represent escapes from process and homocidal history, or they may create analogues for synchronicity.

Following Vico, both Yeats and Joyce believed that history was the actualization in time of a pattern within the human mind. In the "Ithaca" episode, Joyce finds a metaphor for this pattern in the stars:

an infinity renderable equally finite by the supposititious apposition of one or more bodies equally of the same and of different magnitudes: a

mobility of illusory forms immobilised in space, remobilised in air: a past
which possibly had ceased to exist as a present before its probable spec-
tators had entered actual present existence.[15]

In the work of Louis MacNeice, Derek Mahon perceives more than
mere emblems of timelessness: "The Islands of the Blest, the Hesperides,
Tír na nÓg, the Land of the Every Young—call it what you will, it crops
up regularly in MacNeice's poetry and is usually associated with the West
of Ireland."[16] Even a casual reader of MacNeice has observed as a major
theme eddies of timelessness, when "time was away and somewhere else,"
which afford only momentary pauses in time's flow. Mahon himself, of
course, has created a postcataclysmic landscape where time can register
only in the slow oxidation of civilization's detritus, in "the terminal democracy / of hatbox and crab, / of hock and Windowlene."[17] If the poems
are not situated in a "cold dream / of a place out of time,"[18] they may
muse openly on an otherworld:

> Somewhere there is an afterlife
> Of dead leaves,
> A stadium filled with an infinite
> Rustling and sighing.
>
> Somewhere in the heaven
> Of lost futures
> The lives we might have led
> Have found their own fulfillment.[19]

Distinctively his own, Mahon's setting derives in part from Beckett's,
where we also hear eloquent voices intoning "germinal ironies" in a timeless wasteland.

Heaney's bogland, hoarding artifacts of the past, is an emblem of syn-
chronic history. "Earth-pantry, bone-vault, / sun-bank, embalmer," the
bog is store and restorer of natural energy and of history. "Casket, mid-
den, / floe of history," it is a topos for the unconscious:

> Ground that will strip
> its dark side,
> nesting ground,
> outback of my mind.[20]

In *The Messenger,* Thomas Kinsella creates a complex emblem of the entelechy or time's pattern. Confronting his father's death, he reverses the narrative of the elder Kinsella's life, past the periods of bitter disappointment, to periods of achievement and, finally, to his youthful father's first day of work as a messenger boy. In the course of this reversed narrative, the poet's own alfresco conception is supervised by a dragonfly that contains at this moment the code of its past existences, as larva, cocoon, and imago. The poem's advance through the stages of the poet's recovery—from nightmare of the body's putrescence and vulnerability to the resplendent image of fresh beginnings—has its analogue in the dragonfly's rise from slime into "insect-shimmering beauty":

> Trailing a sunless instinct,
> a saw-jawed multiple past,
> an edible (almost liquid)
> vulnerability,
> and winged!—weightless and wondrous!—
> up from the bloodied slime
> through the arms of a black rainbow
> scooping down in beauty
> he has come, he has arisen
> out of the pool of night![21]

Such emblems and narrative devices may offer the reader a separate perspective on our historical world, but these are not the otherworlds that parallel our world in ancient stories or in the contemporary narratives of John McGahern and Paul Muldoon.

III

Although otherworlds are a constant theme in McGahern's earlier five novels, they are usually represented in psychological terms that obviate the wonder or "otherworldly" quality we find in folktales. Most frequently, characters preoccupy parishes of the past, of drunkenness, or of fantasy that detain them from their actual lives. In *The Pornographer* (1979), for example, while drink ("a change of country") and the past (a "permanent,

impermanent day")[22] offer escapes from reality, the title character's erotic
narratives compete with, and even taint, the actual world where only the
female characters can confront the austerities of birth and death. In one
scene the pornographer observes one of these women being drawn into
his otherworld:

> Warmed by the whiskey, watching the fire catch, I felt time suspended
> as she read. If God there was, he must enjoy himself hugely, feeling all
> his creatures absorbed in his creation; but this was even better. It was
> as if another god had visited your creation and had got totally involved
> in it, had fallen for it. (66)

The pornographer's Wildean editor speculates that "one of the reasons of
art's supremacy is just because of the very limitations of life. There will
be no art in heaven" (25). Meanwhile, the surrogate heavens created by
the literary imagination, implicitly even McGahern's fictions, can distract
us from the business of living. In positing the source of the otherworld as
the verbal or literary imagination, McGahern renews an idea articulated
by Wilde and suggested by Synge when Christy Mahon departs with his
father for a world created in his own imagination.

Presented thematically in the earlier fiction, the otherworld is represented dramatically and experientially in McGahern's two collections of
stories. For example in "The Wine Breath," from McGahern's first collection, a priest approaches a neighbor who is sawing wood:

> Suddenly, as he was about to rattle the gate loudly to see if this would
> penetrate the sawing, he felt himself (bathed as in a dream) in an
> incredible sweetness of light. It was the evening light on snow. The gate
> on which he has his hand vanished, the alders, Gillespie's formidable
> bulk, the roaring of the saw. He was in another day, the lost day of
> Michael Bruen's funeral nearly thirty years before. All was silent and
> still there. Slow feet crunched on the snow.[23]

Through an act of will he withdraws from this otherworld:

> He did not know how long he had stood in that lost day, in that white
> light, probably for no more than a moment. He could not have stood
> the intensity for any longer.[24]

The priest recognizes with what greater frequency and how rapidly he
haunts these dead days, "as if he'd suddenly fallen through time; it was

as if the world of the dead was as available to him as the world of the living."[25] Although to his priestly imagination, these moments "bathed in the eternal . . . seemed everything we had been taught and told of the world of God," in the next sentence he avoids the church gate "with its circle and cross" and detours around the churchyard. His momentary visits to this radiant and timeless world darken the present, which he sees "as a flimsy accumulating tissue over all the time that was lost."[26]

In the charming story "A Slip-Up" the aged protagonist actually becomes abandoned in this otherworld. Having retired from his farm, Michael accompanies his wife to Tesco's market, where he begins his daily imaginary reclamation of his lost farm. Michael's otherworld seems as complete and credible to the reader as his real world, and if we miss his transition into that imaginary world, we share his confusion.

> He still preferred to wait for her outside with the shopping bag against the Special Offers pasted in the glass. By that time he would have already reached the farm between the lakes while walking with her, and was ready for work.[27]

But this day he overextends himself in his imaginary labors and grows petulant:

> He was too weak to work. It must be late and why had she not called him to his meal? He stuck the fork in the ground and in exasperation went over to the barbed wire. The strands were loose. . . . Why had she not called him? Had she no care? . . . It was in this impotent rage that he heard the horn blow.[28]

Agnes has returned to Tesco's where she forgot to collect him hours ago. The story of their "slip-up" is greeted at their pub, the Royal, with quiet elation that leaves Michael ashamed and estranged in this world of the present.

For the duration of the reader's confusion, such relativity of time and space seems marvelous or, in the more precise language of Tzvetan Todorov, "fantastic." As a literary term, the fantastic pervades that portion of a "realistic" narrative when the reader and the protagonist encounter some experience that defies the laws of normal reality. Either the event is uncanny—explicable in psychological terms as a trick of the mind— or supernatural, operating according to nonnatural laws such as those of fairyland. According to Todorov, "The fantastic occupies the duration of this uncertainty. Once we choose one answer or the other, we leave the fantastic for a neighboring genre, the uncanny or the marvelous."[29] In modern Irish literature the clearest cases of the fantastic passing into the marvelous may be Austin Clarke's romances and Flann O'Brien's novels, *At Swim-two-birds* and *The Third Policeman*. Although these fictions finally settle into supernatural domains, as they hover temporarily in the fantastic they also cast psychological and philosophical shadows.

In the examples at hand, the story from the Blue Stack Mountains about the magical boat and McGahern's "A Slip-Up," we could nearly time the duration of the fantastic, as the reader adjusts to the marvelous universe of the fairies or recognizes that Michael's memory and imagination have become more vivid than his actual life. McGahern's forays into an otherworld, which soon reveal themselves as uncanny, achieve several effects. First, McGahern reminds us that we are citizens of collateral worlds: for Michael, the world of memory and the mundane world or, for the hero of *The Pornographer*, the actual world and the world of erotic fantasy that, because of its compulsive nature, cycles endlessly. Second, by evoking a supernatural otherworld, "bathed in the eternal,"[30] and then suggesting its origins in memory and imagination, he offers the reader a morsel of his protagonists' disillusionment. Sharing a disbelief in their otherworlds, McGahern's characters remain exiles from these worlds that they nurse in the mind's dark marsupium. The heroine of *The Barracks* realizes that the "world of hers wasn't the whole world; each person was a world; and there were so many people."[31] Because McGahern's characters can live in their own pasts, they are separated from each other not by time so often as space. For example, toward the opening of "Parachutes" in McGahern's new collection, the protagonist notices how

> The long hand of the clock stood at two minutes to eight. It did not seem to move at all. She was gone, slipping further out of reach with every leaden second. . . . Outside she was nowhere in sight.
>
> I could see down on the city, its maze of roads already lighted in the still, white evening, each single road leading in hundreds of directions.[32]

Following the Irish writer's tendency to spatialize time, McGahern would convert Lear's "Never. . . ." or the Raven's "nevermore" to "nowhere." The otherworld of memory offers a location for the lost loves as well as for the dead.

IV

Even beyond McGahern, among contemporary Irish writers Paul Muldoon evokes most deliberately the themes and experiences of stories of the otherworld. Although the first two volumes, *New Weather* (1973) and *Mules* (1977), contain only one snippet of an *immram*, these volumes, like the subsequent three volumes, can be read in light of the basic themes of otherworld narratives. Such readings may even complement poststructuralist interpretations, such as William Wilson's fine essay on Muldoon in *Contemporary Literature* (Fall, 1987). From the early poem "Identities," which concludes with these three lines—

> I have been wandering since, back up the streams
> That once had flowed simply one into the other,
> One taking the other's name. [33]

—Wilson derives the following paradigm for much of Muldoon's work:

> The woman, seen either as mother or lover, is the keeper of duplicitous words, while the father, dead or otherwise absent from the scene, is the meaningful center of an old relationship with the natural world, a traditional pastoralism that seems irretrievably lost in the poet's own life, and one that he perforce elegizes. [34]

With the father's elemental unity irrecoverable, the poet moves toward the woman's complex world which, as Wilson points out, is always associated with literature:

> To fall into the textual realm is to fall from idealized unity into division, into the play of signification and *différence*. In Muldoon's poetry, there are losses which nothing, let alone words, can restore. [35]

If we substitute for "idealized unity" and "the play of signification and *différence*" the folklorist terms "identity" and "metamorphosis," we may draw closer to Muldoon's sources and his intention. Elliott Gose has recognized that, in ancient Irish tales, trials and riddles in the otherworld allow the hero to achieve his identity. In the process, however, he frequently must undergo metamorphoses in which he risks losing his sense of self and even his humanity. Gose then quotes Heinz Lichtenstein:

Metamorphosis and identity are the two limits of human existence, incompatible with one another, but complementary in that human life exists in a movement between these two limits.[36]

Muldoon's five volumes can be characterized in relation to these polarities within the otherworld quest. As Wilson suggests, the first two volumes concern identity, expressed as a gravitation between Lawrentian parents, "a servant boy" and "the school-mistress." *Immra* appear overtly only in "Armageddon, Armageddon," the sequence that concludes *Mules*. From the impending disaster of Armagh, the seven poems offer only false escapes into the stars or myths or into the fictional otherworld of Lawrence Durrell. The second section of this poem suggests that should one escape, one's repatriation, like Oisin's when he was drawn home "To be one again with the mountains, / The bogs and the little fields,"[37] would be a death and disintegration.

In the third volume, *Why Brownlee Left*, Muldoon associates the entrance into the otherworld with themes of identity. As Muldoon has said in an interview:

One of the ways in which we are most ourselves is that we imagine ourselves to be going somewhere else. It's important to most societies to have the notion of something out there to which we belong, that our home is somewhere else . . . there's another dimension, something around us and beyond us, which is our inheritance.[38]

Within this volume, this "somewhere else" may be the mysterious place of conception, the land of lost possibilities, irrecoverable innocence, or the destination of a cancelled journey. As in folktales, where otherworldly encounters may occur at various boundaries—at the edge of spring, fall, or nightfall, at two river's confluence, at a crossroads or a stile—borders abound as poetic voltas into otherworlds: an unbroken furrow in "Why Brownlee Left," MacNeice's mysterious window ledge from his poem "Snow," which the poet violates in a sexual initiation ("History"), and an avenue in "The Avenue." Several poems celebrate entrance or breakthrough, and two, at least, "The Bishop" and "The Boundary Commission," evoke the *feth fiada*, an invisible curtain surrounding the otherworld of the Tuatha de Danann, who became the Irish sidhe.[39]

Muldoon acknowledges his re-creation of voyage tales in "Immrama." This poem recounts an aborted voyage in which the man who later would become his father "disappeared / And took passage, almost, for Argentina. / . . . That's him on the verandah, drinking rum / With a man who might be a Nazi, / His children asleep under their mosquito-nets" (WBL, 23).

This small voyage into the otherworld conditions us for "Immram," a voyage through thirty ten-line stanzas into a Raymond Chandleresque Land of Cockayne. Hardly a translation of *Immram Mael Duin*, the similarities between Muldoon's and the eighth-century tale, which resides in fragments in the *The Book of the Dun Cow,*[40] enlarge the otherworld theme in *Why Brownlee Left*. In the tale, the hero, an illegitimate son of a heroic warrior, is raised in the foster home of the queen. Learning of his true lineage from the taunts of a schoolmate, he embarks for knowledge and for revenge on a marauder who murdered his father. Muldoon's poem begins with the anticipated "ball," the predictable rhyme for "hall," as truant as the missing father:

> I was fairly and squarely behind the eight
> That morning in Foster's pool-hall
> when it came to me out of the blue
> In the shape of a sixteen-ounce cue
> That lent what he said some little weight.
> "Your old man was an ass-hole.
> That makes an ass-hole out of you."
> My grand-father hailed from New York State.
> My grand-mother was part Cree.
> This must be some new strain in my pedigree.
>   (WBL, 38)

As in the original tale, the son embarks to find not his father but his father's destroyer who, in both tales, is forgiven. In his quest for knowledge and revenge, he drives "west to Paradise" (38), wanders "into the wild, blue yonder" (39), and feels he will "forever be driving west" (40). Like the original Mael Duin, the hero visits a terrain guarded by a magical cat—in this version a "black cat" from Harlem wearing "a full-length coat of alligator" 943)—and the Tír na Mná, island of beautiful women, "bronzed, bleached, bare-breasted, / Bare-assed to a man," chanting "The Lord is my surf-board. I shall not want" (45). In "Immrama" the road-not-taken leads the father to another gene-pool and the annihilation of the poet-son. In "Immram" a Howard Hughes–like godfather has converted the father into a mule, a drug courier and a sterile future, who assumes disguises in a life of endlessly differed identities. When discovered, the destroyer of the hero's father has taken on the appearance of Hughes during "the hidden years" and of the hairy Man of Ireland whom Mael Duin encountered. This adversary inverts his role and forgives the hero who can then only return to his foster home.

In this volume, we can perceive a metaphorical or psychological intention within most evocations of "somewhere else" or of the voyage to the Otherworld. The brief lyric "Bran," for instance, alludes to an *echtrae* or *immram*, which may date from the seventh century,[41] in which Bran encounters a beautiful woman who invites him to an otherworld of women, where they conjugate blissfully and timelessly. At the urging of one of his mariners, he returns home, but the repatriate crumbles to dust, like Oisin, at his first footfall. In the inversion of the poem's long sentence—

> While he looks into the eyes of women
> Who have let themselves go,
> While they sigh and they moan
> For pure joy,
>
> He weeps for the boy on that small farm
> Who takes on oatmeal Labrador
> In his arms,
> Who knows all there is of rapture.
>   (WBL, 12)

—the erotic otherworld has been replaced by innocence and childhood to which we can never return. If Bran is the dog's name, as Muldoon has suggested,[42] then the possibility of "rapture," transportation to heaven, is denied or limited to a Labrador's love. Otherworlds are evoked, therefore, to depict the phenomenological truth that we are drawn to other realms, the possible existence of which are often denied by the poems.

Whereas we can contemplate the nonexistence of this otherworldly state, we cannot contemplate the state of nonexistence, the volume suggests, without populating or hypothesizing it imaginatively. The early poems on the poet's own conception and the *immra* in which his own existence is erased in the rerunning of his father's life are metaphors for the possibility that we create art to enliven nothingness, an idea on which I elaborate in my conclusion.

It may be, as Wilson has suggested, that women lead the poet into literature, complexity, and *différence*, and away from the primal unity of the father. Conveyed through poetry, however, even this binary distinction must dissolve into a recognition that the polarization is qualified—the mother has read only one volume of Proust; the father can cure farcy—and that as seed-carrier, the father bears the infinite variations of the poet's self—one source of the *immra*—and that as chthonic spoor tender, he is an unconscious ministrant at the mushroom-induced transformation and vision of "Gathering Mushrooms." In *Quoof*, the otherworld is evoked by metamorphoses and visionary changes of state, rather than *immra*: women become trees; unicorns become East Village innocents; butterflies from *New Weather* become destroying angels; the poet becomes his own Pegasus. Within one poem, "The Salmon of Knowledge," a master metamorphoser transforms from semenlike lymph to informant of Finn MacCool, to icon of Christ, to culinary delight—changes inherent in the legends of salmon. In this volume's concluding sequence, a protagonist drawn from the Trickster cycle of American-Indian legends mutates through various forms as the stanzas themselves ring changes on the sonnet form.

As with preceding volumes, the title poem of *Quoof* directs us toward the book's theme: the importance of language in these metamorphoses. In "Quoof," what for his father was an object has become for the poet a secret, functional word, employed to make something happen, to effect separations or penetrations with lovers. In one case, in an encounter "with a girl who spoke hardly any English," the nonce word loses the linguistic background that gives it uniqueness. By equating the poet's groping advance to the yeti's spoor, and therefore the poet to the marginally existing yeti, "Quoof" displaces the poet himself outside the boundaries of language, where he will have to reinvent himself and his relation to society through words:

> my hand on her breast
> like the smouldering one-off spoor of the yeti
> or some other shy beast
> that has yet to enter the langauge.
>
> (Q, 17)

In Muldoon's most recent volume, *Meeting the British* (1987), the variability of words vaults us into various states of mind, if not otherworlds. After a prefatory prose poem, the first lyric, "The Coney," treats the

inexplicable transformation of the father from life to death, which the
poet imagines only through the metamorphosis of words and their images
("which made me think / of something else, then something else again,"
he says in a later poem). In the first two stanzas, the poet assumes the
dying father's roles of mowing the dead garden and honing the scythe,
which he does badly, reducing the whetstone, usually stored on a plank
in his father's cap, to two lop-ears. In the final two stanzas, the inter-
mediary whetstone becomes a wet rabbit in a swimming pool, the plank
a diving board, the cap bathing togs, and the honing the poem's most
memorable image:

> "Come in"; this flayed
> coney would parade
> and pirouette like honey on a spoon:
> "Come on in, Paddy Muldoon."
> And although I have never learned to swim
> I would willingly have followed him.
>
> (MtB, 12)

This invitation to enter another element, surprisingly addressed to the
father, the poet himself would accept, in order to follow "him," who is
also his father. The elision of these words, which transport us into a comic
otherworld, can be reasonably traced, yet the poem evades explication.
The whimsical equation of garden, or perhaps septic tank, with swimming
pool and the animism projected as Disney animation remain mysterious
or, in Todorov's term, "fantastic."

For two reasons, Todorov might have withheld this designation from
Muldoon's poetry. Terming the fantastic "the bad conscience" of a pos-
itivist ear, Todorov argues that the fantastic depended on a belief "in an
immutable, external reality" and "a literature which is merely the transcription of such a reality."[43] He assumes this belief has vanished in
Western culture. Yet, Muldoon plays off against a society that is, by his
characterization, less mobile and more limited in experience than other
modern societies. He says, "It's a fairly homogenous country in which
everybody's experience is pretty much the same, and the same images just
tend to turn up".[44] As in the oral tradition a sense of the otherworld must
have depended on a stable and unanimous sense of this world, so Muldoon's
variability of language and of points of view arise from, and are mollifying
to, a calcified sense of language and history.

Second, Todorov argued that poetry was insufficiently narrative to be fantastic. With an outmoded sense of poetry even for 1970, at time of writing he had not yet encountered contemporary experiments in narrative poetry—compressed and fragmentary poetic narratives—which one critic has defined in terms of Muldoon's recent poetry:

> Reflexive, aleatory, and cornucopian, the New Narrative deploys its fragmented and ramifying fictions to image the unpredictability of life, and its continuous shadowing of What Might Be.[45]

I would argue that this characterization of Muldoon's poetry, poised between reflexion and prediction, extends to poetry Todorov's genre of the "fantastic":

> The classic definition of the present, for example, describes it as a pure limit between the past and the future. The comparison is not gratuitous: the marvelous corresponds to an unknown phenomenon, never seen as yet, still to come—hence to a future; in the uncanny, on the other hand, we refer the inexplicable to known facts, to a previous experience, and thereby to the past. As for the fantastic itself, the hesitation which characterizes it cannot be situated, by and large, except in the present.[46]

Much of Muldoon's poetry remains poised in a present, yielding neither to an understanding of the uncanny nor a credence for the supernatural. This position can be maintained only dynamically, as Todorov would recognize, through the play of signification and a purposeful fragmentariness within the poems and a circuitry of reference among the poems we might characterize with Muldoon's own phrase from *New Weather*: "Carefully appointed mirrors / create the illusion of depth."[47] When asked thirteen years later about this thematic play among his poems—"Is there a risk of the poems becoming rather hermetic . . . a hall of mirrors?"—Muldoon responded: "That depends whether you feel lost or enlarged in a hall of mirrors."[48]

Poised between the uncanny and the marvelous, Muldoon's version of the fantastic induces in the reader the effect of wonder tales on an auditor. Gose reminds us that "mankind's continuing attachment to disorder, to the violation of boundaries is shown . . . by pleasure in hearing tales about tricksters. . . ."[49] In language that reminds us of Muldoon's startling violations of decorum in poems such as "Blewits," "The Unicorn

Defends Itself," and "Beaver," Mary Douglas argues that the violation of taboos in ceremonies or in tales forces the audience

> to turn around and confront the categories on which
> their whole surrounding culture has been built up
> and to recognize them for the fictive, man-made,
> arbitrary creations that they are.[50]

The Rees brothers ascribe a similar effect to tales of the otherworld:

> The storyteller, like the juggler and the illusionist, by convincingly actualizing the impossible, renders the actual world less real. When the spell is over, the hearer "comes back to earth," but the earth now is not quite so solid as it was before, the cadence of its time is less oppressive and its laws have only a relative validity.[51]

By inculcating on an experiential level a relative sense of time and law, the wonder tale, like Muldoon's "fantastic" or evocations of the otherworld by McGahern and other contemporary writers, can undermine absolutist views of history or manifest destiny, strengthen a sense of lived history, and, thereby, serve a political end. We might even submit these otherworld narratives to the Name-That-Fifth-Province contest, promoted fairly recently by certain Irish periodicals. In the now defunct *Cranebag*, Mark Hederman has characterized this "notion of a 'fifth province' " as

> an aesthetic analogy which describes a space which is neither physical, geographical, nor political. It is a place which is beyond or behind the reach of our normal scientific consciousness. It therefore requires a method and a language which are sui generis both to reach it and describe it. The only method available to us at the moment is a certain kind of art.[52]

The editorial seems to direct us toward the strain of Irish literature I have been describing: "In the Celtic tradition there has always been a penchant towards or a hankering after this other dimension, an intuitive awareness of 'the fifth province.' "[53]

In 1967 Jacques Derrida characterized the literary act, for reader or writer, as "a departure from the world toward a place which is neither a *non-place* nor an *other world*, neither a utopia nor an alibi, the creation of 'a universe to be added to the universe,' " in Focillon's phrase. He goes on to define "the consciousness of having something to say as the consciousness of nothing . . . upon which all consciousness of something enriches itself. . . ."[54] Six years earlier, working from Celtic tales of the otherworld, perhaps with a nudge from Heidegger, the Reeses struck this Derridean note:

> There is in the concepts of the boundary, the centre, intercalary time, "today," betwixts-and-betweens, . . . multiple names, multiple skills, puns and, we may add, metaphors, an ambiguity, or a multiplication or concentration of meaning which makes them fitting symbols of the unmanifest, which is itself the world of chaos and at the same time the ground of all being.[55]

To simplify, this most contemporary statement and this characterization of ancient tales of the otherworld both suggest that creativity occurs at the edge of doubt and the undisclosed rather than on the secure plateau of safe assumption or some peak of "knowledge." Specifically, McGahern investigates the fragility of current life, the seductiveness of adjoining worlds of the past or fantasy; Muldoon re-creates the variable states of the present as the chance confluence of infinite variations that excludes uncountable lost possibilities. The creative process they enact is not peculiarly Irish. We recall that Shelley's rhetorical question when tracing the life-giving waters of imagination to the undiscovered country of Mount Blanc—"What . . . / If to the human mind's imaginings / Silence and solitude were vacancy?"[56]—is an implicit affirmation of "gleams of a remoter world." In conveying or re-creating the mystery and drama of the human situation in time, however, the Irish writer inherits an advantageous spatializing concept by which he represents a movement out of the present as an entrance into an otherworld, by which Clarke's modernized ancient hero, for example, may ask, when his love slips from the present into the otherworld, as she must, "But why was everything next to nothing?"[57]

Notes

1. Austin Clarke, *The Sun Dances At Easter: A Romance* (London: Melrose, 1952), 105,114.

2. Myles Dillon, *Early Irish Literature* (Chicago: University of Chicago Press, 1948), 67. This book misprints the date of the inscription of The Book of Fermoy

as "fifth century." The date "Mainly 15th cent." is offered by the *Catalogue of Irish Manuscripts in the Royal Irish Academy Fasciculi xxi-xxv* (Dublin, 1940), 3091.

3. Proinsias MacCana, "Mythology in Early Irish Literature," in *The Celtic Consciousness*, ed. Robert O'Driscoll (Portlaoise: Dolmen Press, 1982), 145, as quoted in Elliott B. Gose, Jr., *The World of the Irish Wonder Tale* (Toronto: University of Toronto Press, 1985), 5.

4. Jeremiah Curtin, *Irish Folk Tales*, ed. Seamus O Duilearga (Dublin: Talbot Press, 1941–42), 170.

5. Gose, *Irish Wonder Tale*, 106.

6. Séan Ó hEóchaidh, *Fairy Legends from Donegal*, trans. Maire Mac Neill, ed. Seamas O Cathain (Dublin: Comhairle Bhealoideas Eireann, 1977), 22; Tzvetan Todorov, *The Fantastic*, trans. Richard Howard (Cleveland: Press of Case Western Reserve University, 1973), 139.

7. Alwyn and Brinley Rees, *Celtic Heritage: Ancient Tradition In Ireland and Wales* (London: Thames and Hudson, 1961), 324.

8. Ó hEóchaidh, *Fairy Legends*, 22; Rees, *Celtic Heritage*, 325.

9. Christa Maria Loffler, *The Voyage to the Otherworld Island in Early Irish Literature*, vol. 2 (Salzbury: Institut fur Anglistik and Amerikanistik, 1983), 426.

10. Loffler, *Voyage to Otherworld*, 12.

11. Rees, *Celtic Heritage*, 343–44.

12. Ó hEóchaidh, *Fairy Legends*, 287.

13. Ibid., 289.

14. MacCana, "Mythology in Early Irish Literature," 145.

15. James Joyce, *Ulysses*, corrected text (New York: Vintage Books, 1986), 575.

16. Terence Brown and Alec Reid, eds., *Time Was Away: The World of Louis MacNeice* (Dublin: Dolmen Press, 1974), 121.

17. Derek Mahon, *Poems 1962–1978* (London: Oxford University Press, 1979), 74.

18. Ibid., 65.

19. Ibid., 59.

20. Seamus Heaney, "Kinship," in *Poems 1965–1975* (New York: Farrar, Straus and Giroux, 1980), 197–98.

21. Thomas Kinsella, *Peppercanister Poems 1972–1978* (Winston-Salem: Wake Forest University Press, 1979), 129.

22. John McGahern, *The Pornographer* (New York: Harper & Row, 1979), 142, 147. Other references to this work will appear within parentheses in the text.

23. John McGahern, *Getting Through* (New York: Harper & Row, 1980), 97.

24. Ibid., 98.

25. Ibid., 99.

26. Ibid., 102.

27. Ibid., 29–30.

28. Ibid., 31.

29. Todorov, The Fantastic, 25.

30. McGahern, Getting Through, 100.

31. McGahern, The Barracks (London: Panther Books, 1972).

32. McGahern, High Ground (New York: Viking, 1987), 11.

33. Paul Muldoon, New Weather (London: Faber & Faber, 1973), 22.

34. William A. Wilson, "Paul Muldoon and the Poetics of Sexual Difference," "Contemporary Literature 28, no. 3 (Fall 1987): 319.

35. Wilson, "Paul Muldoon," 324.

36. Gose, Irish Wonder Tale, 31.

37. Muldoon, Mules and Early Poems (Winston-Salem: Wake Forest University Press, 1985), 84.

38. John Haffenden, Viewpoints: Poets in Conversation (London: Faber & Faber, 1981), 141.

39. Muldoon, Why Brownlee Left (Winston-Salem: Wake Forest University Press, 1980), 23. Hereafter, this volume will be cited parenthetically in my text as WBL with page numbers. Subsequent volumes by Muldoon—Quoof (1983) and Meeting the British (1987), also published by Wake Forest University Press—will be similarly cited as Q and MtB with page numbers, respectively.

40. Dillon, Early Irish Literature, 125.

41. Ibid., 104.

42. Clair Wills, Nick Jenkins, and John Lanchester, "An Interview with Paul Muldoon," Oxford Poetry 3, no. 1 (Winter 1986–87): 16.

43. Todorov, The Fantastic, 168.

44. Wills, "Interview with Paul Muldoon," 17.

45. John Kerrigan, "The New Narrative," London Review of Books, 16–29 February 1984, 22–23.

46. Todorov, The Fantastic, 42.

47. Muldoon, New Weather, 40.

48. Wills, "Interview with Paul Muldoon," 14.

49. Gose, "Irish Wonder Tale," 101.

50. Ibid., 103.

51. Rees, Celtic Heritage, 342.

52. Mark Patrick Hederman, "Poetry and the Fifth Province," Cranebag (1985): 111.

53. Ibid., 113.

54. Jacques Derrida, *Writing and Différence*, trans. Alan Bass (Chicago: University of Chicago Press, 1978), 8.

55. Rees, *Celtic Heritage*, 348.

56. P. B. Shelley, "Mont Blanc"

57. Clarke, *Sun Dances at Easter*, 128.

Irish Elegiac Tradition in the Poetry of Máire Mhac an tSaoi, Caitlín Maude, and Nuala Ní Dhomhnaill

Maureen Murphy

"A woman fiannaí or a crowing hen" is a proverbial expression of the traditional poetic division of labor in the Irish countryside. Fionnscéalta (or hero tales) were the prerogative of the men; *caointe* (or laments for the dead), the prerogative of the women. Three contemporary poets, Máire Mhac an tSaoi (b. 1922), Caitlín Maude (1941–1982), and Nuala Ní Dhomhnaill (b. 1952), have taken elements of the *caoine* and transformed a traditional form in elegies that express their own poetic voices. All of the poets share some similarities in background, a commitment to the Irish language and to the Gaeltacht, and a sympathy for outsiders that is, perhaps, a reflection of their own sense as poets—women as witness.

Máire Mhac an tSaoi was raised in Dublin; she spent several months of every year of her childhood in Dún Chaoin, however, in the Kerry Gaeltacht. Her uncle, Monsignor Padraig de Brún (1889–1960), successively professor of mathematics at Maynooth, President of University College, Galway, and Chairman of the Institute for Advanced Studies, was an accomplished translator as well as poet. Mhac an tSaoi translated his collection *Miserere* into English (1971).

While she had hoped to be an actress and attend the Abbey School of Acting, her parents disapproved and she enrolled, instead, at University College, Dublin. A brilliant and versatile scholar, she did postgraduate work in Paris and in Celtic studies at the Dublin Institute for Advanced Studies; she was called to the Irish Bar and later joined the Department of Foreign Affairs, from which she was granted leave to assist Tomás de Bhaldraithe with the *English-Irish Dictionary* (1959).

141

Caitlín Maude, born and raised in Connemara Gaeltacht, traced her gift for poetry to her mother's side of the family. She took a degree in Irish and French at University College, Galway, where she was active in the College dramatic society and in Galway's Taibhdhearc Theatre. She later won international praise for her portrayal of Máire Ní Chathasaigh in Mairéad Ní Ghráda's An Triail (The Trial), in the 1964 Dublin Theatre Festival. Playwright as well as actress, she wrote "An Lasair Choille" (The Gold Finch) with Micheál Ó hAirtnéide (Michael Hartnett). She was also an accomplished musician whose record of sean nós singing, "Caitlín," was produced by Gael-Linn in 1975.

Like the others, Nuala Ní Dhomhnaill claims poets as forebearers. Her grandfather Pádraig Ó Domhnaill translated Old Irish poetry into Modern Irish; on her mother's side she is related to Seán Ó Duinnsléibhe, the Blasket poet Dunleavy who keeps Tomás O Criomhthain from his work in An tOileánach (The Island Man).[1] Although born in Lancashire to Kerry people living in England, Ní Dhomhnaill was fostered out at five to her aunt's house in Cahiratrant, a village near Ventry in the Corca Dhuibhne Gaeltacht. She too studied Modern Irish formally at university level, was seriously interested in drama—as both an actress and as a playwright—and has, in recent years, become known to Irish television audiences for "I m'Aonar Seal."

In traditional rural Irish society, death was the central ritual and the caoine the unique expression of grief. Travelers to Ireland from the seventeenth to the nineteenth century recorded their horror of it; descriptions served to reinforce the stereotype of the Irish as barely civilized. Thomas Crofton Croker said in Researches in the South of Ireland (1824):

> The Irish funeral howl is notorious and although this vociferous expression of grief is on the decline, there is still, in the less civilized parts of the country, a strong attachment to the custom, and many may yet be found who are keeners or mourners for the dead by profession.[2]

The travelers' reports suggest that these keeners, who were always women, were simply a claque of criers; however, the cry was not a wail, but a spontaneous, yet traditional, poetic form that addresses the genealogy, property, and character of the deceased and his ancestors, and suggests something of the community's values: family pedigree, family relationships, physical grace, courage, and generosity. "Caoineadh Airt Uí Laoghaire" (The Lament for Art O'Leary), attributed to Eibhlín Dhubh Ní Chonaill, is at once the best known of the traditional *caointe* and one of the most passionate love poems in Irish.

Mhac an tSaoi, Maude, and Ní Dhomhnaill have each appropriated some of the formal elements of the *caoine*: the direct address to the deceased, the formulaic language, the praise for the deceased and the sympathetic response of nature.[3] Above all, the *caoine* has provided the poets with an emotional context for their elegaic poetry.

Máire Mhac an tSaoi's "Caoineadh" places conventions of the *caoine* into the spare and compressed quatrains of Old Irish lyrics. She describes the landscape mourning the early death of a young woman: the crying wind, the gray sky. In the final stanza she simply enumerates the qualities lost to death: the gentle ways, the generosity, the agile mind.

"Inquisitio 1584" is an elegy for a Kerryman hanged in Limerick, no doubt for his part in the Desmond rebellion that was suppressed in 1583:

> In the year of our Lord
> 1584
> or early in the next,
> Sean MacÉamonn MacUlick
> was hanged at Shannonside.

Mhac an tSaoi marks the loss of MacUlick's land to strangers and, therefore, the loss of his name in his own parish; however, she does not curse those responsible, as in the traditional *caoine*. Instead, she counsels MacUlick to sleep undisturbed:

> Don't disturb your peace,
> Sean MacÉamonn MacUlick,
> on the banks of the wide Shannon
> when the winds from the sea
> blow west from your home country.[4]

Mhac an tSaoi turns tradition on its head in "Lament for Seamus Ennis, Late Champion Piper of Ireland." In fairy legends a mortal piper is frequently abducted by the music-loving sídhe; however, in this "Lament," Ennis is taken from the supernatural as well as from the mortal and natural worlds and all keen "an rí-phiobaire Éireann," the King of Irish Pipers. There is a mixture of musical and mythological allusions: Donn, the old Irish god of death, spreads the news; Ennis is compared to Orpheus in the magical ability of his music to transform—till all is silenced by death:

White flowers of repentance the barren staff knew;
The pillar-stones danced to hear Orpheus' tunes,
But King-piper of Ireland, voice is withheld from you-Ever![5]

    (trans. Máire Mhac an tSaoi)

Máire Mhac an tSaoi's bleak vision of death: an irrevocable loss in the "Lament," and a final betrayal in "Bás Mo Mháthar" ("My Mother's Death") is relieved in the poet's ironic antiphon to the traditional *caoine* in "Harvest of the Sea." While the mother laments:

"Oh little son, age was not your portion,
And it is the nature of youth to be wild and scapegrace—
And Ochone!"

The poet describes the ugly "whelpish" boy twice drowned—in the sea and in his mother's grief:

We have drowned the ugly fledgling a second time—
Once in the tide-race and once submerged in flattery
And Ochone!

But, finally, the poet too surrenders to ceremony:

. . . let them have it their way—
Set up the waxen image among the candles,
The Phoenix arrayed after his corpse washing

concluding that death covers all:

And the hare-lip was hidden below the coffin-lid!
And Ochone![6]

While Mhac an tSaoi's lyrics are characterized by intensity controlled by craftmanship, and by love and family as frequent themes, Caitlín Maude's poetry is less restrained, while social and political issues are often the object of her muse. A strong sympathizer for the Republicans on hunger strike in Long Kesh, Maude's elegy for Bobby Sands, MP for Fermanagh—South Tyrone, who died 5 May 1981, speaks in Sand's own voice:

> In my own place up North,
> life is like the stormy weather—
> far more rain than sun,
> but there was a sunburst over my cot
> and I never gave in to the dark sky.
> Look at me—
> not able to find rest in my own country,
> nor could any saint.
> I walloped stones
> along with every schoolboy,
> understanding that it wasn't
> a street game at all—
> and I was the Indian.[7]

"Caoineadh na Mná Tí" (The Housewife's Keen) reveals Maude's deeply spiritual side. The poet addresses a ruined house of the sort one sees in rural Ireland which when it is abandoned, and its fire extinguished, its thatched roof collapses. The house is a metaphor for all that is destroyed by neglect; however, Maude promises hope:

> You shelter your fairy furnishings
> waiting for the day
> that the wild radiance will be teased
> into a peaceful light.[8]

That consolation with its echo of the Beatitudes takes one by surprise, for neither the traditional *caoine* nor those of the contemporary poets offer the reassurance of eternal life given by Christian orthodoxy.

Nuala Ní Dhomhnaill, on the other hand, sings outside the choir of Christian orthodoxy and social convention, trusting instead to experience and to her unconscious to provide the powerful images that inform her poetry. Two of her early elegies were written for women who shaped her early life. Nature joins with the poet to mourn Máire Nic Aodha in "Caoineadh Mháire Nic Aodha." The sun is an orange glow in the drab winter landscape:

> Winter has come to us,
> an unlucky season—
> a lean time, dull
> except for the color of oranges.[9]

A metaphor for Máire's brightness, the orange of the season—the color of the early winter sunset in the lonely West Kerry countryside—shares shape as well as color with Máire's breast. Both are warm, full-bodied and life-nourishing.

"In Memoriam Elly Ní Dhomhnaill, 1884–1963," helps chart Ní Dhomhnaill's psychological development as a woman and as a poet. Like Máire Mhac an tSaoi and Caitlín Maude, her sympathy is for the outsider; however, Ní Dhomhnaill goes beyond sympathy to count herself one of their number. Her poem "Táimid damanta, a dheirfearcha" ("We are Damned, my Sisters") celebrates the natural, spontaneous, life-affirming women who prefer:

> . . . to be shoeless by the tide
> dancing singly in the wet sand
> the piper's tune coming to us
> on the kind Spring wind, than to be
> indoors making strong tea for the men.[10]

Ní Dhomhnaill would count her aunt Elly Ní Dhomhnaill one of her "sisters" not for the public virtues of lineage, physical courage, and generosity, but for the private ones: integrity, autonomy, moral courage.

> She took an honors degree
> in biology
> in 1904
> then came home
> to her own townland,
> a windy place
> on the slope of a hill,
> and stayed there till she died.

> She never married.
> No one around was good enough.
> And when her brother married,
> she thought the woman
> unworthy,
> so she sold the land on them.

She fought with her father.
She fought with her brother.
She fought with the parish priest,
for, to her, it wasn't right
to read the dues aloud at mass. ✳
It set rank among the poor
who paid beyond their means—
leaving their children hungry.
Therefore—

She would sit in her pew,
her hand on her blackthorn stick,
her hat on her head,
satisfied to hear from the altar,
"Elly O'Donnell-nothing."

My father was the one person
who visited her—
the *Pious Aeneas* of the clan.
When she died,
she left the house to him
that was sold because of the damp.
I promised I would write her a letter,
a thing I didn't do.
Perhaps it is letters
that I've written since
addressed to her proud spirit
that couldn't be
with a man her equal.

My husband was put on his guard
for fear of the same bad blood.
He said I'd be like herself,
a stranger to her own kind.
She'd no other heir.

Long ago,
there was a bitter wind blowing from Binn os Gaoith
and our ancestors going with cattle to Macha na Bó.[11]

Elegiac figures like Máire Nic Aodha and Elly Ní Dhomhnaill counteract
the destructive female force that made her early appearance in "Máthaír"
(Mother, 1977) which begins:

> You gave me a dress
> and you took it back again.
> You gave me a horse
> and you sold it when I was gone.
> You gave me a harp,
> and you asked for its return.
> You gave me life.

and concludes:

> What would you say,
> if I tore up the skirt?
> if I drowned the horse?
> if I ruined the harp
> by strangling the strings of happiness
> and the strings of life?
> If I walked the edge
> of the cliff at Cuas Cromtha?
>
> I know your answer,
> with your middle-aged mind.
> You would declare me dead,
> and write in the medical report
> these words:
> Ingrate. Schizophrenic. [12]

Ní Dhomhnaill recognizes hostile forces not only in her own immediate
environment but in the world of Irish speakers in the Gaeltacht and shares
her concern about them with Mhac an tSaoi and Maude. While none has
made her home in the Gaeltacht, it has provided the psychic location for
each poet and each has been actively interested in its survival and has
been openly critical of the indifferent or antagonistic forces in the government and in public institutions like Radio Telefís Éireann.

Mhac an tSaoi's "The Role of the Poet in Gaelic Society" is, in part,
a *caoine* for the Gaeltacht. She describes its demise not in linguistic or

cultural, but in human terms. Speaking of the local people, who know their way of life is an anachronism, she says:

> Those who can adapt to the new, adapt—
> many with startling success, some
> with deep traumatic lesions—those
> who cannot adapt, die—of the want
> of the will to live. This is literally true;
> easily two-thirds of my school mates
> and near contemporaries in one such district
> are dead—all in their forties and fifties.[13]

Nuala Ní Dhomhnaill concludes "Wounded Knee Irish Style," her own elegaic description of the "beleagured minority" who wake up the same Corca Dhuibhne Gaeltacht, saying she can not do other than rage when ". . . what I know to be one of the richer spoken vernaculars in the known world is being bled to death daily before my eyes and when with it an integral part of myself is dying."[14]

In the tradition of Myles na gCopaleen's *An Béal Bocht* (The Poor Mouth), Caitlín Maude's criticism of the government policy toward the Gaeltacht takes the form of satire. She celebrated the 1977 visit of Scottish poets and musicians to Rosmuck with her "Amhrán Bréagach" (Lying Song), a parody of an *aisling* or vision poem:

> I awoke one morning and saw a great wonder
> Jack Lynch on Cnoc Mordán chasing after the cattle
> Liam Cosgrave on a donkey going to collect the dole
> and Ritchie Ryan having a good time begging cap in hand.[15]

The poem continues describing the deputies asleep in the Dáil and Maude's Cill Briocáin neighbors, who live near Patrick Pearse's cottage in Rosmuck, picketing the GPO shouting "Give us the Cruiser so we can put a stamp on his nose."[16] There is a satirical poke at RTE, an institution notorious for its lack of sympathy for the Irish language and its programming needs, making the media a significant factor in speeding the demise of the Gaeltacht. Finally, Maude's last stanza describes the EEC in the language of Mac Conglinne's vision of The Land of Cockaigne—a palace of butter and cheese set in a sea of milk. Maude's allusion to *Aislinge Maic Con Glinne* reminds one that Irish poetic tradition is bound to the survival of the Gaeltacht.

Folklore suggests other risks to poetry. In Munster there is a saying that when poetry passes from the women of the family it is gone forever from the men.[17] Máire Mhac an tSaoi, Caitlín Maude and Nuala Ní Dhomhnaill all claim poetry as an inheritance and have used traditional forms, particularly the *caoine*. They have also brought to their work the compassion that has come of being twice an outsider: as poet and as woman. At the same time each poet has developed her own voice: the lapidary perfection of Mhac an tSaoi, the passion of Caitlín Maude and the psychological power of Nuala Ní Dhomhnaill. One can not now say whether their poetic gifts will be lost to the male heirs in their families, but it is certain that all men and women of future generations will inherit this moment in Irish life and letters to which their poetry is witness.

Notes

1. Michael Durkan and Lucy McDiarmid, "Q. & A.: Nuala Ní Dhomhnaill," *Irish Literary Supplement*, 6, no. 2 (Fall 1987): 42.

2. Thomas Crofton Croker, *Researches in the South of Ireland* (London: John Murray, 1824), 172–73.

3. Sean Ó Tuama, *Réamhaiste, Caoineadh Airt Uí Laoghaire* (Baile Átha Cliath: An Clóchomhar, 1963), 21–24 and Rachel Bromwich, "The Keen for Art O'Leary, its background and its place in the tradition of Gaelic Keening," *Éigse*, 5, no. 4 (n.d.): 236–252.

4. Máire Mhac an tSaoi, "Inquisitio 1584," in *Margadh na Saoirse* (Baile Átha Cliath: Sáirséal agus Dill, 1971), 26. Unless otherwise indicated, the translations are my own.

5. Máire Mhac an tSaoi, "Lament for Séamus Ennis. Late Champion Piper of Ireland. Slow Air," in Maureen O'Rourke Murphy and James MacKillop, eds., *Irish Literature: A Reader* (Syracuse: Syracuse University Press, 1987), 365.

6. Máire Mhac an tSaoi, "Harvest of the Sea," in Carol Cosman, Joan Keefe, and Kathleen Weaver, eds. *The Penguin Book of Women Poets* (New York: Penguin Books, 1979), 377–79. Translated by Máire Mhac an tSaoi.

7. Cáitlín Maude, "I m'áit dhúchais ó thuaidh," *Dánta* (Baile Átha Cliath: Coiscéim, 1984), 70.

8. Maude, "Caoineadh na Morá Tí," p. 67, ll. 7–10.

9. Nuala Ní Dhomhnaill, "Caoineadh Mháire Nic Aodha," in An Dealg Droighin (Cork: Mercier Press, 1982), 42, ll. 1–4.

10. Michael Hartnett, trans., "We are Damned, my Sisters," in Dermot Bolger, ed., *The Bright Wave* (Dublin: Raven Arts Press, 1986), 135.

11. Ní Dhomhnaill, "In Memoriam Elly Ní Dhomhnaill," 69–70.

12. Ní Dhomhnaill, "Máthair" p. 28, ll. 1–7, 10–23. This nemesis appears in a later incarnation as a *cailleach* or hag she calls *bean an leasa* (woman of the fairy fort) and who is the subject of a cycle of poems that opens with the lines:

> Bean an leasa strode
> into my poems.
> She didn't close the door.
> She didn't ask permission.

("Fuadach," *Suaithinseach* (Maigh Nuad: An Sagart, 1984), p. 65, ll. 1–4).

13. Máire Cruise O'Brien (Mhac an tSaoi), "The Role of the Poet in Gaelic Society," Robert O'Driscoll, ed., *The Celtic Consciousness* (Dublin: Dolmen Press, 1981), 243.

14. Nuala Ní Dhomhnaill, "Wounded Knee Irish Style," in *Ireland of the Welcomes* 32, no. 3 (May–June 1983): 28.

15. Maude, "Amhrán Bréagach," p. 61, ll. 1–4. Jack Lynch was Taoiseach from 1966–73 and from 1977–83. One of the most unpopular decisions he made during his administration was to close the National School in DúnChaoin. Mac an tSaoi and Maude were active in the public protest against the closing. Liam Cosgrave was Taoiseach from 1973–77. Richard "Ritchie" Ryan was Minister for Finance in the 1977 Lynch government.

16. Maude, l. 12. Conor Cruise O'Brien was Minister for Post and Telegraph from 1973–77.

17. Mac an tSaoi, "Role of the Poet," 247.

Diarmaid Ó Súilleabháin:
Literature and Political Commitment

Charles B. Quinn

When readers look back on modern literature in the Irish language of this period, Diarmaid Ó Súilleabháin (1932–85) will have a special place. The number, substance, and strength of his writings, particularly his prose, will be recognized, as well as what he once styled his "missionary zeal" to bring the Irish language into the mainstream of modern European literature.

His vocation as a writer was for him a serious lifelong commitment, and the self confidence and certainty with which he pursued his literary career were apparent. The variety of subject matter and style illustrates how conscientiously he pursued his literary aim as he saw it and with what diligence he tried to give shape and substance to *an duine eile ann* (the other self), the one who sought freedom and fulfillment. There are many themes in his work: alienation, class distinction, hatred of hypocrisy, love of nature, love of country. His willingness to face the moral problems in an Ireland adrift from its traditional and cultural moorings makes his work distinct in Irish fiction. He believed that the writer must be engaged, with a duty to examine and comment on political and social matters. Tradition, dúchas (heritage) and ethnic identity were centrally important, and for him they were identical with the republicanism to which he remained faithful throughout his life. This essay examines the nature of this political commitment particularly as delineated in his novel *Ciontach*[1] (Guilty), a jail journal of his three months' incarceration for political offenses against the state.

Ó Súilleabháin would concede that many might say that the writer who engaged in politics was wasting if not destroying his literary talents. True, perhaps, if involvement was for personal advantage. But against this position he argued that the course of Irish history and the current problems of Northern Ireland placed an obligation on the writer to oppose injustice and speak out.[2]

Diarmaid Ó Súilleabháin was born in the historic Béarra peninsula, West Cork, where the principal occupations were farming and fishing and where the Irish language had recently been but was no longer the daily medium of intercourse. Surrounded on three sides by the Atlantic, this windswept peninsula infused in the young Ó Súilleabháin a love of the sea in all its moods, a love that remained a central point of inspiration for him in his writing. He entered the teaching profession and spent most of his adult life as a teacher in the town of Gorey, County Wexford.

There was a strong republican tradition in Béarra. Five of Ó Súilleabháin's maternal uncles were involved in the struggle for independence that led to the founding of the Free State and the unnatural division of the country by which six northeastern counties remained under British control. He viewed the struggle for an united Ireland as a continuous one, having its roots in the physical force movements of the nineteenth century and embracing and validating the present republican campaign in the North. He was convinced that the idealism and suffering of the 1919–21 campaign had been forgotten by the politicians of the Free State who had been rewarded with jobs and pensions. He was also convinced that, like his forebears he, too, could play a part in the historic struggle, and it was no surprise to find him in the Sinn Féin organization, a member of its Ard-Chomhairle, and the spokesman for their campaign of renewed resistance in the Six Counties.[3] In 1972 he was arrested, imprisoned in Mountjoy jail, and eventually tried and sentenced by the special criminal court for a speech soliciting guns and ammunition.

Ciontach is not a political tract but an autobiographical novel on prison life. We are told that he spent many years in determining the proper frame and tone, finally settling on the second person narrator as in his earlier novel, *Caoin Tú Féin*.[4] In a way all the aspects of his life and work come together in *Ciontach*: the social and political statement, the contemplation of man as a living being, and the study of the effects of imprisonment both on mind and soul.

There are many forms of servitude but according to Ó Súilleabháin incarceration within the bleak and forbidding walls of Mountjoy prison was not the worst kind. In an interview he stated that it was part of his intellectual training to tolerate any place but agreed that it would be very difficult for one lacking the requisite intellectual control to suffer imprisonment.[5] At times, however, deprivation of freedom did bear down hard on one as imaginative as Ó Súilleabháin, who styles it a living hell. The quiet of the prison was deceptive, concealing as it did pent up emotion and violent anger. He visualized it as looking at a tempestuous sea through the window of a train—the roar and fury of the elements were there but unheard. His later description of the prison outbreak confirmed this judgment.

Enveloping the whole prison was a feeling he personified as *Gruaim* (despondency). The gloom of stone walls, iron bars, institutional prison coloring and prison smell, darkness and shadow, the bareness of the narrow cells—all combined to bewilder an inmate and break his spirit. The habitual criminals, the regular Mountjoy inmates fared worse than the political prisoners in Wing B₁, where Ó Súilleabháin was placed. Life was hard on the former, the product of slums and social neglect. There was little hope that they could break from the circle of poverty and crime. The chains that bound the political prisoners, on the other hand, were more than actual physical chains: they were chains that linked them to patriots of the past. The sight of the initials "J. B., Westport, I.R.A., 1923" recalled for the author the long list of those who had fought for freedom:

> Cinnte Dia ach go raibh craos mor folach ag Éirinn nó shlog sí siar a sá den chuisle ab fhearr dá chuid. Ar bhealach aduain d'fhéadfá ar an ala úd an ghráin dearg a thiomsú d'aigne istigh ina haghaidh . . . ar cailleadh léi; ar fealladh orthu mar gheall uirthi, ar díbríodh, ar briseadh, ar bascadh, ar cuireadh dá mheabhair léi, ar maslaoídh, ar maraíodh, ar díbríodh, ar deoraíodh, ar lomadh go hurlár balbh taobh spride dhe . . . ar claochlaíodh ar bhealach gur iompaigh siad go nímneach in aghaidh a leannán spioradálta . . . For they died for Ireland.[6]

On his arrival Ó Súilleabháin was uncertain of his place in the nationalism movement, but he found that imprisonment was for him a paradoxically liberating experience. Becoming one of the band of these political prisoners was something that made him understand and feel in the depths of his being the affirmation they and he gave of their political credo: "Ba shaoránach go fíor tú anseo—duine iomlán, duine foirfe saor. Bhain mar a bheadh blaiseadh breise dúchais, comhfhiosú níba dhéine tíre, le do bheatha anseo. Mar a raibh easpa cheana bhí comhshlánú anois."[7]

The idealism, camaraderie and self discipline of the group enabled them to rise above the depersonalization of prison life. The author meditates on the extraordinary commitment of Alfo, the OC of the prisoners, in this idealized portrait: "B'iomaí duine a bhi ann. Fear fileata an anama: fear dian danartha na réabloíde . . . B'shin rud nár tuigeadh riamh do na Gaill go ropfadh fir de shíor ar aghaidh ina n-aghaidh dá mbeadh orthu Gaeil a nádúr a chlaochló le beith míthrócaireach, feidmiúil, *faustach* fiú, ar mhaithe céim chúise nó an leathchéim féin a thógáil lena ré."[8] Among the prisoners were many Northerners. Although their aims were the same as those of their cellmates from the South, half a century of partition had affected them in ways that the author himself did not fully understand. Partition created borders other than the political ones: there were borders of educational philosophy, borders of years of political, social, and economic oppression. But both North and South were at one in their hatred for the twenty-six county republic that they contemptuously referred to as the "Free State." Ó Súilleabháin emphasizes a clear distinction between the dedication and selflessness of the political prisoners and the external world of Free State *ábharchas agus mé féineachas* (materialism and selfishness): "Rith sé leat go minic go raibh Muir Meann na Mioscaise idir Poblachtachas Éireann uile agus an iarlaislathas a bhí sásta postú is saibhriú laistigh de theorainn na bhFiche Sé."[9]

This theme of spiritual bankruptcy in an ever more affluent Ireland is one that Ó Súilleabháin raised in his writings before. He views with particular distaste those who are concerned with the making and application of the laws: politicians, officers of the court, the Special Branch, the Gardaí and the wardens. There is, however, a mixture of scorn and pity in his estimation of the latter two categories, the gardaí and warders: "Ar bhealach mhothaigh tú trua doíbh is ar caitheadh de mhaslaí leo amhail dá mba fhórsa eachtranach iad—ní nárbh ea. Dá olcas é mar scéal ba ghnáth-thuathánaigh a bhformhór gardaí, muintir a d'éalaigh isteach san éide ó chinnteacht an bháid bháin féin. D'fhéadfá féin a bheith ina measc."[10] It is with a certain irony he views his own status as a paid employee of the state he is opposing.

As is usual with Ó Súilleabháin a more confident and integrated sense of being is linked with an awareness of membership in a large community—witness his reflections on the prison mass on Saint Patrick's Day (136). He finds it difficult to participate in the baiting of the warders but he does understand how necessary it is for the prisoners to protest, to defy rules and regulations, to plan escapes. The banter and persiflage were a kind of psychological safety valve: "I bpríosún duit níor mhór duit gáire a dheánamh fút féin . . . níor mhór duit dul ar foráil is an fán le do staid a dhífhosú, le do sprid a sheachtrachu nó rachfá an bealach dubh eile, lonnófaí tú i ngleann do gheilt ná ní thiocfá as go brách."[11] The games and tricks played could be cruel if not actually sadistic as evident by the kangaroo court on the two newly arrived republican prisoners (101–4).

There comes in prison a certain realization of self that the author finds it difficult to explain—a certain diminishing of the humanity of the individual. Although the enforced confinement in the cell and the quiet of the prison enabled Ó Súilleabháin to continue his writing (he completed a novel—still not published), he found himself becoming too introspective. Whatever his reluctance initially to conduct an Irish class or later to assume the responsible post of adjutant of the political prisoners he eventually found in both assignments a sort of healthy release. The hesitation and doubt provided him with, as it were, a mirror in which to see shortcomings and deficiencies. He feared he lacked the necessary firmness of temperament in one who commands because as a literary man he had too great an understanding of and sympathy with human weakness.

The delivery of a parcel of new books to his cell reminds him of the fever of anticipation with which he received galley proofs of his books in the past, of how he proofread each well-known syllable and word (100). He asks what is this mystery of creative writing. Why be an author? Was it just an attempt by him and fellow writers to anesthetize themselves, to create a fictional world removed from the harsh realities of life? Who appointed them to be "moulders of humanity," to be accuser, defender, and judge of others, to stamp an inky mark on other individuals?

The hermits and the anchorites of old in their self-imposed solitude had in some paradoxical way a clearer vision of humanity by the very fact of being isolated from man. In solitude one best knows oneself, an important step in the knowing of others. If prison confined and cramped the writer physically, it had the saving dimension of permitting him to concentrate on examining his own soul and mind and of coming possibly to judge others without personal or worldly bias.

In prison, Ó Súilleabháin says, one is gifted with greater keenness of vision and deeper understanding of those forces that pertain to ordinary external things that happen to be free. There arises a deeper insight into life by seeing two mating crows on a rooftop with nesting materials in their beaks. Even well-known landscapes and seascapes possess a beauty hitherto unknown—so states the author of his trip under police guard to the courthouses of Wexford and New Ross. He sees from his narrow cell window a tree in all its month-of-May beauty, a tree that represents a glorious symbiotic relationship of grace and beauty with nature and that for him becomes a symbol of peace and freedom. If creatures could reason as humans do, he wonders what the beautiful butterfly that flutters around his prison cell, oblivious of its sinister aspect, would think of the human condition with its wars and prisons and beds of pain and misery. Even the Sunday morning bells of the city intoned the music of civility. Some sense of beauty and permanence attached to these iron tongues that spoke to the people of the past and suggested the future.

Contemplation of these symbols of freedom and normality reminded the author all the more of the reality within the walls of Mountjoy. He found it necessary to distance (he uses the word *seachtraigh*, to exteriorize) himself from the depersonalization of prison life. A fellow prisoner, styled by Ó Súilleabháin as Tír Eoghain, who had spent many years as a political prisoner, explained his own particular method of externalization (156). He would permit his thoughts to roam at will, then try to push the life-force from his body, to etherealize himself as it were, and range over time and space. Initially these attempts would not go beyond the threshold of the imagination; however, one day he felt as if he were translated beyond his body and time. Such occurrences were very rare and filled with such pleasure that Tír Eoghain instinctively sensed the danger of crossing the border of consciousness. Our author does not inform us as to whether or not he imitated such a practice but it must be stated that reveries and dreams form an important part of the book.

Memories of his youth and his *muintir* (people) are those most common in his dreams: "Fiú is tú faoi thaibhreamh b'fheasach duit go ndúiseófá uathu is fós go bhfillfeá nó go bhfilleadh uaráin áirithe den Duine-Cuimhne is gurbh iad cuimhní mhuintir d'óige ba bheoúla cinnte i measc mhuintir do thaibhrimh."[12] In a long passage (68–70) he wonders about those dream visitants and about his other, his dream self, which he felt was as important as the self of daily living. He often cursed this up-and-downness of his consciousness. Were these others trying to capture and imprison him so that he would come to know more intimately "*do dhoppelganger, do Shéadna beag faustach féin*" (your doppelganger, your own little Faustian Seadna).

The final third of the book, *Ciontach*, is concerned with the prison riot and the author's trial by the special criminal court. The leisurely pace of the narrative with its stream-of-consciousness musings now quickens into discursive prose. Ó Súilleabháin's position as adjutant forced him into an active role during the course of the riot and the negotiations that followed. He ably defended himself before the court. The verdict of three month's imprisonment was set aside in view of his three months' incarceration while awaiting trial.

The very title of the book, "Guilty," suggests the nature of Ó Súilleabháin's political apology. By casting the narrative in the second person the author dramatizes his theme, directly calling on and challenging the protagonist. The reader who expects a sustained explication of political philosophy will be disappointed. The republican influences of his youth were strong and he retained the Irish fidelity to tradition so that he was never satisfied to neglect it nor turn his back on it: "Rinne tú machtnamh faoi seo, iniúchadh agus féinscrúdú . . . Arbh é gur bhain ceangal éigin aduain idir an duine agus na chéad tarlúintí ina shaol?:[13] Nowhere does he question his political beliefs because he is convinced of their rightness. While one can appreciate the uncompromising honesty of a stand that placed him at variance with the great majority of his countrymen one must regret the petulance and acerbity of his tone when discussing the politicians, officers of the state, and the media. National affairs are never so black and white as the author wishes us to see them. A writer commenting on the novels written about the present struggle in the North accuses Ó Súilleabháin of having a superiority complex, of damning all who disagree with him.[14]

A certain ambivalence is apparent in the author's thinking. In an earlier novel, *Dianmhuilte Dé*, the protagonist, Ceilpí, patriot and father of three patriot sons, mourns his daughter who has rejected their republicanism but who still had her ideals: "Grá a bhí agat, grá do do mháthair is do do chuid deartháireacha . . . grá a bhí chomh láidir leis an ngrá eile, an grá nár tuigeadh duit . . . an grá tíre."[15] In thinking back on his own youth Ó Súilleabháin criticizes his father for the latter's total indifference to the claims of nationalism but concludes by saying: "*Is fós b'athaiar caoin cneasta é ar an uile bhealach*" (He was a kind honest man).[16]

In a recent article in which she speaks of Ó Súilleabháin's hidden politics Máirín Nic Eoin examines his attitude to class distinction as a social phenomenon and of the conflicts that arise because of differences.[17] She accuses him of a certain social and economic determinism that is hard to explain in a revolutionary dedicated to ending class distinction and the political power associated with certain classes. While the author has a sharp eye for the atmosphere that fosters differences, his political prospective is a narrow one. He was convinced that the habitual criminal in Mountjoy had little chance of rehabilitation, that the working classes were unlikely to make an effort to improve themselves, and if they did, they would still be looked upon as "Runners-in." His earlier novel *Maeldún*[15] is a scathing indictment of the classes with wealth and power. Nic Eoun also adverts to the simplistic attitude Ó Súilleabháin (and republicans generally) has toward women. They see women in the traditional role of homemaker who must perforce be conservative, bourgeois, antiintellectual, and antirevolutionary. She tends the home and children while men pursue their dreams, republican and otherwise. If the abstract concept of the significance of the family is important for Ó Súilleabháin, then how narrow, confined, and depersonalized is his impression of the role of women.

As noted earlier *Ciontach* is not a political tract. Although it was not as a writer Ó Súilleabháin was jailed it was as literary man that he meditated on and refined his prison experience to produce this autobiography. It is an important work by an insider for the light it throws on the republican mind. When other writers chose silence he elected to speak out on a vital national issue. Even if one does not agree with Ó Súilleabháin one must acknowledge the depth of his commitment and the steadfastness with which he pursued his dream of a united Ireland.

Notes

1. Diarmaid Ó Súilleabháin, *Ciontach* (Baile Átha Cliath: Coiscéim, 1983). All references are to this edition; translations are by the writer.

2. Nollaig Ó Gadhra, "Diarmaid Ó Súilleabháin-Agallamh," *Feasta* (Meán Fómhair 1985: 15–21.

3. Seasamh Ó Murchú, "Diarmaid Ó Súilleabháin: Nóta Beathaisnéise," *Irisleabhar Mhá Nuad* (1984): 7–20.

4. Pádraig Ó Snodaigh, "Diarmaid Ó Súilleabháin-Duine, Ealaíontóir," *Comhar* (Nollaig 1986): 14.

5. Ó' Gadhra, "Diarmaid Ó Súilleabháin-Agallamh," 20.

6. Ó Súilleabháin, *Ciontach*, 44. "Surely to God but Ireland had a great hidden maw because she had swallowed enough of her best. In some strange way it was possible to summon up in your mind a deep hatred of her . . . of all that were lost because of her, of those betrayed, banished, broken, crushed, driven insane, abused, driven out, exiled, stripped bare of spirit . . . so transformed that in a way they turned in hatred from their spiritual loved one."

7. Ibid., 46. "You were truly a citizen here—a full person, a perfectly free person. There pertained to your life here a greater sense of heritage, a more intense consciousness of your country. Where there was a deficiency before, there was fulfillment now."

8. Ibid., 120. "He was many persons. An imaginative man of the spirit: a hard cruel revolutionary. That is something the English never understood that men would eternally rush forward against them even if they, the Irish, had to transform their nature to be merciless, forceful, *faustian* even to advance the cause a step or even a half-step during their lifetime."

9. Ibid., 117. "It often occurred to you that there was an Irish Sea of Hatred between all-Ireland Republicanism and the worthless establishment that was satisfied with place-seeking and getting rich within the borders of the twenty-six. . . ."

10. Ibid., 86–87. "In a way you pitied them because of the insults showered on them as if they were a foreign force—which they weren't. However bad, the guards were ordinary country folk, men who slipped into uniform to avoid the emigrant ship. You yourself could well be one of them."

11. Ibid., 38. "In prison you must laugh at yourself . . . you must let yourself go to destabilize your status, to exteriorize your spirit or you would go another dark way, you would settle into a depression of insanity from which you would never escape."

12. Ibid., 62. "Even when dreaming you would know that you would awake from them, that you and some well-spring of People-memories would return, and that the memory of the people of your youth were most alive among the people of your dreams."

13. Ibid., 207. "You made your meditation on this, your scrutiny and your self-examination . . . was it that there was some strong link between the person and the first happenings on his life?"

14. Pádraig Ó Siadhail, "Na Sé Chontae, an Saorstát agus an tUrscéal Gaeilge, 1975–1986, Cuid 1," Comhar, (Meitheamh 1987): 28–33.

15. Diarmaid Ó Súilleabháin, Dianmhuilte Dé (Baile Átha Cliath: Sáirséal agus Dill, 1964), 192–93. "You had love, love for your mother and for your brothers . . . love that was as strong as the other love, the love you never understood . . . love of country."

16. Ó Súilleabháin, Ciontach, 92.

17. Máirín Nic Eoin, "An Pholaitíocht faoi Cheilt," Comhar (Nollaig 1986): 24–28.

18. Diarmaid Ó Súilleabháin, Maeldún (Baile Átha Cliath: Sáirséal agus Dill, 1972).

John Banville: Portraits of the Artist

George O'Brien

I

Doctor Copernicus and *Kepler* take a biographical approach to their subjects, while *The Newton Letter* and *Mefisto* are autobiographical. Or: Banville's "science" quartet is a diptych, each panel of which has two complementary portraits. Yet, *Mefisto*, the concluding work of the quartet, contains numerous thematic and dramatic echoes of *Birchwood*, the quartet's preamble. Meanwhile, *Birchwood* is an operatic treatment of the anxieties expressed in the Gothic ballad that gives Banville's first book, *Long Lankin*, its title. And in *Long Lankin* we first meet Ben White, protagonist of *Nightspawn*. At the end of "The Possessed," the novella that concludes the first edition of *Long Lankin*,[1] Ben White says: "I think I might write a book. I could tell a story about the stars and what it's like all alone up there . . . there are all kinds of things I could do. Join a circus maybe." The thought irresistibly occurs that the character is not merely sketching his own vague plans but is anticipating the development of his author's output (Gabriel Godkin, protagonist of *Birchwood* does join a circus). Ben White's sketchiness cautions against anticipation being taken for a synonym of prophecy. And in any case, as Banville's astronomers discover, anticipation is never the whole story.

The notion of tentative unity (typical of Banville's sense of play and paradox) suggested by his output as a whole is more easily discernible at the level, or within the framework, of each unit of the output. Each Banville work is an elaborate and idiosyncratic structure. And each novel's uniqueness is usually premised on the ostensible sanity of number (a tactic confirmed by *Mefisto* where artist and mathematician are synonyms). Thus, *Nightspawn* consists of three parts, each divided into twenty-seven sections, an arbitrary number, arbitrarily arrived at (by means of white space, exclamations and single-sentence confidences), yet a number that loses its arbitrariness through repetition. Or, there's the two-part invention of *Mefisto* that formally accommodates that novel's numerous motifs of the binary. Or there's *Kepler*:

> . . . constructed in five sections, the number of chapters in each of the sections corresponding to the number of sides of each of the five polygons [which, the astronomers believed, "could be inserted within the intervals of the six planets of the solar system"], and all of the chapters of equal length within the section. Also, the narrative structure itself is closely worked. Time in each of the sections moves backward and forward to or from a point at the centre, to form a kind of temporal orbit. But no section comes back exactly to its starting point, since, as Kepler discovered, the planets do not move in circles, but in ellipses.[2]

And the story isn't bad, either!

The above interview's expository blandness, however, is obviously merely a gloss on what in the novel in question is rendered as need and drama. The eponymous hero of *Kepler* knows only the desire to posit his own strategies and objectives with the conclusiveness of his author. If, as Banville goes on to say in the same interview, "I can only maintain that for me this is what art is about: form," then his novels enact a quest for form on the part of his protagonists, a quest fraught with uncertainty and imprecision, a quest requiring the resources of artifice in order to decode the real (though perhaps successful only in temporarily recoding it). Banville's genre is the romance, the text of journeying to other worlds, to the world of the other; the text of desire, where the ideal called harmony is implored to realize itself; the text of the spirit's ardor and of the heart's vagaries.[3] Banville's imaginative idiom is the baroque, with its grandiloquence, its emphasis on the tension between unity and disparateness, with its play of light and shade (particularly evident in *Doctor Copernicus* and *Kepler*, where minds feel heavy, black wings impinge on them and the sky is enigmatically, piercingly clear).

The Banville type is the artist, the seeker, the risk taker, the man (typically) without glibness, the nonconformist, the ignoramus well versed in old knowledge, the enemy of history, the loveless one ("cold") whom love does not appease. The artist is the one willing to live out whatever Ben White means at the end of *Nightspawn* by "I love words and I hate death. Beyond this, nothing." The artist accepts, in the spirit if not necessarily the style of Gabriel Godkin, the series of two-faced findings with which *Birchwood* inconclusively concludes:

> I began to write . . . and thought that at last I had discovered a form which would contain and order all my losses. I was wrong. There is no form, no order, only echoes and coincidences, sleight of hand, dark laughter. I accept it.

Neither form nor order for Godkin the author, perhaps, but what do the mirrors, twinnings, repetitions, and circularity of his narrative support but the possibility of order and form? Neither form nor order, but the necessary fiction of it.

II

Ben White is the prototype of the artist according to Banville. Partly, this is a matter of temperament. Like Doctor Coppernigk he is "cold"; yet, like the anonymous writer-protagonist of *The Newton Letter*, he is a lover who mistakenly identifies whom it is he loves. Kepler and Coppernigk are caught up in, and distracted from their work by, revolutionary historical events whose meaning they imperfectly grasp; the same is true of White in *Nightspawn*, set in Greece on the eve of the Colonel's coup. His successors in the Banville canon are to a decisive degree dreamers, theorists, rhetoricians of possibility, unworldly, deficient in action, ditherers. White is frequently called a fool and a coward by the conspirators with whom he is will-nilly involved.

Yet being an artist is not simply a question of temperament. Nor is it a question of aptitude or cultural lineage. White is not necessarily an artist because, "I just want to write a little book, that's all." While his narrative's opening words may echo the first sentence of Dostoyevski's *Notes from Underground*, they seem more to propose a posture than to invoke a tradition. It may be that "There's magic to combat any force," as he tells his virtually inseparable companion, Erik Weiss ("not knowing what I meant"), but the magic is not written on the mysterious but crucial document that White carries around in a silver box.

Over and above the details of posture and prop, behind the transparent theatricality of much of the novel's action, a sense of White the artist is sustained through his personification of coherence problematically considered. In a novel as self-conscious as *Nightspawn*,[4] which contains a character named Aristotle Sesostris, not to mention a certain Weiss who is something of a doppelganger, it seems safe to assume that the protagonist's name has been chosen deliberately. The world inscribes itself on his blankness, a condition of neither stupidity or innocence and one manifested in the strikingly unconditional quality of his presence in the world—the precondition, perhaps, of the "accept" of Gabriel Godkin. Another way of describing this condition might be to call it an unjudging givingness to experience, a romantic incapacity to avoid immersion and Wertherish weltering, a givingness fuelled by being conscious of its own helplessness. Ben says, "Accidie was my greatest fear."

As *Nightspawn* implies, the critical instance of blankness is the transcription of its occasions: "I had a vertiginous sensation of planes of awareness slipping and sliding uncontrollably, running into each other and locking, like loose, shuffled pages of a book." The text of the narrative reproduces the character of the experiences that are its pretext. Or at least the fiction is that this act of reproduction, or creation, takes place unmediated: that's how the material is intended to be perceived. The fiction's reality, its formal distinctiveness, relies wholly on the fact that it has been made to exhibit such effects.

From the standpoint of the plot of *Nightspawn*, Ben White is a double agent, eddying uncertainly between contending camps of plotters, apparently finding the overall design of their efforts incomprehensible, asking: "Do you really think all this is necessary here in Greece now? This whole revolution thing . . . it's not real. . . ." His erratic, unpredictable, experimental, un-Byronic involvement in a nation's destiny, an involvement without specific personal value and whose issue is heartbreak, functions as a metaphor for his being an artist.[5] The artist feels the brutalities of history, the puerility of reason, the impermanence of love, just like everyone else. But unlike everyone else, the artist sublimates the essentially time-known and time-bound quality of experience into his work, into the permanence of form. Ben White notes: "Only here, in these sinister pages [blank, presumably], can time be vanquished. These little keys on which I dance transfix eternity with every tap." No marks for originality here.

It seems rather callow to obscure the pain of Greece with Ben White's self-dramatizing narcissism. Yet, it is precisely at a time of turmoil, when confident agents act in the name of the possibility of an order superior to the status quo, that problems of coherence arise. Politics redefine the context of existential questions: the questions themselves are neither answered or silenced. And in the present case, when the ideal of order is ultimately entrusted to "Papa Dop's" police, there must remain someone— even if, "You find no answers, only questions"—willing to say (incapable of saying other than): "I am talking about the healing of wounds. I am talking of art."

Thus it is, too, in the "war of attrition between imagination and time,"[6] with Gabriel Godkin in *Birchwood*: "Such scenes as this I see, or imagine I see, no difference, through a glass sharply–if I provide something otherwise than this, be assured I am inventing." To invent would be to impart consistency and regularity to an even more problematic country than the Greece present in *Nightspawn*: the past. Gabriel's belief—while he was living, so to speak, not writing—is that he had discovered "harmony" in seeing his parents make love al fresco:

> How would I explain, I do not understand it, but it was as if in the deep wood's gloom I had recognised, in me all along, waiting, an empty place where I could put the most disparate things and they would hang together, not very elegantly, perhaps, or comfortably, but yet together, singing like seraphs.

Nothing in Gabriel's experience confirms the dispensation of "this new music," except his need of it, which misleads him into a world polarized between trivia (Prospero's travelling show) and horror (famine, rape); a need that has the time-related context of Gabriel wanting to secure the truth of his lineage. Like Ben White (and the repetitiousness of the terms is one of the drawbacks of Banville's tightly integrated corpus), Gabriel ends up abjuring, even as he seems to solicit, the stabilizing power of the word:

> This world. I feel that if I could understand it I might then begin to understand the creatures who inhabit it. But I do not understand it. I find the world always odd, but odder still, I suppose, is the fact that I find it so, for what are the eternal verities by which I measure these temporal aberrations? Intimations abound, but they are felt only, and words fail to transfix them.[7]

To imagine is to falsify, but for Gabriel what is the alternative? "I invent, necessarily," he admits: it's either that or totally succumb to contingency.

III

Ben White, in particular, and Gabriel Godkin, with his vigilance and obsessiveness, suggest special, even decadent, cases of Henry James's description of the artist as someone on whom nothing is lost. The matter of loss is preeminent in their narratives, and while narrating contains an irresistible sense of recuperation, it cannot overlook the flaws in the project:

> The literary artist, like the infant he once was, must learn how to speak in order to assimilate the world . . . to leap the chasm between the name and the thing named—to leap *and not look down* . . . The problem for the writer, if he is honest, if he is an artist, is that his set lesson is twofold. He must learn, and unlearn. He must leap, executing graceful somersaults as he goes, but look down, always, no matter how vertiginous the view.[8]

The text, then, is the bridge across the chasm, a structure intended both to keep lines of communication open and to create a sense of marvel about the difficulty and success of doing so. Assuming none of this is lost on the artist, the designer, the question of what is gained remains. Or, to exhaust the metaphor, what material would be sufficiently durable for the bridge? This is the question that Banville takes on in the wake of the formative yet rather adolescent experiments of his early work and that occupies the science quartet.

One of the most notable shifts of emphasis marked by the quartet—the second phase of Banville's career—is from person to world. The urge to find form in creation, rather than to find it in one's responses to creation, represents a welcome change from the excessive introspection (tantamount to narcissism) of Godkin and White. In other respects, being captivated by Arthur Koestler's *The Sleepwalkers*, Banville's initial inspiration, has been liberating, enabling him to make a distinctive contribution to the contemporary revival of interest in the historical novel and to excercise his imagination's pictorializing capacities. "What the heart desires, the world is incapable of giving" is an apothegm offered as a tin lid to cover the events of *Nightspawn*. Beginning with *Doctor Copernicus*, the same statement is a point of departure, not arrival. Now chasm is subject rather than conclusion.

Not that the privileged, cursed, precarious status of the artist is thereby dispensed with. Banville's subject matter in the quartet may be astronomers and mathematicians but they are no less artists because of their medium of expression. It certainly seems legitimate for Kepler to think his principle of harmony to be "a perfected work of art." The opening sequence of *Doctor Copernicus*, with its unmistakeable echoes of the opening sequence of *A Portrait of the Artist as a Young Man* (and of the tension and desire born there of being aware of the gap between word and thing), leaves no doubt as to the protagonist's lineage.

The scientist-artist authenticates himself not by means of his credentials, however, but by his optic, by keeping faith with his view of the world, for all that society may object. The optic harbors the ideal that the world is amenable to comprehension, that it can accommodate the perceiver's desire and the perceived's disposition for what is referred to throughout the quartet as "harmony." If, as was discovered in *Nightspawn* and *Birchwood*, the world, antiromantically, declines to vouch for self, the romance of Copernicus and Kepler is in their proceeding as though self may underwrite world. The hubris of this attitude—a hubris that seems ironically natural, uncultured, unaffected—is the saving grace not vouchsafed to Gabriel and Ben White, although Gabriel has glimpses of it:

> Listen, listen, if I know my world, which is doubtful, but if I do, I know it is chaotic, mean and vicious, with laws cast in the wrong moulds, a fair conception gone awry, in short, an awful place, and yet, and yet a place capable of glory in those rare moments when a little light breaks forth, and something is not explained, not forgiven, but merely illuminated.

Now it is not themselves that these scientific questers seek, but a thing. It is not in order to negotiate his well-founded existential dread that Copernicus works toward his theory of cosmic integrity. It is "to save the phenomena," by which he means to adjust respectfully the myth of order enshrined in the Ptolemaic model of universal harmony. The creative project is to evince form, rather than express self. Thus, Copernicus:

> If the sun is conceived as the centre of an immensely expanded universe, then those observed phenomena of planetary motion that had baffled astronomers for millenia became perfectly rational and necessary. . . . The verification of the theory . . . would take . . . years, perhaps, to complete, but that was nothing. . . . What mattered was not the propositions, but the combining of them: *the act of creation* [emphasis in original]. He turned the solution this way and that, admiring it, as if

he were turning in his fingers a flawless, ravishing jewel. It was the thing itself, the vivid thing.[9]

Form is the fiction to which Gabriel and his forerunner will not subscribe, the fiction that their author establishes on their behalf. Their experience causes them to dissent from the idea of order while it fuels their desire for it. In the case of Copernicus, form—the coherence of thought which theory denotes—offers the possibility of integrity that "the grimy commonplace world" cannot support. The politically indifferent astronomer brings about a revolution of far greater moment than anything resulting from the ugly sectarian violence of his day. This revolution is, appropriately for the artist, a revolution in consciousness. It works its way by thought. It embraces difference, its weapons are patience, clarity, and language. It triumphs by rectifying and augmenting, by not despoiling creation's necessary complexity, by being the dream of one man. Its alter ego is play: "all is play," says Kepler, himself a casualty of his times, and one who, like Copernicus, was no good at politics, hence fully qualified to appreciate how his devotion to harmony (and to Copernicus: "There was for Kepler something almost holy, something redemptive almost, in that vision of an ordered clockwork of suncentred spheres"), whose subtext is song, is a worthy counteractivity to history, whose subtext is death.

IV

Like his great avatar, however, Kepler is haunted and appalled by his awareness of human limitation. The painful, seemingly callous, deaths of loved ones is in *Kepler* the counterpart of Copernicus's loveless life. As Kepler writes: "That, so I thought is our task here, I mean transformation of the chaos without, into a perfect harmony and balance within us. Wrong, wrong: for our lives contain us, *we* are the flaw in the crystal, the speck of grit which must be ejected from the spinning sphere." And historically speaking, both Copernicus and Kepler exemplify an arresting embodiment of a connection between attainment and failure. The magnitude of both these path-breakers' accomplishments is premised upon a good deal that has subsequently been proved wrong. Yet their incorrectness is for Banville perhaps more illuminating than their incontrovertibility, because in it lies the necessary fiction of all theory. Were it not for the flaws there would be no theory: were it not for the fiction that there were no flaws there would be no theory. Form, unwittingly born of fallibility, achieves its perfection and harmony (in Kepler's mind: "The heavenly motions . . . are nothing but a continuous song for several voices, perceived not by the ear but by the intellect, a figured music which sets landmarks in the immeasurable flow of time") on the basis of a fiction of completeness. Kepler's song metaphor expresses the truth of that fiction.

Perhaps in order to posit his own fiction of completeness, Banville concludes the science quartet by moving from historical to contemporary settings, by replacing the biographical approach with the autobiographical, and—reverting to the interests of his prequartet fiction—by rendering the truth of failure rather than the fiction of success. "Words fail me, Clio," the anonymous narrator of *The Newton Letter* confesses at the outset; but they are not all that fail him. His inability to read correctly the signs of life around him, which is no less than his compulsion of perfection, confirm the gap between narrator and subject, mind and thing, text and life. The narrator-historian is waylaid by the "inimitable" ordinariness of his love object, Charlotte Lawless—a surname that, besides being the same as that of Gabriel Godkin's mother in *Birchwood*, suggests boundlessness ("she was all potential") and lacking susceptibility to form:

> When I search for the words to describe her I can't find them. Such words don't exist. They would need to be no more than forms of intent, balanced on the brink of saying, another version of silence. . . . I must concentrate on things impassioned by her passing. Anything would do, her sun hat. . . . The very ordinariness of these mementoes was what made them precious . . . it was a passion of the mind. I gave up all pretence of work on the book. You see the connection.

This imaginative passion for Charlotte is sustained despite the amply adequate physical satisfactions that the narrator receives from Charlotte's niece, Ottilie; despite the fact that Charlotte's husband Edward is dying of cancer; despite the whole fabric both of family life and the life of the immediate environment being a tissue of unpredictabilities. The narrator, charmed by the possibilities of his own idealizing, suspends work on his biography of Newton to appropriate the *ordinary*, that strangest and most elusive of enigmas."[10]

Up to this point, "Newton was my life." But Newton too underwent a crisis of faith:

He was fifty; he went a little mad. . . . Because he had to have certain
absolutes of . . . space, time, motion, to found his theories on. But
space, and time, and motion . . . can only be relative, for us, he knew
that, had to admit it, had to let them go, and when they went . . .
everything else went with them.

Newton declined the alternative of a necessary fiction. And in order to
underline his refusal, Banville fabricates a letter from "the astronomer"
to John Locke attempting to explain his overwhelming *weltzschmerz*, a
condition that Newton imagines may be relieved in time by communicating in "a language none of whose words is known to me; a language
in which commonplace things speak to me." The letter's crucial influence
is heavily underlined; it is given the same status as *The Newton Letter* itself
has in the narrator's biography: "He [Newton] wanted so much to know
what it was that had happened to him, and to say it, as if the mere saying
itself would be redemption." The fictional letter clarifies Newton's reality;
the real letter—the text of Banville's novella—illuminates Charlotte's
world: "Ferns . . . its daily minutiae, was strange beyond expressing,
unreal, and yet hypnotically vivid in its unreality." The author makes,
and in the process is unmade: the historian relinquishes his craft for the
sake of an alternative imaginative territory—love—only to find what
cannot be named in the first scientific, distant instance even more press-
ingly elusive in the emotional present. In the two-faced text, which suc-
essfully articulates failure's presence lies the essence, the chasm and how
to bridge it.

As though to make more explicit the reality of failure, and to remove
from it some of the aesthetic gilt attached to it in *The Newton Letter*, the
final work in the science quartet, as its title perhaps suggests, considers
the question of evil—evil being thought of in *Mefisto* as the failure of the
world. In keeping with the light and shade motifs throughout the science
quartet, *The Newton Letter* is set in a dazzling summer. *Mefisto*, on the
other hand, is dark: a theme for cello. It also is the most obsessively binary
of Banville's works, the binary being the dual number that Gabriel Swan,
the mathematician-narrator, recognizes as his natural idiom but one that
he cannot use as a language to live by. While one and zero exist, to
Gabriel, as mutually dependent coordinates of experience, denoting sin-
gularity and its other (negation), it remains existentially inconceivable to
oscillate at random between them. His ideal is to redeem one from its
negation: to rescue Sophie, the sluttish mute, to purge Adele of her drug
addiction, to love, with its ideal of the unique, the complete, the united.

The counterpointing of the romance of creativity with romance more conventionally regarded is one of the numerous, subtle grace notes that make both *The Newton Letter* and *Mefisto* such dazzling performances. These two novels' obviously romantic protagonists help counterpoint in turn what are referred to in *The Newton Letter* as "all those high cold heroes who renounced the world and human happiness to pursue the big game of intellect"—Copernicus, for example. It hardly needs saying that he fails, that he cannot help himself from being tempted into antiworlds of squalor, pain and waste by Mephistophelian Felix, his doppelganger. How can he refute "chance," the term with which his narrative begins and ends?

The familiar answer is, by belief in theory; by the consolatory "sense of order I felt, of harmony, of symmetry and completeness" resulting from feats of mathematical prestidigitation. And in view of this novel's over-statement, if anything, of the flesh's frailties, the note of rededication at the end is more poignant than ever, not merely because it echoes similar notes in Banville's work, initially sounded by Ben White in *Nightspawn*: "Stop. Stop, and go on, it is the only way." In addition, for Gabriel Swan, the prospect of renewal is viewed in the light of an experience of newness and rehabilitation that has led him to acknowledge himself inundated by "things . . . mere things themselves"; and to the realization that, "About numbers I had known everything and understood nothing." The second part of his narrative, beginning with a virtual rebirth resulting from being badly burned, deepens and makes more dreadful the hopelessness of the first part. The deterioration is matched, however, by an intensification of Gabriel's faith:

> From the start the world had been for me an immense formula. . . .
> But what was different now was that it was no longer numbers that lay
> at the heart of things. Numbers, I saw at last, were only a method. . . .
> The thing itself would be more subtle, more certain, even, than the
> mere manner of its finding. And I would find it. . . .

All Gabriel finds, however, is its absence—or, the fiction of seeking. Gabriel's gift achieves nothing. Yet, it is his keeping faith with his vision that preserves him. Without it, he is Felix, manipulator of contingency, inventor of plots for other people, exponent of a sense of order that limits and diminishes. The least obviously artistic of Banville's protagonists, Gabriel exemplifies most economically the cost of that most inevitable of all fictions: "I have begun to work again . . . it will be different this time. . . ."

Now in his forties, John Banville has already produced a substantial body of work that, quite beside the point of its undoubted intrinsic merit, raises interesting questions about the development of Irish fiction, about tradition and originality, about the genres of the Irish novel. However those questions may be investigated, Banville's oeuvre exists as imposing exemplification of imaginative freedom. His stylistic aplomb, his book-ishness, his range and ambition make his presence a particularly refreshing one. Not that his work is without blemish: sometimes his concerns seem too modishly indebted to antirealists such as Nabokov, Borges, and Beckett. None of his works avoid preciousness; and they frequently exhibit an overindulgent degree of formal self-consciousness. Clearly, he has done his utmost to live up to his own hope for

> . . . an art which is honest enough to despair and yet go on; rigorous and controlled, cool and yet passionate, without delusions, aware of its own possibilities and its own limits; an art which knows that truth is arbitrary, that reality is multifarious, that language is not a clear lens.

This hope is enshrined in Banville's portraits of the artist. The artist as Thales in Plato's story, who, stargazing, falls into a well. The artist who fills the celestial and subterranean spaces between which we live with indispensable artifice.

Notes

1. *Long Lankin* (London: Secker and Warbury, 1970). As the "Author's Note" to the second edition (Dublin: Gallery Press, 1984) reminds us, "The Possessed" and another story, "Persona," have been dropped. Added is "De Rerum Natura," a story rather uncharacteristic of the original collection's moodiness but representative of the author's increasing lightness of touch.

2. Rudiger Imhof, "An Interview with John Banville," *Irish University Review* 2, no. 1 (Spring 1981): 6.

3. Considering Banville as an exponent of romance is a useful way of placing his work in the context of Irish fiction where the genre occupies pride of place. A revealing glance at the implications of this point is given in Ronan Sheehan. "Novelists on the Novel: Ronan Sheehan talks to John Banville and Francis Stuart," *The Crane Bag* 3 (1979): 76–84.

4. In the author's view, "the most honest thing I have done . . . a kind of betrayal of the reader's faith in the writer's good faith, and also . . . of . . . the novelist's guild and its secret signs and strategems." Rudiger Imhof, "Interview," 6.

5. This phrase comes from Seamus Deane's superb discussion of *Long Lankin*, *Nightspawn*, and *Birchwood*: " 'Be Assured I am Inventing': The Fiction of John Banville," in Patrick Rafroidi and Maurice Harmon, eds., *The Irish Novel in our Time* (Publications de l'Universite de Lille III, 1975–76), 329–39.

6. This is one of the implications perhaps of his saying: "Pisces my sign. The fish is a noble animal, and recognized as such is given, like man, a singular plurality." The artist is spreadeagled at the axis of the paradox, in pain and slightly ridiculous.

7. Compare *Nightspawn*: "I am not god, I did not invent human beings. Why is it expected that I should understand everything?"

8. John Banville, "A Talk," *Irish University Review* 2, no. 1 (Spring 1981): 13. His emphasis.

9. Identification with "things" is prefigured in the story "A Death" in *Long Lankin*: "The things around him as he looked at them began to seem unreal in their extreme reality. Everything he touched gave to his fingers the very essence of itself." In *Nightspawn*, when asked what he writes about, Ben White replies: "Things . . . I write about people too . . . But you have to be careful with them. They always want to have meanings, or be symbols, always something more than they are." In neither text, however, is there an adequately developed sense of, or commitment to, the character and dispensation of "things."

10. Emphasis in the original.

Aidan Carl Mathews: Three Snapshots and Two Commentaries

John Unterecker

All of the photographs—some seventy or eighty of them, if I could assemble them in one heap—are a consequence of the Yeats International Summer School, where I first met Aidan in August of 1973 and where, for five different (but not consecutive) summers, we would expand our friendship, track the history of other friends, and critique each other's poems.

Of that first summer, when Aidan was a UCD student recently turned seventeen but looking, at best, a cherubic fifteen, I have only three clear memories (and no photographs): a memory of Aidan and me sitting in the front parlor of the Imperial Hotel in Sligo, reading through a stack of his poems, and of my desperate straining to hear his whispered response to my comments; a memory of his whispered reading (a little louder than in the Imperial's parlor) at the student poet's session and my very abrupt realization that his poetry showed extraordinary promise; and finally a memory of an awed girl telling me and two of her friends, "He can actually *converse* in Latin!" I've no idea if the latter is or ever was true; but I do know that Aidan as a boy had been taught to love literature and the arts, to search in philosophical speculation for something he could accept as truth, and, in travels with his godfather, to observe both nature and human nature with a valuing, accurate eye. He had been, perhaps, a scholar-linguist born, muttering Greek and Latin (and Irish) in his cradle; but he was also, toward the end of his adolescence, well on his way to becoming a Renaissance man.

The next summer, in August of 1974, Aidan's adolescence did not so much come to an end as erupt into frenetic displays of comic invention. And here we need snapshot no. 1: Caitriona (Belfast born but studying at St. Mary's College in England), Susan (a Wellesley undergraduate), Aidan, Doug (a student from the University of Texas at Austin). Their heads are lined up in that order, left to right, but torsos and legs are wildly interwoven with feet (left to right, with owner's initials) set up in this diagram: CL, AL, SL, CR, DL, AR, SR, DR. The effect is vaguely like Siamese quadruplets with everyone joined to everyone else somewhere between hip and ankle. The design, choreographed toward the end of our stay at the Yeats School, was Aidan's, the photography mine.

This was the year Aidan had decided to put off childhood and put on the costume of poet. He had a brand new beret perched jauntily on the side of his head; he whispered still, but almost audibly; and he overflowed with projects: a planned trip to Egypt, a passionate romance, magazines to be edited and distributed. The immediate project, however, was romance. He was at the Yeats School. He was, like Yeats, a poet in need of inspiration, preferably from a mortal muse. Tall Maud Gonne had inspired Yeats. Susan was a good two inches taller than Aidan. The answer seemed, to Aidan at least, obvious. Within a day or two all of us—except possibly Susan—knew to the tiniest detail Aidan's constantly shifting fantastic schemes to put Susan on her proper pedestal. Though the schemes varied, the climax speech was always to be the same: "Susan, it is your destiny to be Maud Gonne to my William Butler Yeats!" When Aidan finally got around to making his speech, Susan, as Maud Gonne before her, turned down her would-be suitor. Aidan, more inventive than Yeats, settled on second best: a "mystical marriage" of the whole quartet: hence, snapshot no. 1. "Mystical marriages," after all, being purely spiritual, could brook no refusals and could expand and contract as needed, incorporating any number within reason. It was an extraordinarily happy summer for all of us and particularly for Aidan, who reworked old poems and wrote new, firmer ones, and whose ironic wit and flair for "events" sent us piling into my rented car and off to picnics on beaches or mountains every time the sun would break through the off-and-on drizzle. At school's end, we gave ourselves a farewell weekend tour up into Donegal: Killibegs, Renvyle, Ardara, and particularly the area in and around Glencolumbkille. At Malin Beg, the four of them spelled out our names in gigantic letters on the "Golden Strand" so that I could stop time from the cliff top before Aidan led them into a dance, pummeling the twenty-foot-high names— CAITRIONA, JACK, SUSAN, DOUG, AIDAN—into sandy oblivion. We specialized in beaches, dolmens, mountaintops, and souterrains: "There's nothing so nice as a hole in the ground," Aidan remarked, thinking perhaps of *Alice in Wonderland,* as he led the pack down the well-like shaft and along the unlighted tunnel that cut under Glencolumbkille churchyard's burial ground. But Aidan, last out, seemed pleased to be back with the rest of us to watch an above-ground sunset.

Aidan's planned trip to Egypt never got past England where, according to a letter from Susan, Aidan "picked up a lot of big words" and forced her to consult her dictionary four times. In writing to her, however, he did not once refer to her as "sphinx-like Maud Gonne."

The next year was crucial to Aidan's development as a poet. He had had a chance to travel on the Continent—to France and Germany—and also to Greece, where, in another letter to Susan, he said he was "getting closer to the truth than ever before." But a different kind of truth had already opened to him in the summer of that year, for he spent the months working in a mortuary, a job that was to provide subject matter for work in both his first and second books.

The manuscript for that first book, *Windfalls*, was finished in 1976, when it won the Patrick Kavanagh Poetry Award, and was published in 1977 by Dolmen Press in a handsome paperback edition. As might be expected, it reflected Aidan's travels. Joyous experiences in Greece balanced disappointing trips to Chartres and Koln cathedrals where faith was commercialized and "Nothing is as it ought to be." At Chartres, where he had "expected awe," he found himself "tempted To a nervous scrutiny of hands Expertly fondling a girl's bottom." At Koln, where a guide made faltering jokes and tiredly whipped up fake enthusiasm, Aidan found a distraction parallel to that at Chartres:

> A young girl bends across a pew,
> Jeans taut in the candle-light. Need
> Tenses to an old hurt. The church,
> Toil of an alien passion, crumbles.

This conflict between spirit and flesh marks many of the poems in *Windfalls*, poems that are frequently visceral in intensity. The conflict is a real one. The game of romance that Aidan had invented for our amusement two years earlier is replaced by the harsh need for prayer and the equally harsh and shuttling demands of lust.

"Night," one of the most powerful poems of the book, brilliantly demonstrates that conflict not just in statement but in form and technique as well:

> I switch off the light, afraid
> Of what comes after night prayer.

Even on knees by the bedside,
Half-way through a Hail Mary,
No crucifix can halt
The thought or the suggestion.

I think of bulking rock,
The blunt knock of mallets.
A soldier threw the dice,
Another picked his nails.
A shape slung on a cross;
Wrists, ribcage slackened.

In the distinct darkness,
Other pictures gather.
Suburbs in the distance
Slope to a camp brothel.
Raucous laughter, loiterers;
Merge of damp bodies.

What of the pitted forehead,
Lips that had spoken love,
Feet lashed to a splinter?
No need to reckon why
The night brings perspiration,
Two beckoning impulses.

If we glance at the neat six-line stanzas, all seems symmetrical. But if we track placement of accent in the fundamentally trimeter pattern, you realize rhythmical tension is deliberately built into lines of greatest emotional tension. In the fourth line, for example, the lineup of spondee, anapest, and trochee ("Half-way through a Hail Mary") unbalances the rhythm precisely as the erotic thought we have not yet heard of intrudes on the prayer. As in most of Aidan's poems, rhyme—usually either hidden within lines or buried in the form of partial rhyme within words themselves—creates patterns of subtle concord or dissonance as the sense demands. Consider, for example, the principal sound patterns in the first stanza. The one full rhyme (light / night) is hidden toward the ends of the first two lines. But a whole set of other repeating sounds "disturb" the stanza by being locked into words that put an edge on feelings because we both do and do not "hear" them. If we spell out the sounds as words, however, we can make them visible. In the first two lines, for example, there are four "inaudible" rhymes: *I, lie, nigh,* and *sigh*; but our eyes fail to listen to them because (with the exception of *I*) they are hidden in other words: *light, night,* and *bedside.* For similar reasons our eyes fool our ears into not noticing the partial rhyme at the ends of the second and fourth lines—*prayer* / *Mar*(y)—or the third line's echoing *E* rhyme in *Even* and *knees* that picks up another echo in the unaccented final syllable of the following line (*Mary*). A similar agony-laden sound linkage ties the fourth and fifth lines together in the words *through* and *cru*cifix; and, in a slightly different fashion, the consonance of hal*t* and though*t* painfully binds lines five and six.

Many nineteenth- and early–twentieth-century scholars would have called—as they frequently did the rhythmical and sound structures of Emily Dickinson and Gerard Manley Hopkins—such poetry barbaric. Contemporary critics, depending on their sensitivity, describe it as either "arythmical and unrhymed" (the tone-deaf ones) or "ingenious" (the "new" prosodists).

Knowing Aidan, I am inclined to guess the grander effects are deliberate but that others were lucky accidents that, simply because they sounded right, got poked into the poem or kept in it as other phrases were discarded. I doubt, for instance, to cite my earlier analysis of the fourth line, that Aidan said to himself, "I'll now create a bit of tension by following a spondee with an anapest and give it a little zing by finishing with a trochee." On the other hand, I'll bet he was well aware of and liked the way alliteration balanced out a line that opened with a pair of strong beats ("Half-way") and ended with another pair of strong beats ("Hail Mary"), while, in between, a couple of unaccented beats ("through a") hold up the see-saw design by a kind of unemphatic fulcrum. In other words, the way anyone (Aidan included) achieves a strong line, strong stanza, strong poem is partly by choice and partly by chance; but the good poet—and Aidan is conspicuously one—consciously or unconsciously hears what he is doing and, with a great deal of deliberation, accepts it when it finally locks sound and sense into a mutually supportive system. It is called "having a good ear," is it not?

Because of that good ear, though all but one of the poems of this first book are clearly traditional in structure, Aidan is able to stretch form virtually to the breaking point. As a result, the tone is uniquely his own. Influence hunters will, I think, be hard put to locate Aidan's models. The best they might come up with would be a line or two reminiscent of the urgent / ironic quality Eliot managed in such early work as "Preludes" or perhaps—and this seems to me far-fetched—the bittersweet wit of some of John Crowe Ransom's early poems. But as soon as I say this, I reject it. The "influence" does not exist. What does exist is a parallel attempt of young poets of very different eras to sound old beyond their years.

In a number of the best poems, a gorgeous "Love Poem," say, full of lyric grace, or an "Earthworm" meticulously observed in its career as "soil sifter," its dangerous emergence into the foreign world of light where plover and sparrow threaten an "assassin's precision," and its return to the darkness of our abandoned past, "the debris of decades. / Porcelain chips, a copper coin; / Spear point and polished rib," Aidan seems neither young nor old, merely accurate. What could be more accurate, for example, than "Remembering Synge," perhaps the strongest of a series of portraits scattered through the latter half of the book?

> Moorhen, pheasant thrust
> From the tilted stone,
> Abruptly beautiful.
> Turns of the road promised
> Greetings, a bonfire,
> Light on the prongs of a pitchfork.
>
> He refused respite. Needing,
> His eyes narrowed
> To seas the height of pulpits.
> His nostrils accepted
> Damp sacking, burnt herring.
> Solemn, he stood as in a church.
>
> Resting on faces, he felt grief:
> The pathos in a joke,
> The lonely on their own in bars;
> Sadness of mere circumstance.
> Comedy costumed darkness
> Nights when sleep would not come.
>
> Dreaming of seabirds, a thin
> Inkblot on the green sky,
> Death came like a stage aside.
> Outside the hospital,
> Orphans were waving
> White handkerchiefs to the trams.

Accuracy here is not just that of carefully evaluated historical information, although such accuracy is in the poem, but, more importantly, the accuracy of a truth that is absolute: the artist's recognition of the interdependence of human mortality and the reality of the imagination that, surviving, becomes the work of art.

Snapshot no. 2: August 1978: a fragment photograph, the last incomplete frame on the roll. Aidan, like a cheerful, half-disembodied genius of the place, ascends from an island in the middle of Loch Gill. It is a Saturday, the eighth day of the Yeats International Summer School, a day of brilliant sunlight, literally idyllic.

We had reached the island in two rowboats, Aidan, of course, having made all arrangements so inconspicuously that it seemed all eight of us had merely arrived at the dock—though, needless to say, food and drink had somehow been assembled; all of us had one way or another been routed out of bed; knives and forks, knapsacks, cameras, film, books, paper, notebooks stowed in the boats. We all wore jackets and sweaters against the morning chill; but rain, which we were prepared for, never got closer than a few white puffs of cloud on the most distant horizon.

My boat included Ann (a scholarship student from British Columbia), Richard (a young lawyer from San Francisco), and Tim (a friend of Aidan's who had come up from Dublin for the weekend).

Aidan, whose boat was filled with women and who gallantly insisted on doing most of the rowing, had with him Henrietta (a visitor from England), and Sara and Megan (childhood friends who found themselves reunited as they stood in line registering at the school after more than ten years without hearing from or seeing one another).

When we set out, some of us had had visions of rowing all the way up the Garravogue into Loch Gill and on to Innisfree; but once we fought our way into the stiff current of the river and finally out of it into the relative calm of the lake, we were happy to settle for the first island we came to, a big island as Loch Gill goes, perhaps a mile long and half a mile wide, uninhabited except for four black bulls that were content to keep to themselves, casting no more than an occasional cold eye in our direction. Boats tied to the remains of a dock, we spread out on a sunny little hillock to picnic and to talk.

If Yeats's Innisfree is famous for its "bee-loud glade," our island should become infamous for its bee-stinging knoll; our opened wine bottles brought in swarms, and, as bad luck would have it, the only one of us to be stung was Richard who, severely allergic to bee and wasp stings, instantly developed a bump on his upper arm the size of a goose egg. The women took turns trying to suck out the dab of poison; then someone remembered that "something" applied to the sting would "draw" it. My memory is hazy as to what we applied—perhaps peaches, perhaps tomatoes, perhaps mud: everthing handy, I think—but whatever it was, one of the "somethings" worked. After half an hour of anxiety on everyone's part, the swelling began to go down, Richard stopped sweating, and a radiance set in that lasted not just for the day but for the rest of the week and that, in fact, is with me still. Except for Megan and Sara, we had started out as casual acquaintances; abruptly we were a community, proud of ourselves for Richard's triumph over the insect kingdom and more than half in love with each other. There was a shine on everything, as if the gold sun wove its magic into the fabric of our souls. We broke up into shifting groups to explore the island—a broken-down church, the foundations of a house and what might have been a shed, a bit of a wall beginning nowhere and going nowhere, and on the upper part of the island dense groves of trees and vines, rays of gold light cutting through here and there to illuminate Aidan and Henrietta perched on distant boulders and caught up in an intensity of words; nearer, Richard, one hand pressed tight around a bough as if he were taking the very pulse of nature itself; far in the distance, Megan and Sara stopped in a meadow of wildflowers; Ann, a few yards behind me, about to ask if I could identify a leaf—and Tim, whom we had left stretched out for a nap, out of sight of all of us in the full rustling glory of gold grass, gold sun, gold light that, echoing up over everything from the reflecting little wavelets of the lake, cast over his sleeping face and throat a gold-leaf-thin transparency of shimmering air.

For the rest of us, there was a dance of shifting partners in the changing light, so elegant, so full of grace, I wondered if perhaps we were no more than projections of Tim's wavering dream. We had used up words, toward the end, and moved silent and casual as the four grazing bulls that, accepting us at last, drifted off into a far brightness of late, horizon sun. We picked up picnic remnants, settled in the boats, and cast off.

That should have been enough, more than enough. There was no need to row, and we floated downstream, our boats perhaps a hundred yards from one another in the silence. Then I heard Aidan's soft voice and Megan's light reply. An accomplished musician, she had brought her recorder, and soon the whole darkening landscape was alive with music Shakespeare might have listened to beside another river in another time. Maeve's Cairn was outlined in the last light beyond Knocknarea. We tied up at the dockside in Sligo well after dark, had supper somewhere, perhaps picnicking still, and settled into the hotel parlor for late drinks and even later talk.

Except for Tim, who returned to Dublin, we were together for the rest of the week and rode the train together back to Dublin. We promised to write each other and, for years, did. Sara, Megan, Richard, and I met in Berkeley for a reunion several years later, where our talk was of Aidan and his catalytic gift for sharing friends.

Snapshot no. 3: Connemara, 28 August 1979. Aidan and Trish, the woman he would marry, had come to Sligo for the last few days of the Yeats School—probably the wettest in history, for from opening day to the final farewell party Sligo had had literally uninterrupted rain. Sometimes it thinned to a mist and once, I think, there was a glimpse of pale sunlight through rain. But for two weeks, I had walked with, talked to, played among, lectured for, read poetry to, and every weekday afternoon led a seminar of damp, damp, damp people not even beginning to dry off in the omnipresent soggy air. Sunday morning, 28 August, when everybody said farewells and headed back to each separate elsewhere, dawned cloudless, a flame of rinsed sunlight blazing on the brim-full river.

I assume Aidan and Trish had invited me to visit his family's cottage on the south shore of Connemara as a kind of chaperone since they were still not officially engaged. (Or perhaps *because* they were not officially engaged: the neighbors might talk!) The drive from Sligo to Galway was a desperate one: Aidan had the smallest and possibly the oldest car ever manufactured, and I had enough luggage for a family of four. Every thirty or forty miles we stopped to stretch, nibble on cheese and crackers, and, most crucially, check the tires, which were virtually flat from all of the weight. The problem, of course, was that if we added more air they would have exploded on even the smallest bump; if they lost any air the wheel rims would have cut them to ribbons. We wormed our way through Galway, then, as we headed out through the barren beautiful landscape, used every excuse we could invent to romp among roadside boulders. I had entered my rock-photography phase that summer and Connemara was made for me. Aidan and Trish are in the photographs because I am incapable of not photographing friends, but the other reason for their presence is to lend scale to the boulders. "Thin soil, worn rock," I would think as I snapped the shutter, "and transient shadows." Then I would tell myself not to be pretentious.

In snapshot no. 3 it is already late afternoon, a gust of wind whipping Aidan's straggly hair. Both Aidan and Trish are smiling, tired, happy. Soon we will stop at the village store to buy milk for breakfast and a few provisions for supper, though Aidan assures us the cottage is well stocked with food. And indeed it proves to be. And beautiful. Perched on the slope of a little hill, it looks out over the bay and, in the early evening light, catches reflections from tide pools that by midnight will be well under water.

Our project for that evening had been to read through our newest poems. But a phone call after supper changed all that and accounts for my being able to date my visit to the cottage so accurately. Aidan called his mother to say that we had arrived—and learned what everyone else was already talking about. While we had been merrily checking tires and eating crackers and cheese, Lord Mountbatten, enjoying sunlight as much as we after two weeks of rain, had gone boating twenty miles north of Sligo. An assassination explosion had torn him and his boat to shreds.

Aidan seemed literally in shock, and we sat huddled by the radio twisting the dials for the latest news. What we heard was disorganized and fragmentary. Aidan, whom I had always thought of as apolitical, kept talking of the senselessness of the murder, the horror of a pointless terrorist attack on one of the world's most generous humanitarians. We finally gave up on the radio, drank a fair amount, and talked of faith, violence, and the irrational. Aidan was in turn eloquent, angry, morose.

The next day was cloudless as Sunday had been, and Aidan led us on all of his favorite walks. We covered high ground and skimpy pastureland, and then tracked the tide in its afternoon retreat. That evening we did read and talk about poetry far into the night, but our poems seemed to take on unexpected shadows from the news. It was as if the words of the poems, rather than being prompted by life, were responding to it. The next day, after we returned to Dublin, I went on to London where I had several days' wait before sailing back to New York and then flying to Honolulu. In London, I spent a long afternoon watching Mountbatten's funeral cortege on a friend's television and the funeral ceremony itself: that reading of the moving statement he had written to be used on the occasion of his death.

Since then, I've seen Aidan a number of times, all of them brief meetings: a luncheon in 1980 and once, by pure chance, a quick out-of-the-car-window conversation with him and Trish as I was waiting for the number 14 bus on Sanford Road in Dublin. That sort of thing. Neither of us are good correspondents, though I did write him a note (and misaddressed it, so it came back) during the time he held a two-year writing fellowship at Stanford University. While he was there, a number of the poems in *Minding Ruth* (Gallery Books, 1983) were composed or revised.

All of the Aidans I knew—mischievous, witty, affectionate, compassionate—show up in this book as well as those I had only a passing glimpse of: the Aidan outraged at human brutality, or tender in the presence of children, or attempting to sort out the complex emotions of family love.

When I spoke of the poems of *Windfalls* as formal in nature yet achieving tensions and releases by stretching form to its limits, I might have dealt with the same general notion by speaking of the dramatic interaction in Aidan's poetry of intensity and decorum. This is especially true of *Minding Ruth*, I think, where in poem after poem readers find that extraordinarily powerful feelings, feelings they vicariously share, are not so much "tamed" by the carefully wrought verse but rather made visible, audible, and, in a sense, serviceable. In *The World's Body*, Ransom writes of the function of ceremony—a funeral, say—as a way of freeing us from otherwise raw and destructive feelings. Ceremony allows us, he insists, to control grief by giving it a memorable, public, and, perhaps, ironically, "satisfying" form. For the same reason, it seems to me, letters of condolence lock both writer and reader into a healing dialogue. They define loss and, in doing so, give enough shape to pain to make it at least momentarily therapeutic. In freeing pain from privacy, such letters offer the possibility of transforming the ache of grief into the liberation of eulogy.

The larger ceremony of the poem also shapes, controls, and transforms feelings—not just of grief, but of joy, of love, even those of a mind at work. In the title poem of *Minding Ruth*, all of these are present (even the pun on "minding"). The extraordinary element in this poem, which in 1981 won the Ina Coolbrith Poetry Prize at Stanford and which is dedicated to the Irish poet / scholar Seamus Deane, is neither the tender valuation of the child or even the shock at the end when she misreads the monstrous behavior of man to man during World War II but rather the nature of the writer's brief delight in accepting what it is to be a member of the community ("the city itself"), which he enters "as a civilian," the noun carrying the whole weight of civility, of civilization, and of what is entailed in being a true citizen: this contrasted to the photograph of "happy soldiers" at the end of the poem who glory in their brutality and "die laughing" at an "old rabbi squatting in turds":

> She wreaks such havoc in my library,
> It will take ages to set it right—
> A Visigoth in a pinafore

Who, weakening, plonks herself
On the works of Friedrich Nietzsche,
And pines for her mother.

She's been at it all morning,
Duck-arsed in my History section
Like a refugee among rubble,

Or, fled to the toilet, calling
In a panic that the seat is cold.
But now she relents under biscuits

To extemporise grace notes,
And sketch with a blue crayon
Arrow after arrow leading nowhere.

My small surprise of language,
I cherish you like an injury
And would swear by you at this moment

For your brisk chatter brings me
chapter and verse, you restore
The city itself, novel and humming,

Which I enter as a civilian
Who plants his landscape with place-names.
They stand an instant, and fade.

Her hands sip at my cuff. She cranes,
Perturbedly, with a book held open
At plates from Warsaw in the last war.

Why is the man with the long beard
Eating his booboos? And I stare
At the old rabbi squatting in turds

Among happy soldiers who die laughing,
The young one clapping: you can see
A wedding band flash on his finger.

Perhaps it is enough merely to read so remarkable a poem, for we share the evolution of emotions without, I think, any need for analysis. But the complexity of feeling is not accidentally achieved. And the ironies are prepared for us as carefully as the history lesson it teaches. The affectionate celebration of the little girl in the "History section" of the speaker's private library is handled in terms of history (and Germanic history at that). She's a "Visigoth in a pinafore" who "wreaks such havoc" that it will "take ages to set it right." We need to have read the poem at least once to see how efficiently Aidan prepares us for what is to come, even to her choosing to plonk herself down on the works of Nietzsche. In presenting her careless charm, which is charm, she plays the roles of victor and vanquished, Visigoth and victim, Nazi and "a refugee among rubble," sketching a child's aimless images of war, "Arrow after arrow leading nowhere" yet panicking that her toilet seat is cold.

But if she is destroyer and destroyed, she is peacemaker as well. Cherished "like an injury," she brings—in the form of "brisk chatter"—language, the W / word, "chapter and verse." She is able to "restore / The city itself" and all the connotations of city / civilian / citizen / and civilization I have already touched on. The brute complexity of history, though, is not really the province of a little girl in a pinafore who, even though she wreaks havoc in a library and restores the city, is baffled by a photograph in a book that, if I read the poem right, also baffles both reader and author. For her question is, after all, never answered. Maybe because it is unanswerable. Do we know why and how civilization so swiftly uncivilizes itself, more swiftly than the length of a life, even of a generation? The speaker of the poem—let us call him Aidan—looks only at a photograph of Warsaw in World War II. But every reader, I suspect, adds up the barbarism since that time: American farm boys turned killers in Vietnam, the God-fearing young assassins of Mountbatten, the boys and girls in Lebanon and Ghaza on both sides of their hatreds, the adolescent Latin American mercenaries hired by the United States and the Soviet Union to bomb each other's villages, shoot American and Russian bullets into each other's sisters, parents, grandparents . . . all of the little boys and girls who will grow up to murder and betray. Minding Ruth— irritated by her, taking care of her, bearing her in mind. Minding Ruth— the child and all the connotations of her name: "compassion for misery of another; pity; mercy"; "Sorrow; grief; sadness, especially sorrow for one's own faults; repentence; regret; remorse"; "Something causing sadness, especially, cruel action"; "That which is the occasion of pity or compassion; a pitiful sight; a sad thing." These are dictionary definitions. No, there is no answer to Ruth's question, since there is still compassion and grief—luckily, no adequate answer so long as we mind, so long as we escape a completely ruthless world.

The tone of the whole volume is richly varied, as varied as the title poem itself. There are five extraordinarily compelling elegies, four poems that uncoil memories of Aidan's eight-year-earlier experiences as a mortuary technician, a group focused in on his mother and father, and a whole sheaf toward the end of the volume of witty, tender, gently erotic love poems all too long to be quoted and far too good to be quoted in part.

The last poem in the book—a sequence of thirty-four short, haiku-like lyrics, each separately titled—delights me not just because it is delightful (and it is), but because its impudence and freshness and jollity, its bouncing good humor, its sly self-dramatization, prove that Aidan and his new live-in muse (whom he did, after all, marry) can kick up their heels and frolic as well as or better than he could fifteen years ago when, merrily lovelorn, he bounded like a ground squirrel out of souterrains, led us a dance through Donegal, and planned what has indeed transpired: his life as a poet people want and need to listen to. Though I cannot—for obvious reasons—quote all of "Basho's Rejected Jottings," here, for the finale, is a sampling:

1. *How to Read Them*
You could do worse
Than begin like children
By smelling the pages.

4. *Libraries*
Culture, calm, and so forth.
I could go on.

Two desks down,
She's kicked off her shoes.

5. *Basho Makes his Move*
When she looks up,
Her head breaks
Water like silence.

8. *Spring*
Grass through the pavestones
The short hairs
Curling from her cut-offs.

11. *Courtship*
Her feet were cold all night.

Another
Figure of speech sent packing.

16. *Hollows*
Her left armpit
Chafed from shaving.

I mouthwash
Apricot talcum.

19. *Acts of Love*
In the morning,
My hands smell
Of beaches after storms.

21. *Basho in Love is Prolific*
Two haikus
In a month.
Stop rushing.

34. *Reconciliation*
When you come back,
Your hands smell
Of walking gloveless.

The Contemporary Fe / Male Poet: A Preliminary Reading

James McElroy

Peter Porter has suggested in an *Observer* review that Medbh McGuckian writes "like a less loquacious Ashbery."[1] Michael O'Loughlin, writing in *Books Ireland*, has extended this piece of criticism by informing his reader that McGuckian can sometimes become "fey and mannered"; can often lack "Ashbery's wit" and "intellectual slyness."[2] What both of these critics clearly believe, then, is that McGuckian does not measure up to John Ashbery's high textual standards. What neither of them explains, however, is why McGuckian should be measured along an Ashbery or, for that matter, any other male line. Indeed, the fact that both of them find it necessary, and sufficient, to engage the same male principle appears to hide, behind its own coincidence, an initial hegemonic move: any comparison between McGuckian and any other female poet like H. D., Edna St. Vincent Millay, Marianne Moore, or Sylvia Plath is written out of the question.

In the same way, whenever James Simmons writes in *The Belfast Review* that McGuckian indulges in "alluring nonsense" and "comes on as a tease," his priapic terms of reference decode the more beguiling but no less dismissive remarks of Porter and O'Loughlin.[3] Even the consideration that Simmons exchanges their leading man for another and, arguably, more convincing male starting point—Dylan Thomas—does nothing to distinguish the masculinist sense that underwrites all of their criticism. Thus when the same Simmons who refers to McGuckian's poetry as "alluring nonsense" openly admits that he has also had problems handling several of Eiléan Ní Chuilleanáin's poems (poems he selected for inclusion in the anthology *Ten Irish Poets*), the confusion over criterial language and definition only becomes more acute.[4] So acute, in fact, that Simmons actually

189

seems to find it reassuring that he cannot "sense" any real "connections" between the poems contained in *Site of Ambush*,[5] a collection he turns out with a singular quotation from "The Lady's Tower":

> Hollow my high tower leans
> Back to the cliff; my thatch
> Converses with spread sky,
> Heronries. The grey wall
> Slices downward and meets
> A sliding flooded stream
> Pebble-banked, small diving
> Birds. Downstairs my cellars plumb.
>
> Behind me shifting the oblique veins
> Of the hill; my kitchen is damp,
> Spiders shaded under brown vats.
>
> I hear the stream change pace, glance from the stove
> To see the punt is now floating freely
> Bobs square-ended, the rope dead-level.
>
> Opening the kitchen door
> The quarry brambles miss my hair
> Sprung so high their fruit wastes.
>
> And up the tall stairs my bed is made
> Even with a sycamore root
> At my small square window.
>
> All night I lie sheeted, my broom chases down treads
> Delighted spirals of dust: the yellow duster glides
> Over shelves, around knobs: bristle stroking flagstone
> Dancing with the spiders around the kitchen in the dark
> While cats climb the tower and the river fills
> A spoonful of light on the cellar walls below.

This superficial treatment of Ní Chuilleanáin's poetry and the way it dispenses with even the most obvious "connections" between a metaphoric abode like "tower" and any sexual resemblance in the terms "thatch" and "damp" certainly seems to imply (at least from a Freudian angle) that Simmons suffers from a kind of selective amnesia. In fact, his inability to be reflexive and think *through* his own values or countenance the idea that Ní Chuilleanáin's poems might actually represent a viable textual environment tends to postpone any interpretation that might break up the foreplay of language and envision "The Lady's Tower" as an aperture: a poetic opening where writers can begin to organize, protest, and feminize a self-image. This being much the same kind of self-image that Medbh McGuckian "Houses" in her poem "The Soil-Map":

I am not a woman's man, but I can tell,
By the swinging of your two-leaf door,
You are never without one man in the shadow
Of another; and because the mind
Of a woman between two men is lighter
Than a spark, the petalled steps to your porch
Feel frigid with a lost warmth. I will not
Take you in hardness, for all the dark cage
Of my dreaming over your splendid fenestration,
Your moulded sills, your slender purlins,

The secret woe of your gutters. I will do it
Without niggardliness, like food with one
Generous; a moment as auspicious
And dangerous as the christening of a ship,
My going in to find the settlement
Of every floor, the hump of water
Following the moon, and her discolouring,
The saddling derangement of a roof
That might collapse its steepness
Under the sudden strain of clearing its name.

For anyone with patience can divine
How your plasterwork has lost key, the rendering
About to come away. So like a rainbird,
Challenged by a charm of goldfinch,
I appeal to the god who fashions edges
Whether such turning-point exist
As these saltings we believe we move
Away from, as if by simply shaking

A cloak we could disbud ourselves,
Dry out, and cease to live there?

I have found the places on the soil-map,
Proving it possible once more to call
Houses by their names, Annsgift or Mavisbank,
Mount Juliet or Bettysgrove: they should not
Lie with the gloom of disputes to interrupt them
Every other year, like some disease
Of language making humorous the friendship
Of the thighs. I drink to you as Hymenstown,
(My touch of fantasy) or First Fruits,
Impatient for my power as a bride.

It would appear, then, that the notion of reading as a neutral or neuter act (a component feature of phallic criticism) can no longer be entertained. Instead, the kind of impunity that characterizes the thinking of Porter, O'Loughlin, and Simmons, as well as James J. McAuley who, in 1962, criticized Eithne Strong on the grounds that *Songs of Living* enveloped her "in an enigmatic mist of runic chanting," has to be revised.[6] What is more, the unworded premise that drives a critic like McAuley to ignore some of Strong's more feminist poems, but valorize those that keep her in her place as either a nurturing female ("Prayer") or an incurable romantic ("Immutable"), has to be called into question; the kind of question that can relinquish McAuley's assertion that Eithne Strong "leads us off into a world of half-glimpsed will-o-wisps, and shadowy imagery"[7] as readily as it can overturn his opinion (in the same review) that Rupert Strong's *From Inner Fires* suffers from little more than an occasional, and manly indiscretion . . . "lapses in diction."[8]

Even more ironic than the deliberations of McAuley and Co. is the fact that a female critic like Carol Rumens can turn on Eavan Boland for writing in specifically feminist terms only completes the hegemonic circle: "female miseries accumulate—mastectomy, wife-battering and anorexia nervosa, as well as menstruation and the Cosmetic Con—but it all adds up to a pretty familiar statement. There are flashes notably in "Anorexic" and "In His Own Image" of the sensibility that produced the fine title poem of her last collection, "The War Horse," but overall that strong willed, sensuous control of language has slipped into mere stridency."[9]

Here, Rumens's comment that Boland represents a "pretty familiar statement" is not only antifeminist (she later claims that "Boland is working, to the detriment of her talent, in the Anglo-American tradition"), but underestimates how feminism was, and still is, a belated phenomenon in Ireland.[10] What Rumens therefore describes as a familiar list of "female miseries" might, at this critical juncture, be reinterpreted in order to identify the woman poet as a mediate space in language, redress poetic standards, and compel language to work for women at the level of both criticism and poetry. Indeed, Rumens's disdainful aside that Boland's language has "slipped into mere stridency" (another *Times Literary Supplement* critic calls it "bitterness")[11] might actually help to define its own limitation as a limitation that refuses to study linear disobedience and consider the possibility that beauty—both aesthetic and physical—might be defined in far more militant terms:

> Time to start
>
> working
> from the text,
> making
>
> from this trash
> and gimmickry
> of sex
>
> my aesthetic:
> a hip first,
> a breast,
>
> a slow
> shadow strip
> out of clothes[12]

Masculinist critics, and this includes the androcentric Rumens, therefore seem to be caught up in their own right of way. So much, in fact, that they are rarely able to identify aesthetic values as their own and prefer, instead, to work them like universal facts of life or, if that fails, merely to shoot the female poet in an imperfect, incomplete, inferior masculine pose and then read her like an X-rated flick. Either way, of course, the critic still manages to blur any menacing female delivery. Thus when Padraic Colum writes in his preface to Eithne Strong's *Songs of Living* that women's poetry "tends to be self-centered, self-regarding, self-pity-ing,"[13] and supports his claim by citing Christina Rossetti, Elizabeth Bar-rett Browning, and Edna St. Vincent Millay as evidence of this untoward literary practice, his argument is *already* well taken. The one exception to this rule, Strong herself, is favored by Colum precisely because she can write outside this "context": "by going back to something ancient Eithne Strong writes of a woman's life in a way that takes her outside the context that so much of women's poetry has to be read in. We read hers as the utterances of the priestess, the druidess, the sybil."[14]

However, even Colum's desire to redeem Strong, once it is read ec-topically, seems to involve an acute reversal: Strong can either return, compliments of the male sex, to "something ancient" and belated (strike man as mysterious and irrational); or, failing that, become nothing more than a solipsist who is "self-centered, self-regarding, self-pitying" (a mys-tery to both herself *and* man). Indeed, the recognition that Strong will only be taken seriously once she is torn from "the context that so much of women's poetry has"—*has?*—"to be read in," merely indicates how language can hamper critics even when they try to turn things around. After all, the need to turn things around rather than accompany them into their own textual space is, in itself, a means of keeping certain poetic ideas and themes under wraps, especially a theme like the female "self," which is so often pushed aside as the sign of a female complex rather than a binomial—at least binomial—signifier of a complex social condition.

Consequently, when Eavan Boland asserts in "Making Up" that a wom-an's sense of identity is a male predicate—"it's a trick. / Myths / are made by men."—her language is deliberately meant to rename the "self" and, where possible, toss the belief that women are made in their own image and likeness. Equally, her argument that a woman's "look" is fashioned by commercial, as well as other forces, is presented as a challenge; an expectation that the female writer can counter an abiding psychological and somatic nuance that the fe / male is made "In His Own Image":

> I was not myself, myself.
> The celery feathers,
> the bacon flitch,
> the cups deep on the shelf
> and my cheek
> coppered and shone
> in the kettle's paunch,
> my mouth

blubbed in the tin of the pan—
they were all I had to go on.

How could I go on
With such meagre proofs of myself?
I woke day after day.
Day after day I was gone
From the self I was last night.

And then he came home tight.

Such a simple definition!
How did I miss it?
Now I see
that all I needed
was a hand
to mould my mouth,
to scald my cheek,
was this concussion
by whose lights I find
my self-possession,
where I grow complete.

Despite this radical talent for signifying the female "self" as a sliding, rather than a fixed and immutable referent—"not myself, myself," "meagre proofs of myself," "gone / From the self I was"—Boland's poetry, at least its "simple definition," still remains off limits. Accordingly, whenever a poem like "Anorexic" approaches "the self" as a fiction, and instills the overwhelmingness of man in wo / man—ushers in the "Anorexic" as not just not herself, but as a crucial representation of how she, *her self*, might be understood—the central point that balance is a split decision gets lost along the way:

Flesh is heretic.
My body is a witch.
I am burning it.

Yes I am torching
her curves and paps and wiles.
They scorch in my self denials.

How she meshed my head
in the half-truths
of her fevers

till I renounced
milk and honey
and the taste of lunch.

I vomited
her hungers.
Now the bitch is burning.

I am starved and curveless.
I am skin and bone.
She has learned her lesson.

Thin as a rib
I turn in sleep.
My dreams probe

a claustrophobia
a sensuous enclosure.
How warm it was and wide

once by a warm drum,
once by the song of his breath
and in his sleeping side.

Only a little more,
only a few more days
sinless, foodless,

I will slip
back into him again
as if I had never been away.

Caged so
I will grow
angular and holy

past pain,
keeping his heart
such company

as will make me forget
in a small space
the fall

into forked dark,
into python needs
heaving to hips and breasts
and lips and heat
and sweat and fat and greed.

Almost, but not quite, as unremitting as Boland's "Anorexic," Medbh
McGuckian's "Saint Sophia" also leers into another "small space" or, as
she would have it, "the slim space of man":

My interest is in disappearing, flattening—
The fuller figure, fasting to a plan,
Occupies the slim space of man.
The almshouse book of comfort illustrates
The true functions of mouths. But the doctor
Is part of the problem, my hunger will never be felt.

If only I could understand the pain
Of building myself up, the feather
Of my thin precarious life to blow away,
The burnt-out calories of my body
Would show me up, highlight my invisibility:
When morning comes, I'd be as good as new.

Clearly, both of these poems renounce masculinist definitions. Not only
that, but they both detest all the attendant myths that induce a "thin
precarious life" of "burnt-out calories." Eiléan Ní Chuilleanáin, much like
Boland and McGuckian, not only regards these myths as unclean but
anticipates nothing more than a "Woman and world not yet":

Wash man out of the earth; shear off
The human shell.

Twenty feet down there's close cold earth
So clean.

Wash the man out of the woman:
The strange sweat from her skin, the ashes from her hair.
Stretch her to dry in the sun
The blue marks on her breast will fade.

Woman and world not yet
Clean as the cat
Leaping to the windowsill with a fish in her teeth;
Her flat curious eyes reflect the squalid room,
She begins to wash the water from the fish. [15]

At this stage an apparent longing to enter and conjugate fe / male, wo /
man, and s / he, inscribes a protest by undoing stagnant social identities,
reorganizing female signifiers, and blowing away the myth of genderless
writing. What it also manages to do—expose the "I" of discourse as a
disposable run on Signifiers over Signifieds—not only works toward the
social matrix in which fe / male selves occur, but the ways in which this
matrix organizes women and convinces them, in some shape or form, to
accept themselves as part of the "conscious uncontrol" Eithne Strong
objects to in her poem "Spirit-Bound":

I am but an empty dull thing,
peering,
prying,
from the furtiveness of my little soul's sneaking;
hating men for the shame
in my wretched privacy.
Weakly,
contemptible,
vacillating in my conscious uncontrol.

The question still remains, though, whether these "lesions" in the fe /
male self will ever be allowed to surface as serious issues in literary criticism.
In fact, the entire question of how to think man's ongoing critical categories—self / other, subject / object, presence / absence, law / chaos, male /
female, and so forth—still has to be written before "Woman and world"

can become an authentic, possible theme; the very same theme that Virginia Woolf poses in unusual, and unusually somatic terms when she writes in her essay "Professions for Women" that telling the truth about her own experiences "as a body" remains unsolved:

> I doubt that any woman has solved it yet. The obstacles against her are still immensely powerful—and yet they are very difficult to define. Outwardly, what is simpler than to write books? Outwardly, what obstacles are there for a woman rather than for a man? Inwardly, I think, the case is very different; she has still many ghosts to fight, many prejudices to overcome. Indeed it will be a long time still, I think, before a woman can sit down to write a book without finding a phantom to be slain, a rock to be dashed against.[16]

This thoughtful measure of the fe / male writer's self and her somatic predicament ("telling the truth about my own experiences as a body") is certainly in direct contrast to the masculinist critic's almost total indifference toward the same subject. Indeed, the intermediate consideration that many critics never talk about the male poet's general *somatic absence*, never recognize that male dominance works through this, and never question the inflexible nature of "the man and woman metaphor" largely means, as Eiléan Ní Chuilleanáin makes plain in her critical remarks, that sexual / textual roles are resistant and predetermined:[17] "Is it that Seamus Heaney needs the vague and remote like MacPherson or early Yeats? I don't think so; it is more that in these poems ("Ocean's Love to Ireland," "Act of Union") he is treating male and female as fixed and recognizable starting points to be used in getting one's bearings on a wider scene. These poems lack the ironic awareness that he shows elsewhere of the inescapably fragmentary nature of such comparisons."[18]

Of course, Ní Chuilleanáin is right. Even a brief extract from each of the aforementioned poems shows how Heaney's male personae simply *assume* their positions as first, aggressive ("drive inland / Till all her strands are breathless"), and then dominant ("I am the tall kingdom over your shoulder") male types:

> Speaking broad Devonshire,
> Ralegh has backed the maid to a tree
> As Ireland is backed to England

And drives inland
Till all her strands are breathless:
'Sweesir, Swatter! Sweesir Swatter!'

He is water, he is ocean, lifting
Her farthingdale like a scarf of weed lifting
In the front of a wave.
                              "Ocean's Love to Ireland"

To-night, a first movement, a pulse,
As if the rain in bogland gathered head
To slip and flood: a bog-burst,
A gash breaking open the ferny bed.
Your back is a firm line of eastern coast
And arms and legs are thrown
Beyond your gradual hills. I caress
The heaving province where our past has grown.
I am the tall kingdom over your shoulder
That you would neither cajole nor ignore.
Conquest is a lie. I grow older
Conceding your half-independent shore
Within whose borders now my legacy
Culminates inexorably.
                              "Act of Union"

This same sexual trace found in Heaney's poems from *Death of a Naturalist* to *The Haw Lantern* is, to borrow one of his own phrases, "imperially / Male." Regardless of Ní Chuilleanáin's protest, then, the male writer still does not have to explain his somatic signature, justify its twists and turns, or fret over its predefinition as a narrative insert unless the male establishment deems it necessary. In fact, even the most cursory glance at the contemporary literary scene provides ample evidence that the somatic grammar Ní Chuilleanáin calls "the man and woman metaphor" still holds. And holds, as Alicia Suskin Ostriker notes in *Stealing the Language: The Emergence of Women's Poetry in America*, for very specific and macho reasons:

Distance remains a virtue in the male poetic establishment, almost like
a corollary of the training which defines the masculine body exclusively
as tool or weapon, forbids it to acknowledge weakness or pain, and

deprives it accordingly of much potential sensitivity to pleasure—a sensuous man is an "effeminate" man—apart from the pleasures associated with combat or conquest. Control—of mind over matter, of orderly word over disorderly emotion—remains a literary desideratum. The discourse of male bonding may derive from big and little game hunting and the tennis court, or from allusions to the responses of women in bed. These are the safe, sane, blushproof topics.[19]

From the very beginning, then, it appears that the "poetic establishment" prefers "Distance" and "Control"—the "blushproof topics"—over the intimacy of Boland's "slow / shadow strip / out of clothes," or the vacillation of Strong's "conscious uncontrol." This is not too surprising when we consider that any change in these categories will not only entail a shift in the critic's line on female poetry—missed "connections," "alluring nonsense," "runic chanting," and "stridency"—but will pressure him, or her, to take a second and quite different look at the "self," and most especially the somatic self, as a facade: a social signifier that does not have, and does not have to have, a specific form of poetic expression. On the contrary, it can become, as it does in a poem like Medbh McGuckian's "The Return of Helen," a somatic twist that takes place as and "where you least expect":

> Being stored inside like someone's suffering,
> Each piece of furniture now begins
> To interpret every eye as sunlight:
> And that smallness in me which does not vibrate
> Is moving none the less towards
> The white and unworked wool of the corded bed.
>
> The old year in his mimic death
> Is my husband like a child unlooked-for
> Moistening the wrong turnings I make
> Myself take, till the path into my body
> And out of it again is a sea-place
> Opening where you least expect.
>
> As from an irresponsible
> Brood of ten, my love of twenty years
> Might oversweetly part your fingers
> To count the points, telling why you ravish her.

Notes

1. Peter Porter, "Out of the Anteroom," *Observer*, 18 July 1982, 31.

2. Michael O'Loughlin, "Twenty-One Today," *Books Ireland* 66 (September 1982):148.

3. James Simmons, "A Literary Leg-Pull?" *Belfast Review* 8 (Autumn 1984):27.

4. James Simmons, review of *Site of Ambush*, by Eiléan Ní Chuilleanáin, *Books Ireland* 3 (May 1976):74.

5. Ibid.

6. James J. McAuley, *Kilkenny Magazine* 2, no. 3 (Autumn-Winter 1962):61.

7. Ibid., 59.

8. Ibid., 61.

9. Carol Rumens, "Kinds of Irishry," *Times Literary Supplement*, 17 October 1980, 1180.

10. Ibid.

11. Michael O'Neill, "Epiphanies and Apocalypses," *Times Literary Supplement*, 11 May 1984, 516.

12. Eavan Boland, "Exhibitionist," in *In Her Own Image* (Dublin: Arlen House, 1980), 31.

13. Eithne Strong, *Songs of Living* (Dublin: Runa Press, 1961), 7–8.

14. Ibid., 8.

15. Eiléan Ní Chuilleanáin, "Wash," in *Acts and Monuments* (Dublin: The Gallery Press, 1972), 9.

16. Virginia Woolf, "Professions for Women," in *Collected Essays*, vol. 2 (New York: Harcourt Brace & World, 1962), 288.

17. Eiléan Ní Chuilleanáin, review of *North*, by Seamus Heaney, *Cyphers* 2 (Winter 1975):50.

18. Ibid.

19. Alicia Suskin Ostriker, *Stealing the Language: The Emergence of Women's Poetry in America* (Boston: Beacon Press, 1986), 120.

Two-Part Invention:
Reading into Durcan and Muldoon

Eamon Grennan

Prelude

Paul Durcan and Paul Muldoon are two of the strongest and most idio-syncratic poets currently writing in Ireland. One is from north, the other from south of a border that, in both direct and oblique ways, registers in their work. But that work, in very different ways, is a continual crossing of borders—of the psyche, of the emotions, political and metaphysical, national and international, personal and public. Both poets are decisive, intriguing, important presences in contemporary Irish poetry, whose work invites and can sustain a wide variety of critical responses. In the double-jointed essay that follows, I have chosen not to give a broad survey of their work, nor to offer some comparative view of their quite distinct imaginations and poetic habits, even though such accounts might forge solid reasons for their prominence among their contemporaries. Instead I want to attempt the more modest task of opening up a little the particular texture of each poet's work, giving as exact hints as I can about the experience of reading these poems. The enterprise, of its nature, is intro-ductory; but it may give reasons for reading further. That, at any rate, is its purpose.

A World of Difference: Reading Paul Muldoon

"On the Edge but Implicated"

Often hard to get a firm purchase on, reluctant to surrender its meanings, the poetry of Paul Muldoon is nonetheless enormously attractive. There's a remarkable openness about it, an agnostic accommodation of many worlds, of multiple points of view. It is at once genial and cool, intimate and oddly remote, both revealing and discreet. At one moment it can be a hall of allegorical, distorting mirrors that reflect in their own unlikely way political or psychological or metaphysical truths. At another it can be a simple gesture of direct emotional power. Many of its best moments manage to be both of these, and more, at once. It has distinct narrative ambition, not just in the longer poems like "Immram" and "the More a Man Has, the More a Man Wants" but also in the way many of the shorter poems are implicit narratives, miniature stories, or the way poems in a single book can echo one another and accrete into larger units. It is also, however, intensely committed to lyrical minutiae and lyrical fragments: an impressive sense of design never throttles an acute, compelling sense of detail. Muldoon's is also a poetry that believes in the efficacy of fiction, well and truly grounded in factual data. His imaginary gardens are hopping mad with real toads. After five books (and he is still an enviable distance from his fortieth birthday)—each energetically different from its predecessors and with its own distinct unity—his original, idiosyncratic, entertaining, and disturbing voice has to be one of the most notable features on the landscape of contemporary Irish poetry.[1]

Having chosen to write about Muldoon's work, I was immediately presented with a large number of possible topics. Should I concentrate on his inventive way with traditional Irish material, for example—his witty revision of the vision poem, the *Aisling*; his splicing of Gaelic narrative with American detective story; his fusion of contemporary events in Northern Ireland and Native American trickster tales? Should I concentrate on the metamorphic nature of his verse, whether in the narrative or lyric mode? The interweaving of political and sexual areas of experience, often with violence as common denominator, also caught, and held, my attention. The proximity of violence and ordinariness in the Northern situation—the way Muldoon lets us feel the true texture of that situation in such conjunctions—was also a possible subject, as was the presence in the poems of apparently hallucinogenic experience. The theme of the father also presented itself, a figure recurring in many of the poems and in many different masks. Or, on the more strictly formal level, should I deal with Muldoon's metrical individualism, his wonderfully sure ear for the right music of a line or his extraordinary use of the sonnet form, the myriad changes he rings on it with the ecstatic abandon of an intoxicated Quasimodo? Any one of these offers itself as a perfectly reasonable and proper topic.

As I considered my own reactions to the poems, however, I decided to explore in more depth a topic that seemed to me simpler and in a way more fundamental than any of those I have mentioned. This was the point in most of the poems where I located my own primary pleasure and fascination, a point preceding and underlying other, more cognitively explicit elements in the poems and responses in myself. On reflection, of course, this observation of mine should have come as no surprise (although almost everything in a Muldoon poem comes as a surprise). For what I kept noticing in the early stages of my encounter with any of these poems was what any strong poet will make me notice—namely his or her handling of the language. In the present case that general consideration had to be even more deliberately refined: the particular elements of language that insisted on my earliest, startled attention here were grammar, syntax, and tone of voice. It was Muldoon's peculiar handling of, or behavior in, these three areas, I discovered, that first began to shape my response to, and understanding of, the experience offered by the poem. In these three areas of language (syntax is technically a part of grammar, but for the purposes of my discussion I have divided them), I believe, it is possible to discover— almost before it becomes conscious of itself—Muldoon's instinctive apprehension of the world.

Grammar, syntax, tone of voice: I have chosen, pretty much at random, one poem in which to observe how these three elements operate. I would imagine it is more or less representative. From *Why Brownlee Left* (1980), it is called "Making the Move."

> When Ulysses braved the wine-dark sea
> He left his bow with Penelope,
>
> Who would bend for no one but himself.
> I edge along the bookshelf,
>
> Past bad Lord Byron, Raymond Chandler,
> *Howard Hughes; The Hidden Years,*
>
> Past Blaise Pascal, who, bound in hide,
> Divined the void in his left side:
>
> Such books as one may think one owns
> Unloose themselves like stones

And clatter down into this wider gulf
Between myself and my good wife;

A primus stove, a sleeping bag,
The bow I bought through a catalogue

When I was thirteen or fourteen
That would bend, and break, for anyone,

Its boyish length of maple upon maple
Unseasoned and unsupple.

Were I embarking on that wine-dark sea
I would bring my bow along with me.

Before I get anywhere near the meaning of this poem I am struck, slowed down, by its curious grammatical action. The sentences have an odd, unorthodox, slightly refracted quality. For one thing, the subject—usually the most anchoring aspect of a statement or sequence of statements— keeps shifting. Beginning as Ulysses, it quickly becomes Penelope (or does the *who* refer, however oddly, to the bow? In either case what I have to experience is the sudden transformation of an object, a grammatical object, whether direct or indirect, into a subject). Then *I* is the subject, giving away, in a subordinate clause, to *Blaise Pascal*. This in turn cedes to *such books* (following that slightly enigmatic use of the colon), which gives way as subject to the impersonal *one*, then to *primus stove, sleeping bag*, and *bow*. On closer inspection, however, these last three turn out most likely to be indirect objects of *I edge . . . Past*. Then *I* becomes subject again, followed by, in the subordinate clause, the understood *bow*. Finally, bringing the poem full circle, the *I* is the subject of the last sentence, in a context that has this last subject usurping the action of the first subject, Ulysses.

While I am still trying to get a grip on subject, I notice—with a slight heightening of unease (or a certain sort of wary exhilaration?)—that its shifty mobility (apt enough in a poem called "Making the Move" and invoking the archetypal voyager) is repeated in the way the verb behaves. For both tense and mood are marked by extreme inconstancy. The first four lines, for example, have three verbs in the indicative mood, two of them in a simple past tense and one in a simple present. The mood and tense of the other verb—*would bend*—are indeterminate. Is it a conditional mood or a past continuous? At some level it has to be a sort of future, since at Ulysses's departure Penelope's not bending is in the future. A past future perhaps? The present of *I edge* shifts to a past participle (*bound*), then to a simple past (*divined*). After this there's another shift, this time to a present subjunctive (*may think*) and a series of simple presents (*owns, unloose, clatter*)). From here we are taken to a past (*bought*), a past imperfect, and a past continuous (*would bend*—or is it a conditional?). The final sentence brings the whole poem to ambiguous rest in a subjunctive and an unambiguous conditional.

However brief and rough this account, it is possible to see from it that Muldoon has taken the two grammatical elements to which we look first for our bearings in most sentences—subject and predicate—and has seriously shaken up whatever conventional expectations we might have of them. He will not allow me, as a reader, to settle down with my normal assumptions of how language should behave. A result of this bewildering, almost indecently kinetic nature, of subject and verb is a speedy unsettling of any firm sense of identity, and an equally rapid undermining of any sure sense of time or of the status of action. In the world the speaker brings to life, uncertainty seems a natural law: both the logic of time and the condition of being slip their moorings, and subjective identity itself keeps sliding in and out of the speaker's grasp. But this grammatical unsteadiness never seems to overcome the world of the poem, never reduces it to merely chaotic randomness; rather the world is constituted by such unfixed elements. However much it may disorient the reader, this grammatical indeterminism implies on the part of the speaker a way of knowing experience that is both clearsighted (each detail lucidly observed) and tolerant of confusion (the void, after all, is *divined*). And because grammar always adumbrates an epistemology, this particular grammatical variety reveals—perhaps involuntarily—a radically skeptical epistemological posture. The world, that is to say, is known in a number of different ways at once, no one of these excluding or taking precedence over another. And since grammar, as what we take to be a definitive given of language, is one of language's most decisively social attributes (i.e., unquestioningly shared; incorrect—as we say—usage normally has social or sociological implications), its unorthodox (not "incorrect") activity here suggests a certain estrangement on the part of the speaker, a sense of being removed from a community of assumptions, isolated, exiled from the center to the edge, at sea. Before ever touching the *apparent* (surface or narrative) meaning of the poem, then, I can know a considerable amount about the experience it contains and embodies.

The poem's syntax has an equal part to play in shaping my primary (pre-"meaning") response. Technically, of course, it is "the second part of grammar" (OED), dealing with "the established usages of grammatical construction" (OED). For my present purposes, however, I want to separate it from "grammar" and deal with it on its own. Syntax is a spatial and temporal energy governing the shape of the sentence, disposing the (grammatical) elements in a certain way. Put simply, it is where (and therefore when) the words are in relation to one another. I suspect it is less socially determined than what I have been calling grammar, more malleably responsive to idiosyncratic manipulation by the individual writer / speaker. It suggests more emphatically the operation, or at least the collaboration, of the individual will in the production of meaning, in the effort to make particular sense in language of a given world, a given "being."

The syntax of the first three lines, the first sentence, of "Making the Move" is unexceptional. This is so in spite of the way the third line skids away from the upright organization of the first two, just enough to give the reader a small pause, a brief hesitation, minor perplexity. The following fifteen lines, however, which make up a single sentence (showing Muldoon's muscular control of line / sentence relationships), put a number of syntactical dubieties in my way. The comma at the end of the first line, for example, sets the inaugural statement off from what follows. After this slight, almost subliminal, oddity, the syntax proceeds in a normal way for four lines, phrase added predictably enough to phrase, the parenthetical extension of "Blaise Pascal" ("who, bound in hide") neatly tucked in. After the colon, however, things begin to go curiously awry. The colon itself is a crucial syntactical instrument: it sets up certain expectations of the way what follows it relates to what precedes it. The first four lines after the punctuation here are unsurprising in themselves and form a syntactically straightforward sentence (subject, predicates, objects—each element deftly and rhythmically fitted to a single line). But what precisely is the relationship between this and the earlier element of the same sentence? I *suppose* it is a species of enlarged apposition, but the peremptory speed with which one of these elements is laid down alongside the other lends a tense, nervous quality to their conjunction. The syntax splices the elements together without any facilitating gestures of explanation or connection. It immediately implicates me as a reader in some primal awareness of *something unsaid*. (This is confirmed, I suspect, when I later notice the way philosophical or theological *void* evolves into (inter)personal *gulf*: the syntax tunes me to hear more accurately, more feelingly, what the diction and its imagery hint at.)

The next six lines form the last major unit of the poem's long central sentence. Immediately I read them, their syntax ignites uncertainties in my mind. The largest of these concerns the precise nature of the relation between this unit and what has gone before. These connected statements follow a semicolon, but how do they belong to the sentence as a whole? It takes me more than one reading to see that, like the books and me-tonymic authors mentioned earlier, they are all objects of "I edge . . . past." Syntax works, therefore, to distance object from subject and main verb in an unusual way. It orchestrates a sort of gapped discourse. It forces me to experience a gulf between subject / verb and object (objects, indeed, that seem at first to be subjects themselves). Individual syntactical particles of these six lines compound the unsteady and uncertain state I am left in by the problems of the larger unit. For one thing, the frustrated expectation of a fulfilling verb upsets my reading at the end of the first line and throughout the extended description of the bow. The apparent construc-tion seems to prepare for a statement that never occurs: the objects seem organized for something that never happens, a destination never arrived at. The syntax involved in the description of the bow, then, also bears some peculiar marks. The paratactic disposition of clauses, for example, keeps me reaching for the "point" of the description, which seems to be perpetually postponed. This sense of postponement is intensified by the way the last two lines sound like an explanatory afterthought, with a further syntactical oddity to be found in the fact that the *cause* of bending and breaking for anyone (the unseasoned and unsupple wood) is placed after its effect. It is also possible to argue that the line, "That would bend, and break, for anyone," bends or breaks the natural syntactic push of the sentence with a kind of parenthetical aside (an aside, however, of central thematic and emotional importance). The disposition of the statement in these last two lines also heightens the syntactical tension of the whole unit, for by postponing the adjectives, placing them after what they mod-ify, the speaker inverts the normal order. The postponement also adds a possible ambiguity as to precisely which noun ("maple" or "length") the adjectives modify. So, on top of everything else, syntax naturally disturbs grammatical understanding.

From all this it is easy to see that these six lines are, to say the least, syntactically uneasy, a fact accentuated by the rather curious punctuation (an instrument of syntax): no comma where I might expect one, after "fourteen," and the decisive presence of two commas where they might not have been expected (before and after "and break"). But in the last two lines of the poem, syntax is restored to something straightforward and firmly controlled. The compound sentence, meticulous in its observance of syntactical norms, brings the poem to a strong full stop. Couched in conditionals as it is, there is about the syntax itself a kind of unflinching steadiness, a firmness of resolution.

What, in syntactical terms, have I learned from the poem? First I learn something about the poet's sense of the relationship between things. No element in itself is difficult to understand. But the precise nature of their coexistence, the way they add up to a larger unity of complex sense, is problematic. Syntax also suggests the nature of the poet's own particular power over the world he has invented. In Muldoon's case that power lies in maintaining cool control over shifting elements, elements related to one another in unlikely, unpredictable ways. And although relations between objects in the world he offers are dynamic, changing, complex, often strange, the world itself does have design. By means of his syntax the poet comes at sense in this world, both by ordering things in orthodox ways and by upsetting conventional expectations. Muldoon's syntax suggests a doubled sense of being-in-the-world: on one level things are in their usual places, it is a normal world; on the other, things are unusually located, joined in unexpected ways. The dynamics of the verse derive in part from shuttling between the two levels, more or less at home in both of them. Syntax, too, is responsible for the rhythm of the poem (emphatically in evidence in the penultimate couplet), for the way the lines beat, the phrases engage one another. It is the means by which the poet's apprehension of the world and of being (this apprehension being fundamentally an interior rhythmic reality) becomes willed, articulate. So what Muldoon's musical (i.e., deliberately rhythmic) syntax amounts to is a twofold fact: his awareness of a world in which the relations between things is not what is expected, and his assertion of his own right to arrange the elements as he wishes to suit his purposes. Syntax is power, the poet's authority. In this case it reveals a problematic world *and* the poet's sense of his own autonomous power to respond to that world in his own way. So world and self—poetic self—are both embodied by this syntax, both given their due. In the way it registers a mode of being, then, Muldoon's syntax adumbrates an ontology.

Molded by grammar and syntax, a reader's initial experiences of a Muldoon poem can be unsettling. Syntax and grammar make the familiar (as all the elements are in themselves) strange. As instruments of estrangement they imply that such an estranging sense of things persists in the very grain and fiber of Muldoon's apprehension of experience. An analogy for this process of estrangement, this rattling of the known and the familiar, may be found in his inventive handling of the sonnet form. In poem after poem—especially in *Mules*, *Why Brownlee Left*, and *Quoof*—he dissects the convention, ranging over a multitude of its formal possibilities. In strictly formal terms, that is, the poet again locates himself "on the edge" in deft, fairly radical experimentation but "implicated" in the conventional source itself. Another analogy—this time a purely linguistic one—may be seen in his use of cliché. Perpetually retreading their balding familiarity, he gives new and curious life to such bland formulations as "best of both worlds," "as the crow flies," "I would give my right arm." Doing this, he at once stands at the very center of linguistic habit and on its cutting and renewing edge.

The third quality or element in my initial response to most or all of these poems tempers the unsettling experience of grammar and syntax. For, in the midst of their odd, unconventional activity, the tone of voice is ordinary and beguiling, building up my confidence in the normality of the poem's world. The tone of voice reassures me that a certain steadiness is to be found in this world; that whatever the problems attaching to things, it is all right for them to be that way. No matter how grammar bewilderingly shifts or how syntax unsettles my sense of expected relationships, the tone of voice remains even, just telling me, in a way that is both reserved and intimate—unemphatic and detailed, no odd tonal gestures, no sudden shifts of register—a few apparently personal facts. This voice embodies a kind of unflappable sanity among slightly skewed circumstances. It creates a tone at once intimate and formal, moving between the mannerly impersonality of "Such books as one may think one owns" and the more relaxed, personal "myself and my good wife." it can distance into impersonal narrative, as the first lines do; take us closer to the spectacle of personal action ("I edge along the bookshelf"); startle us into an awareness of an emotionally charged situation ("this wider gulf / Between myself and my good wife"); and end on an almost plangent note of personal feeling ("I would bring my bow along with me"). But, different as they could be, these three registers slide easily, unobtrusively into one another, each one of them striking the reader as something familiar, something with the resonance of direct address that is intended to convey information and feeling but in an unsurprising, even genial way. Muldoon himself has referred to "a range of tones," and he singles out "that sweet, inveigling voice" in which "the speaker quite often says, 'Come on in. Please come in, and sit down and make yourself at home.' Usually what happens then is that the next thing you know you get a punch in the nose. In fact, you know there's been some shift, some change, some dislocation."[2] But for all its minutely graduated shifts, changes, and dislocation, and in spite of that punch in the nose, it is this carefully controlled and impeccably, almost pedantically, modulated tone of voice that continues to reassure us as readers that we are in a knowable, even local world, no matter how its elements behave or relate to one another, no matter how metamorphically strange or alien it may become. As distinct from the more palpably designing tones of argument, exposition, demonstration, interrogation, celebration, lamentation, the tone of "Making the Move"—as almost always in a Muldoon poem—is basically the inviting and assuaging one of *narrative*, of telling a story, sharing an anecdote, proffering a confidence. The absence in this particular case of contextual information or explanation has a double effect: it makes of Muldoon's a *new kind* of narrative, and it makes me, as a reader, even more grateful for and dependent on that reassuring tone of voice.

The tone of voice is what contains my other two primary elements, grammar and syntax. I mean "contains" in two ways: the tone is an envelope and the other two elements exist inside it; and tone neutralizes the risk of their reducing the presented world to a chaotic question, a swirl of unresolved relations. Such a tone of voice allows for a continued *civil* existence in the face of a world that shifts about in unsteady, unsettled, and unsettling ways. The air of the poem, generated by its tone of voice, is benign. In it, the other oddly disposed elements can abide, without reducing the whole fabric of this world to meaninglessness. Tone of voice is the suffused nature of the speaker, an *achieved* nature that rises out of a full, unflinching awareness of the complexities represented (and dramatized) by grammar and syntax. Tone, that is, represents and dramatizes the speaker's hospitality and openness to the world, even when *what* he says remains enigmatic. So this tone of voice enables me to welcome and take pleasure in what may remain impenetrably private. It lets me be intimate with enigma, to share, with something like communal satisfaction, a family secret. Tone, finally, is the signature of feeling. It is the audible body of feeling that in this case is variable and unspoken, yet presses indirectly into the pragmatic naming of things with intimate personal associations. The tone of the poem indicates the delicate nature of the feeling—its reluctance to name itself, yet its discreet eagerness to be known. And in the last three couplets the tone, although still unruffled and discreet, touches, just, an almost confessional level of personal intensity. It could be said, then, that tone of voice registers *as feeling* (vulnerable but tolerant) that compound experience of perplexity and deliberate will which is lodged in the poem's grammar and syntax. In this way the three elements I have been dealing with are bound together to become one single *primary* (for me) experience of reading the poem. It seems important that this primary response should culminate in *feeling*, both a feeling *inside* the world of the poem, and a feeling *about* the experience in that world. It is as if the poet's various (conscious and unconscious) strategies at what for me is a primary level of the poem's existence— strategies, that is, of grammar, syntax, and tone of voice—are all a means of at once concealing and revealing emotion: concealing its precise nature; revealing its complex range, depth, and variety. So in the very linguistic innards of the poem, the poet is a free agent, odysseying fluently among the inner and outer reaches of his own experience. It is not surprising that this should seem connected to Muldoon's own opinion of "a writer's job," which is, he claims, "So far as any of us can . . . to be a free agent, within the state of oneself, or roaming through the different states of oneself."[3]

"Making the Move" seems to be about parting, fortitude, maybe betrayal, some complicated sense of hurt. It includes a snapshot of the speaker's present interests, and an evocative memory. It glances off the hard facts of a personal relationship. It dramatizes the activity of a curious, hospitable, restless consciousness, feeling its way (as that primus stove and sleeping bag suggest) into solitude, a solitary existence. Half to itself, half to an impersonal audience, it speaks its strange experience in a deceptively mild-mannered way. Full of sharply delineated facts, it remains elusive about the actual emotional condition of the speaker. It leaves a reader sympathetically connected with quite a number of things, but unable to establish, as it were, a hierarchy of commitment among them. Commitment, finally, is to the *unjudged* experience as a whole: that is what the poem gently compels. All this, I believe—what has to be a large part of the poem's "meaning"—is implicit in the fusion of grammar, syntax, and tone of voice.

Such a fusion makes reading a Muldoon poem an exhilaratingly active experience. Such a fusion also allows me to see how the phrase "on the edge but implicated"[4] lies at the very root of the form of life constituted by the poem. The speaker of "Making the Move," for example, is on the edge of his experience, at its periphery, curiously impersonal about it. He is also "on the edge," at some extremity of experience—an end, a beginning. At the same time he is "on edge," as seen in the unexpected and unconventional way he presents that experience. (That he *edges* along the bookshelf lends a literal endorsement to this notion.) "On edge," then, is a bridge from "on the edge" to "implicated." It points to the implicitly perceived difficulty of the world and the emotional pressure of the voice responding to it, both of which reveal how the speaker is necessarily bound to this world, is a feeling part of it, implicated in it: "The move" he is or may be "making" is away from the achingly familiar. It seems fair to say, then, that grammar, syntax, and tone of voice let me know in an immediate and unavoidable way the true depth of meaning in the phrase "on the edge but implicated." They show it to be a basic description of Muldoon's reception of the world, in the grain and fiber of his way of being.

"Making the Move" is a fairly "unloaded" poem. It does not enter overtly into the more significantly loaded zones of sex, politics, or metaphysics the way many of Muldoon's poems do. Its subject matter is not laden with references to obviously important public or private areas of our world. Yet what I have been saying about three of its stylistic features contains a useful general truth about Muldoon's work. The elementary nature of grammar, syntax, and tone of voice throws light on the activity of his imagination in those more substantively sophisticated areas of psychology, metaphysics, aesthetics, cultural commentary, love, sex, elegy, and politics. Ubiquitous witty skepticism; strong and often refracted feeling; esoteric knowledge; politely anarchic refusal of any tribal or narrowly political alignment: these are among the qualities that make him the compelling and considerable poet he is. These, and an endlessly inventive delight in crowding his world with credible fictions, give to his poems their particular and peculiar configurations. But it is his special qualities of grammar, syntax, and tone of voice that underlie and embody the complex nature of his sexual, cultural, metaphysical and political understanding. Estranged and intimate, anarchic and believing in order, tolerant of individual idiosyncrasy, strange and reassuringly familiar, violent and quotidian, utterly factual and depending "on more than we could see" ("Early Warning," in WBL, 16)—Muldoon's poems are a strong, imaginatively confident response to an ambiguous, unsteady, endlessly uncertain sense of experience. In political terms this can refer to the state of Northern Ireland; in emotional terms it can refer to the state of personal relations; in metaphysical terms it can refer to the contemporary state of our world and our being-in-the-world.

No matter what the precise referential nature of Muldoon's subject matter, however, grammar, syntax, and tone of voice will suggest a constancy in his response to, his apprehension of it. Coming awake as a poet in the wake of (especially) Heaney and Mahon, Muldoon has had to find and claim his own poetic space. Looser, more stylistically various, more extravagantly agnostic than they are, he has immersed himself more deliberately in the destructive element. And his work rises out of it speaking—in what are essentially *un*speakable (political, emotional, and metaphysical) states—his own finely tuned contemporary truth. What I have tried to suggest here is the way this truth—whatever its nature or substance—is rooted in his poetic manner, in those rudimentary elements of it that first impress me when I read almost any of the poems. Grammar, syntax, and tone of voice create a sense of being—in many senses—"on the edge but implicated." And growing as they do out of the ground of these enabling elements, his poems make—in every sense—a world of difference.

A Different World: Reading Paul Durcan

"My job is to be present which I am"

Along with Paul Muldoon, Paul Durcan has emerged in the past ten years as probably the most considerable "younger" poet in Ireland.[5] Since 1975 he has published seven substantial collections, as well as two smaller volumes (in 1967 and 1982). *The Selected Paul Durcan*, edited by Edna Longley for Blackstaff in 1982, gave the best of his work a more fixed and influential presence in the world. Since then his reputation has expanded—as enlightened passionate satirist, as savagely humorous deflater of the social, cultural, moral, and political pretensions of the Irish Republic, as outspoken idealist in the unusually spliced realms of the domestic and the erotic, as starkly candid documenter of his own life and psyche (either in locally autobiographical or strangely allegorical modes), cartographer of a landscape of solitary hurt and, at the same time, representative angst. In the forthright and often wildly inventive way the best of his work takes on the world (in both the combative and scapegoat senses of that phrase), Durcan has earned a right to the high esteem in which he is held not only by other poets and by the critics but also, and especially, by an extraordinarily wide spectrum of ordinary readers. His remarkable abilities as a performer (much more than a "reader") of his own poems have won him an audience—at least a live and in-Ireland audience—to rival that of Seamus Heaney.[7] By now the work has achieved a critical visibility that allows Edna Longley to describe it as "visionary," and "in touch with the deepest wells of native Irish spirituality, yet radically

challeng[ing] their pollution"; Durcan, she says, "has developed the conscience of the race."[8] Derek Mahon has praised him as an "Orpheus
ascending into the light, an exemplary sufferer, a hero of art," and Seamus
Heaney calls him "one of the most original and undaunted imaginations
at work in our favor anywhere today."[9] Heaney goes on to say that Durcan,
"with Paul Muldoon and a number of women, are among the ones who
are 'changing the game' (to use Lowell's downbeat phrase) in Ireland."

As with Muldoon, many issues could claim critical attention in Durcan's
work. What are the particular values, for example, that inform his bitterly
satiric account of contemporary Ireland? What is the purpose behind (or
the precise nature of) his poetic treatment of women—both particular
women (chief among them his wife of fifteen years from whom he has
been recently divorced) and the idea of "woman"? Politically it would be
interesting to anatomize Durcan's "a plague on both your houses" in his
pained response to Republican and Unionist violence in the island, a
response that may be the unhappy luxury of a Southern poet. His poetic
antecedents, too, could be a worthwhile study: rooted in the bifurcated
tradition deriving from the two most important Southern poets after Yeats,
he mixes the mundane spirituality of the later Kavanagh (*Agape* in parochial action) with the savage indignation of Austin Clarke's intensely
topical satire (idealism lacerated by the quotidian moral failures of the
actual). Beyond such influences, and in a more explicitly comic realm,
the nature of his inheritance from Flann O'Brien could be investigated,
since Brian O'Nolan's impeccable ear for all sorts of self-betraying Irish
voices has become an unmistakable part of Durcan's gift, producing beautifully eccentric scenarios to rival the best of Myles. The presence of Joyce
in the work—pervasive and, in the best sense, patronizing—might also
be explored, since many of Durcan's poems seem to draw some of their
moral and even formal energy from a (possibly subliminal) memory of the
archetypal clash between the xenophobic vulgarity and brutality of the
citizen and the plain moral and emotional lucidity of Leopold Bloom ("I'm
talking about justice . . . Love, I mean the opposite of hatred. I must go
now").[10]

In an effort to get a little closer to Durcan's specific poetic effects,
however, I have chosen to sidestep these larger issues and concentrate on
a couple of features that first affect me when I read individual poems. In
Durcan's case I find myself again and again being initially startled by
metaphor, and by the poem's movement. (In a general way, that initiating
stir of attention is always caused, I would guess, by some deeply identifying
traits in a poet's mode or craft—a sort of watermark or personal signature.)

Where grammar, syntax, and tone of voice identify Muldoon's work for me, I find that the qualities of Durcan's *metaphors* and the way a poem of his *moves* (the journey it inscribes and forces me to follow) are his most distinctly characteristic and characterizing marks as a poet.

Probably the first things that strike me about Durcan's metaphors are their extremity, their extravagance, their naive and "primary" air. Here are a few fairly random examples winkled out of an abundance of possibility:

> Swags of red apples are his cheeks;
> Swags of yellow pears are his eyes;
> Foliages of dark green oaks are his torsos;
> And in the cambium of his bark juice lies.
>
> ("Polycarp," SPD, 42)

> And I'd sit in her lap with my hands
> Around her waist gulping her down
> And eating her green apples
> That hung in bunches from her thighs
> And the clusters of hot grapes between her breasts.
>
> ("Fat Molly," SPD, 63)

> Under her gas meter I get down on my knees
> And say a prayer to the side-altars of her thighs,
> And the three-light window of her breasts.
>
> ("The Day Kerry Became Dublin", in *The Berlin Wall Cafe*, 25)

> I turn about and see
> Over the windowpane's frosted hemisphere
> A small black hat sail slowly past my eyes
> Into the unknown ocean of the sea at noon.
>
> ("Hat Factory," SPD 38–39)

What all these passages have in common is their benign violence of metaphorical language. In each case Durcan deliberately transfigures the world normally seen, so that it embodies a truth higher or deeper than the one on usual view. In each case the means are simple: the subject becomes something else—an orchard, an oakwood, a fruitful feast, a chapel, a flying ship, an unknown ocean. Stated as fact, none of these "vehicles" is odd or esoteric in itself. There's an almost childlike naïveté about them. Addressed initially more to the eye than the mind, these images speak to something or somewhere quite primitive in us, full of primary colors and sensations (red, yellow, green; bunches, clusters; hot; slowly). When you consider what is being described in such terms, however (a male or female body, a hat, daylight), then the extravagant nature of this "simplicity" (underlined by the undemanding grammatical and syntactical forms, which put no impediments between utterance and understanding) strikes home. In an act of joyous subversion these figures of speech unmake and then remake the known world. They remake the world in the image of the maker's desire; they are the primitive, vulnerable expression of his hope. Insisting on something deeper than the factual layer of reality we call history, they proclaim the truth of possibility, of sensual and emotional possibility. They make a world that surprises us, shocking us into an awareness of such possibility. The fusion of extravagance and naïveté is designed to awaken in us and awaken us to a refreshed version of the world we conventionally inhabit. One aim of Durcan's metaphors seems to be to sway us to embrace the possibility of this new world in ourselves: how can it not be within our grasp when it appears, is offered, in such a simple, almost childlike way? This is how the world could be, were we rightly awake. So something of an evangelical tilt determines metaphors like this, a fact that, if recognized, might open up the otherwise encumbering notion of Durcan's being a "visionary." Metaphors such as those quoted above give concrete point to Derek Mahon's observation that Durcan is "a seeker and, in Rimbaud's sense, a seer."[11] What Durcan *sees* is a world transformed, released from the old limiting laws of singular, inflexible actuality.

In fact, I would say there is something of Chagall (also described as a seer)[12] in Durcan's habits of metaphor, in the way the ordinary world (its ordinariness known in the plain, uncomplicated language, colloquially direct) is altered to become a zone of metamorphic energies. In this colorful and kinetic transfiguration of the world by the word, Durcan activates a Blakean (or, nearer home, a Bloomian) hope for an existence that is all positive energy, all flow, all active peace. As invocations of a latent and fertile goodness in the natural possibility of the world (though human nature, not Nature, is Durcan's subject), these metaphors and their like are an attempt to insert that possibility into the damaged realm of the actual. (Is this a way of fusing, I wonder, the spirits of Kavanagh and Clarke?) Such metaphors achieve some of the same or similar effects as do Chagall's cubist and (mostly) postcubist disturbances of gravity and expectation, his running together of lyrical, narrative, and autobiographical elements, his (seen elsewhere in Durcan) political gestures at once intimate and expansive. (See, for example, Chagall's *The Painter and His Wife* [1969], *The Martyr* [1939], or *Around Her* [1945].)[13]

As with Chagall, the effect of many such metaphors in Durcan is celebratory. Both artists (at their obviously different levels of sheer achievement; my references are to Chagall's artistic means and manners, not to his greatness) embody the extravagance of secular prayer in the comic mode. In work like this the world is renewed, liberated, made over in imagination; the distance between indicative and optative moods is eliminated. The old binding laws of nature are suspended, in deference to the larger laws of feeling. Both Chagall's amazing collocations and Durcan's metaphors testify to this truth of imagination, and the innocent force of their desire is underlined by a kind of naive awkwardness that marks the style in each case, granting it, I suppose, further proof of its own sincerity. The way Chagall invites us to look at a painting may help in the reading of a typical piece of Durcan metaphor-making like the following:

> Our children swam about our home
> As if it was our private sea,
> Their own unique, symbiotic fluid
> Of which their parents also partook.
> Such is home—a sea of your own—
> In which you hang upside down from the ceiling
> With equanimity, while postcards from Thailand on the mantlepiece
> Are raising their eyebrow markings benignly:
> Your hands dangling their prayers to the floorboards of your home,
> Sifting the sands underneath the surfaces of conversation,
> The marine insect life of the family psyche.
> (" 'Windfall,' 8 Parnell Hill, Cork," BWC, 47)

The extended life of this metaphor is characteristic of Durcan's procedures in a number of ways. The fairly simple transforming turn of the first two lines ("swam . . . as if . . . sea") is more and more twisted as the passage continues, implicating more and more elements; the image gains a life of its own, and we are, as we are in a painting by Chagall, in a realm that hesitates between the borders of allegory and dream. The passage from "Our children swam about our home" to "The marine insect life of the family psyche" is a gradual thickening of metaphor, the poet's own surrender to its generative logic. And, as in the earlier examples, the metaphor is an expression of difference, the poet's way of putting an emotional truth that defies or simply eludes more rootedly normative habits of expression. The nature and activity of Durcan's metaphor, that is, imply and give solid body to a hope in the (otherwise inexpressible) spiritual and emotional dimensions of ordinary (in this case, familial) experience. Indeed, as the ordinary is luminously opened up (deepened, set flowing), spiritual and emotional dimensions are made one, identified. Metaphors like this are Durcan's way of getting beyond the limits of representation and touching those of revelation. Among other things, his metaphors are his poetic acts of faith, hope, and charity.

When Durcan's metaphors are employed to express darker realities, their nature *as metaphor* does not change. Many of the recent poems about the breakdown of his marriage (his has been the most poetically public of marriages and divorces, more so than even those of John Montague and of James Simmons) contain such darker realities, metaphorically expressed. He can, for example, describe himself as "Camp Commandant of Treblinka / . . . locked into a tiny white world of pure evil" ("Death-Camp [*after Frankl*]"), or he can portray his wife as

> A Jewish Bride who has survived the death-
> camp,
> Free at last of my swastika eyes
> Staring at you from across spiked dinner plates
> Or from out of the bunker of a TV armchair;
> Free of the glare off my jackboot silence;
> Free of the hysteria of my gestapo voice.
> ("The Jewish Bride [after Rembrandt]," BWC,
> 41)

In this extravaganza of confessional disgust (as if "Daddy" were written not by the victim but the oppressor) the nature and quality of the metaphor (simply its behavior as literary figure) remain what they were in more positive and celebratory circumstances. It is still all primary colors, naive and direct, extreme and simple. One can imagine it as a child's drawing to illustrate / express parental tension, or as a painting by Chagall called "Breaking Marriage." It is a horrendous "domestic interior," composed in a few lurid strokes. The effect lies, just as it did with the lavish and ecstatic descriptions of Polycarp and Fat Molly, in the uncompromising absolutism of the metaphorical vehicle. In this case metaphor is the poet's act not of faith or hope or love, but of self-accusatory despair. The whole poetic procedure here contains the implicit assumption that only the extremity of such metaphor—extending once again into an allegorical sketch, a thumbnail narrative—can contain the emotional / spiritual intensity, and truth, of the subject.

A poetic world of such extremities and such simplicities as those constituted by Durcan's metaphors seems designed to make us see our experience (any experience) with newborn eyes—newborn, that is, in spirit and in feeling. Whether his subject is autobiographical or political, private or public, the nature of his metaphors will always attack those outworn, conventional, and spiritlessly habitual ways of receiving experience that are the death alike of public and private life—of our life as citizens and as beloved and loving creatures. In this way, Durcan's metaphors are at the single root of his double being as a poet, equally fundamental to his satires and his celebrations. They are proclamations of a different world, a world in which good and evil, joy and sorrow, are tangible absolutes, actors in a perpetual psychomachia where—as he says of "the dark school of childhood"—"tiny is tiny, and massive is massive" ("En Famille, 1979," SPD, 116).

In the Irish context—to which they essentially belong—these metaphors are an astringent exhortation to cast off habitual and constricting ways of knowing the world, to be revived in heart and spirit, to embrace the true *possibility* of being. At home in the Republic, an anchored native of one place (in spite of his use of foreign references and environments, of "The Man Smoking a Cigarette in the Barcelona Metro," or "The Berlin Wall Café," even in spite of—as the title of his most recent book announces—*Going Home to Russia*), his work has the certainty and authority of its own firstly human and, only then, national identity (when their coincidence is absolute there will be a brave new republic?). This sense of identity (which might be contrasted with the shifting or quaking grounds of identity in the work of Muldoon) may be gauged by the complete confidence with which Durcan admonishes national mores, public and private, referring, for example, to "the tyrant liberties of Dublin, Ireland, / Where the comedy of freedom was by law forbidden / And truth, since the freedom of the state, gone underground" ("Around the Corner from

Francis Bacon," BWC, 42). No poet since Austin Clarke has had, in this respect, a more natural "national" status. (I'm sure both poets would quarrel with the word, but I don't know another to serve as precisely in delineating that quality of furious belonging, even of speaking for the community—actual or imagined—which they share.) And it is Durcan's metaphors—eschewing any temptation to be artificially or programmatically "Irish"—which are the most revealing signature of that national touch.

What I am calling the "movement" of Durcan's poems is another of the elements that first compels my attention as a reader. I am intrigued by the way a poem opens, proceeds, concludes; how it gets from point to point; how it charts its course. Reading it, listening to it, I am struck by how, in spite of its quick and often surprising shifts of direction, I never lose my way. I am interested in the way the poem can contain a narrative, but the narrative is usually absorbed by, dissolved in, the narrator's feelings— exalted, lyrical, dejected, angry, satirical—about the story being told. This conjunction of story and feeling about it (a condition that also seems to underlie formal and substantive qualities in the painting of Chagall) gives an oddly *radial* quality to many of the poems. Images and metaphors generate digressions, and this trajectory of movement (an operation on and in space) in turn produces a peculiar tempo (operation on and in time). So one is never lulled or (as in the case of a Heaney poem) assuaged or allured by a poem of Durcan's. Rather one is always conscious, sometimes uneasily, of being *moved* (in many ways) from one point or area (or emotion or conviction) to another.

Since this feature of a poem cannot be discussed in excerpts, I will use two poems—both fairly representative—to make and illustrate my point. The first has one of Durcan's most arresting titles. (His genius for remarkable titles is unrivalled: "The Archbishop Dreams of the Harlot of Rathkeale," "What is a Protestant, Daddy?," "Hopping Round Knock Shrine in the Falling Rain," "Irish Hierarchy Bans Colour Photography," "Making Love Outside Árus an Uachtaráin"—each of them conjuring up a weird point of view of the known, familiar world.) The poem in question here is "On Seeing Two Bus Conductors Kissing Each Other in the Middle of the Street":

> Electricity zig-zags through me into the blue leatherette
> And I look around quick and yes—
> All faces are in a state of shock:

By Christ,—this busride
Will be the busride to beat all busrides.

Sure enough the conductor comes waltzing up the stairs—
The winding stairs—
And he comes up the aisle a-hopping and a-whooping
So I take my chance
Being part of the dance:
I say: "A penny please."
"Certainly, Sir" he replies
And rummages in his satchel
Until he fishes out a tiny penny,
An eenshy-weenshy penny,
Which he hands me crooning—
"That's especially for you Sir—thank you, Sir."

So there it is, or was:
Will the day or night ever come when I will see
Two policemen at a street corner caressing each other?
Let the prisoners escape, conceal them in a sunbeam?
O my dear Guard William, O my darling Guard John.

(SPD, 117)

With the title as springboard, the poem gets off to a flying start. The first stanza plunges us into the speaker's responses to this curious and unlikely event. The movement is from stimulus to response to observation to further response (electricity, look, faces, exclamation). Speed is intensified by spoken immediacy, accentuated by the present tense, the "yes," the impulsive "By Christ" (apt, as it turns out, in a tract on brotherly love), and the enthusiastically colloquial "busride to beat all busrides." The movement is itself a quick zig-zag and obliges us to wonder "what next?"; we realize we are in the grip of a hectic teller (resembling many of Durcan's invented speakers). The first six lines of the next stanza form the next phase. Again the movement of the sentence—broken into metrically uneven lines that respond to the segment-logic of the phrase, the telling breath—is a speedy zig-zag, marked by loud rapid rhythmic action (waltzing, a-hopping, a-whooping) and assisted subliminally by the parenthetical reminder of the *winding* stairs. Quick, slightly crazy and maybe-not-there-at-all references (to Yeats in "winding stairs" and "part of the dance," to the marriage ceremony in "up the aisle") further make the movement helter-skelter, yet always forward, coming to rest in the distinct, simple, actual request "A penny please" (what the passenger normally says—or used to say when "a penny" could still buy a bus-ticket, an archaic economic fact that Durcan may be making part of his comedy).

The normality of this exchange (" 'Certainly, Sir,' he replies") then swerves swiftly into the anarchic event, described, however, in a perfectly straightforward anecdotal manner, as the conductor, instead of taking, gives the narrator-passenger a penny. By this time the world is completely topsy-turvy, meanings wind and zig-zag. Then there is another curve, into the parenthetical baby-talk ("eenshy-weenshy"), that retards the narrative but heightens the comic suspense. Finally, the comedy crests over the crooning gesture and the extravagantly solicitous (a trait not common among Dublin bus conductors) manner. As a reader I am being presented here, at high speed, with a series of most unlikely occurrences—all of them unlikely because (*because!*) they are so expresssively charitable. The speed and dodgy trace of the narrative hide its satire in strangeness: awakened by comedy I find, through a rapid mental runaround, that the point is satirical.

The final stanza steps back from the comic event to make the satiric point more decisive, and as a reader I am obliged to leave the field of narrative and enter a more speculative zone. In the longer, steadier lines, movement slows to a more meditative pace, then veers into the subversive possibility of two policemen (much more sinister embodiments of authority than the bus conductors) "caressing each other." This in turn— by means of a grammatical and syntactical skidding that, unusual in Durcan, reminds me of Muldoon—moves into a sort of prayer, thence to a dramatized exchange (but who speaks?) of erotic endearments between the two solidly named Guards. And then, suddenly and surprisingly, it is over.

Even in this brisk description it is easy to see that the motion of the whole poem is rapid, dashing, harelike in shifting direction yet always moving to its proper end. In such a movement I suspect Durcan is appropriating something of the *performative* skill of the oral poet, who can preserve a spine of anecdotal purpose while swerving through strange, abrupt, not immediately explicable transitions. The presence of the speaking performer is what gives unity (and its own acceptable logic) to this variety and speed. And it is this (imagined) speaking presence that makes such movement real and convincing, tuning me (as I listen to the "script") to the subversive satire of the poem even before I begin to deal with it in a more analytical way. The poem's movement, that is, exercises a primary (and, given the suggestion of orality, primitive) power, bringing me to a sort of precognitive understanding. And by responding to it in this way I am participating in its comic anarchy in—from the conventional point of view—a dangerous way. Which is, I would imagine, precisely the effect Durcan wants, as may be gathered from a recent account of his work and his performance of it: "printed words, which can seem flat on the page, come alive in his performances, because he writes for the spoken word, for dramatized dialogue. His strange, mesmerising voice wraps itself around every syllable and texture of his poems, wrapping the audience into its spell, into the very grain of the text."[14]

The second poem I want to use, "At the Funeral of the Marriage," is more serious in theme and more immediately personal. But it too, by its movement, coaxes the reader into entertaining strange, subversive images and ideas. Its movement obliges me to shift ground on some conventional notions, to broaden my way of thinking, to allow into my mental world a much broader set of possibilities about a particular subject. And movement in this case is also the chart of the poet's own attempt to deal with the catastrophe of a broken marriage. The movement of the poem mimes his own imaginative journey in trying to speak about what is close to the unspeakable, to move from one emotional and spiritual point to another. The movement of the poem, in fact, embodies and incorporates the attempt to move.

> At the funeral of the marriage
> My wife and I paced
> On either side of the hearse,
> Our children racing behind it . . .
> As the coffin was emptied
> Down into the bottomless grave,
> Our children stood in a half-circle,
> Playing on flutes and recorders.
> My wife and I held hands.
> While the mourners wept and the gravediggers
> Unfurled shovelfuls of clay
> Down on top of the coffin,
> We slowly walked away,
> Accomplices beneath the yew trees.
> We had a cup of tea in the graveyard café
> Across the street from the gates:
> We discussed the texture of the undertaker's face,

Its beetroot quality.
As I gazed at my wife
I wondered who on earth she was—
I saw that she was a green-eyed stranger.
I said to her: Would you like to go to a film?
She said: I would love to go to a film.
In the back seats of the cinema,
As we slid up and down in our seats
In a frenzy of hooks and clasps,
The manager courteously asked us not to take off our clothes.
We walked off urgently through the rain-strewn streets
Into a leaf-sodden cul-de-sac
And as, from the tropic isle of our bed,
Chock-a-block with sighs & cries,
We threw our funeral garments on the floor,
We could hear laughter outside the door.
There is no noise children love more to hear
Than the noise of their parents making love:
O my darling, who on earth are you?

(BWC, 66)

The first thing I notice about this poem is the particular strategy of its commencement. Offered a conventional metaphor ("the marriage died"), Durcan animates it by taking it literally, then extending it into a miniature allegory. To begin with, the movement of the poem is slow and direct, simply describing a (sort of) factual happening. (Chagall again comes to mind in this image, since many of his pictures seem to be the literalizing of poetic metaphor; I think of *The Anniversary*.) The man and woman pace, the children race—ordinary movements. The image grows more ritualistic as the metaphor extends into the "bottomless grave" (naive, melodramatic expression), and the children are arranged as in an archaic frieze, "Playing on flutes and recorders." The logic of the opening metaphor has been gently and inventively pursued. The movement from detail to detail implies without stating the nature of feeling, in a tone of unemphatic narrative: "My wife and I held hands." At the surprise of this line, which obliges me to revise any clichéd notions of the broken marriage, the movement of the poem begins to swerve. This is signalled by the simultaneous occurrence of a number of actions: while the mourners mourn and the gravediggers dig "We slowly walked away." This new slant is enhanced and made stranger by the parenthetical description, "Accomplices beneath the yew trees." By now the animation of the original image / metaphor has undergone a startling twist. The allegorical nature of the earlier lines can be easily understood as having some reference to an actual event (maybe a visit to a solicitor's office?). In allegorical terms, however, it is not clear how this last image functions. Perhaps it is no more than a veering into fantasy, wish fulfillment.

From here things begin to get weirder and wilder, though the tone remains constant, that of matter-of-fact narrative. Oddity derives from the build-in counterpoint between the naive tone (whereas with Muldoon you always feel some oddity inside the tone itself) and the nature of the events it narrates, as in the mention of that unlikely, but scrupulously located, "graveyard café." The reported talk, about the quality and texture of the undertaker's face, further surprises, and seems to prepare for the next shift of direction, this time with more explicitly emotional consequences, as the narrator takes us into his feelings. Maintaining a straightforward, even naive narrative manner, along with observations verging on the clichéd ("who on earth," "green-eyed stranger") and a blandly repetitious habit of dialogue, the poem stresses at this stage its oral, performative nature. What this unexceptional manner offers in the way of facts and events, however, becomes more and more bizarre, while the feelings expand their complexity. This becomes even more pronounced in the next surprising shift, to the couple tangled in renewed sexual passion (a literal "frenzy of hooks and clasps") and the "courteous" request of the manager, whose mild charity and decent protocol preserves the beat and tone of the mild-mannered narrative, keeping its proper pace. Another swerve increases the tempo to an urgent walking off down "a leaf-sodden cul-de-sac," which turn, in turn, has its own surprise. For the dead end they have come to literally (there is a dream logic about this, in image and movement) suddenly and astonishingly, as if with something of the resurrectional gesture that impels the whole poem, becomes "the tropic isle of our bed," which in turn (the shift is seasonal too) is colloquially redeemed from its cliché by being rudely "Chock-a-block with sighs and cries." The shift in levels of language here augments the surprising moves made by the narrative, while the pace gathers momentum on the parallel actions of tossing the "funeral garments on the floor" and the children's "laughter outside the door." The unexpected rhyme also accelerates the telling here, as well as bringing the original narrative, coupletlike, to its conclusion. But in another surprising twist, a three-line coda is added— two lines of commentary on lovemaking, noise, children (not only a reversal of conventional psycho-Freudian notions of how children react to parental lovemaking, but also, in its excess of delight, a counterpoint to the image of the children playing their ritual funeral music by the grave), and one line of direct addresss. This last may dramatize the scene of lovemaking *or* take the speaker outside the poem altogether, away from the curious narrative mix of allegory and fantasy all couched in an anecdotal mode, away into a resonant full stop that, in the oral performance of the poem would serve to powerful effect as a conclusion with no conclusion, perhaps implying a beginning, perhaps not.

As in the earlier poem, movement in this one has quite a distinct purpose. As I follow it, as it draws me along, it is at the same time reassuring me—this is simply the anecdote of an event; this happened—and sharply unsettling whatever expectations I might have about the subject. Reading it, and even more effectively if I'm listening to it being spoken by its author, I'm likely to suffer a decisive revision of assumptions about the subject. For in this essentially comic movement (from death to regeneration) Durcan manages to incorporate a remarkable spectrum of feeling about this difficult and painful topic. And again, as with the earlier poem, this poem's movement embodies that spectrum before we are analytically aware of the feelings themselves. Such an unsettling movement in such an anecdotal mode leaves the reader / listener in a fairly heightened state of imaginative fracture, one result of which is renewed, refreshed awareness of the limiting effect of fixed assumptions. In an Irish context, where assumptions about marriage and its concomitant facts of life can be especially fixed and unyielding, the swerving, shifting movement of this poem (and many others like it in Durcan's work) is particularly subversive. And this is all the more so in an actual performance, where the performing poet sways a communal body of people—people who are obliged, formally at least, to live within these fixed assumptions about marriage, love, sex— into sharing an explosively antithetical view of the subject, made even more lethal because offered in a mode of comic anarchy. So the movement of the poem shows that even while dealing with an intimately personal issue, Durcan can be a decisively public poet, bringing a difficult and generally affecting truth up from underground. Unsettling expectations by, among other things, moving in unusual and unpredictable ways through a poem, Durcan's mode can release suppressed psychic energies, unleashing them by incorporating them—as spokesman and scapegoat—in himself.

In metaphor and movement, then, Durcan's work manifests a drive toward a different world of expanded moral, spiritual, and emotional consciousness. Even at its most private it can be a public exhortation toward renewal. This condition is identified and aspired to by means of radical satire and celebration, by comic subversion and high but basically simple rhetorical gesture. Both metaphor and movement, at the center of his work as I see it, show the work to be a creative attempt to bully, lovingly, the Republic into becoming a different world. In the animated metaphors and the restless movement of these poems it is possible to detect—through the oddly commanding voice of a comic scapegoat—an enterprising, surprising, courageous drive toward grace. In Durcan's way of "being present" he performs an important job for and in Irish poetry and, more largely, Irish life. As vividly as any, his poetry shows one of the possibilities for a rich and complicated connection between the two.

Coda

In Paul Durcan and Paul Muldoon—no more nor less reliable a guide than my intuition tells me—one may detect a special kind of coming of age of Irish poetry in English. The radical novelty and strangeness of their imaginations; the curiously loose and various ways they inhabit, exploit, deal with the English language; the potentially anarchic, yet in many ways untroubledly native quality of their reception of and engagement with experience, whether local or universal, public or private; in short, their assured confidence and authority of identity (identity may be a shaky concept in Muldoon, but the poet's sense of his own *poetic* self seems impeccably assured)—all these features, a few of which I have shown in action, suggest a poetry caught in the energetic act of freeing itself from traditional (postcolonial?) anxieties, anxieties that have in many ways fuelled the imaginative work of the best of their immediate and more remote predecessors. Among all the striking notes of their work I detect in particular a note of freedom that can do nothing but promise well for the future.

Notes

1. The five volumes, all published by Faber and Faber (London), are *New Weather* (1973), *Mules* (1977), *Why Brownlee Left* (1980)), *Quoof* (1983), and *Meeting the British* (1987). This last was also published, as was *Quoof*, by Wake

Forest Press, Winston-Salem, South Carolina. Faber has published a *Selected Poems*, an expanded version of which has also been published in America, by Ecco Press (1987).

2. *Irish Literary Supplement* (Fall 1987): 37; P.M. interviewed by Kevin Barry.

3. Ibid., 36.

4. From *Viewpoints: Poets in Conversation with John Haffenden* (London: Faber & Faber, 1981), 134.

5. By "younger" I mean after and aside from Kinsella, Montague, Murphy, Heaney, and Mahon—who seem by fairly comon consensus to represent the most accomplished achievement in their respective poetic "generations." Although Durcan (b. 1942), unlike Muldoon (b. 1951), belongs chronologically to the "generation" of Heaney and Mahon, as a poet he seems in a certain sense to come after them.

6. *O Westport in the Light of Asia Minor* (Dublin: Anna Livia Press, 1975); *Teresa's Bar* (Dublin: Gallery Press, 1976); *Sam's Cross* (Dublin: Profile Press, 1978); *Jesus, Break His Fall* (Dublin: Raven Arts Press, 1980); *The Selected Paul Durcan* (Belfast: Blackstaff Press, 1982); *Jumping the Train Tracks with Angela* (Dublin: Raven Arts / Manchester: Carcanet New Press, 1983)); *The Berlin Wall Cafe* (Belfast: Blackstaff, 1985); *Going Home to Russia* (Belfast: Blackstaff, 1987). The smaller volumes referred to are *Endsville* (with Brian Lynch; Dublin: New Writers Press, 1967), and *Ark of the North* (Raven Arts, 1982).

7. I don't mean to strike the competitive note. The fact of Durcan's drawing power is directly aligned with the nature of his verse itself, its performative and public qualities. And, in a world of minisales his recent volumes have been, like Heaney's, best sellers. No doubt an interesting study will some day be done on their respective audiences / readerships.

8. Introduction to *The Selected Paul Durcan*, xv.

9. Mahon, "Orpheus Ascending: The Poetry of Paul Durcan," *Irish Review* (Autumn 1986); 15–19; Heaney: "Three Irish Poets to Watch," *Irish Literary Supplement* (Spring 1986): 27.

10. James Joyce, *Ulysses*, The Corrected Text, ed. Hans Gebler (New York: Vintage Books, 1986), 273.

11. Mahon, "Orpheus Ascending," 16.

12. See Francois Targat, *Marc Chagall* (New York: Rizzoli, 1985), 7. A statement of Mauriac's which Targat applies to Chagall might also be used of some of Durcan's work, of the sense in which its effects seem rooted in a way of seeing: "Under the thick layer of our actions the soul of our childhood remains unchanged" (7).

13. Targat, *Marc Chagall*, numbers 67, 75, 118. I am not arguing for parallels or exact influences (although *"Le Poète Allongé [after Chagall"*], 11 BWC, 10, is

obviously indebted in a direct way). The way I see Chagall simply helps me to read Durcan better.

14. Michael Cunningham, "Paul Durcan: Poet as Public Commentator," *Irish Times*, 28 November 1987.

Real and Synthetic Whiskey:
A Generation of Irish Poets, 1975–85

Harry Clifton

The generation of Irish poets I want to consider began to publish in the 1970s and had formed their reputations by the middle eighties. I came to know some of them personally, but all of them I had already read against the backdrop of a contemporary Ireland I had first to live away from and return to before I could see it in the context of larger forces that were turning it into the same landing-strip as other small countries I had lived in. What kind of society was this? What kind of pool—racial, historical, and spiritual—were the poets fishing in?

The Ireland I returned to in the early 1980s had long since emerged from the mist of a false dawn in the sixties, when all ships had seemed to rise, as its premier Sean Lemass predicted they would, on the incoming tide of global prosperity. Two religious wars had changed all that, the first of them erupting in the north of Ireland in 1969, and the second in the Middle East in 1973. If the effect of the first was to turn us inward and backward, to the tribal, the sectarian, the locally attritional—the effect of the second was to propel us outward to the realization that we too, in spite of ourselves, were citizens of the world, part of a global mesh of marketing, political, and military energies. On the price of international oil our spiritual life would depend, as much as on our local and traditional pieties. Thus Ireland in the seventies and eighties—poised between agnostic pluralism and the conservative backlash against the Filthy Modern Tide.

What was to fill the vacuum? On the one hand patriarchal religion hectoring from the pulpit, on the other the neuroses and addictions of a generation of idle hands and empty hearts. On the one hand state schemes to create illusory jobs, on the other a release of energies in experimental theater, electric music, and surrealistic verses. Organic farms, military splinter-groups, sisterhoods, and sects—a blind groping toward new religious forms, new matrices of relationships. Intermarriage between refugees—Chilean, for example, or Vietnamese—and the sons and daughters of Limerick, Belfast, and Kilkenny. A people, in a word, already streets ahead of the capacity of its intelligentsia—priests, writers, or politicians—to express, let alone legislate for, what was happening to it. If we narrow the context to more immediate influences upon this generation of poets, it would be important to note the freer availability of university education than previously, and the onset of an extensive system of state patronage through the arts councils. Both of these have been mixed blessings and it is probably too early to say whether poetry in Ireland has crabbed or blossomed as a result of them. But most, if not all, the poets have seen the muse trundled through the dissecting room of literary tutorial or creative writing seminar—and have either merged with this imported American system for the sake of earning a living from it or subsequently lived down their intellectualism with a vengeance and taken up a rigidly chthonic stance. It may be that the tentative experiment of bringing a writer-in-residence on campus in a remunerative but creatively untrammeled fashion will heal this particular breach.

With the arts councils, we have to speak the language of projects if we are to describe, in specific terms, what they may be said to have contributed by the middle eighties—the inauguration of an honors system called Aosdána, the funding of a Centre for the Creative Arts at Annaghmakerrig, the financial underpinnings of Irish poetry publishers, as well as individual grants to poets "to enable them to write full-time," that most dangerous of chimerae that dance before the eyes of poets, in Ireland as elsewhere. There is, I am afraid, room for skepticism. To what extent, for instance, could the poetry houses survive without state subvention? And if not at all, does it not imply that they are artificially kept alive rather than being, in a small but authentic sense, a living link with the people? Or again, what is going to be the effect of alienating a young poet from the grind of collective life at an early age, and allowing him to exist in a subsidized freedom? Does our subsidized Irish poet expand imaginatively into the real air of his existence, or collapse inwardly to a bundle of apathy? And finally, what has happened to the prize, award, or fellowship as an indicator of real merit? I ask these questions but leave them unanswered, because they are part of the unresolved atmospheric in which Irish poetry is currently being written. Let me move now from the general to the particular and look at the poets themselves as they stand, laden with distinctions real and illusory, at the entrance to their own and the nation's middle age.

Of this generation, the two who seem to me to have made the deepest impression are Paul Durcan and Paul Muldoon. Superficially (their surreal humor and a certain childlike element in their work) they resemble each other. Actually, however, they are at opposite poles of the same electric field. In them, it could be said, are reconstituted in an Irish context the argument between "cooked" and "raw" poetries, or further back, the distinction Coleridge made between poetry of the imagination (Durcan) and poetry of the fancy (Muldoon). It may be that either or both has done his best work already, and that they are condemned to official recognition and a dispersal of original intensity. Or, on the other hand, either or both may find new points of growth within their imaginative fields. They seem however, in early middle age, to be known quantities, each with a style developed by now almost to the point of parody, and an audience that has caught up with them—or caught on to them, as the case may be. Nonetheless, they are the twin peaks between which a number of others of the same generation but of lesser intensity are currently negotiating their own positions. And if, as seems inevitable, a new synthesis of poetic speech emerges in Ireland in the next decade, it will have coalesced from the thesis and antithesis that these two represent.

In the work of Paul Durcan, we have a realization of Patrick Kavanagh's idea of comedy, or the comic vision, as abundance of life. Kavanagh may have outlined the blueprint for such a vision, but Durcan has filled in the spaces with a colloquial multiplicity of voices undistorted by the feedback of iambic stress. In a sense, he has done in Ireland what Robert Lowell asked of American poetry—namely, achieved "the breakthrough back into life" from a merely Parnassian preoccupation with stanzas that in their enamelled perfection excluded everything else. His forms—and they *are* forms, though ones picked up by the ear rather than the eye—allow for digression, much as the natural consecutiveness and tangential qualities of human speech and thought do. The classic example of this digression, by which life in its unforced state intrudes, is in Robert Frost's "Birches," where

> I was going to say before Truth broke in
> With all her matter of fact about the ice storm

but it is everywhere in Durcan, where his willingness to go off at a tangent is the key to the living inclusiveness of his work—the marvellous enumeration of hats in "The Hat Factory," for instance, not an integral thematic element perhaps, but all the more alive for that, or the visions of Cork city in "Windfall," seen through the windows of his family apartment:

> At home I used to sit in a winged chair by the window
> Overlooking the river and the factory chimneys,
> The electricity power station and the car assembly works
> The fleets of trawlers and the pilot tugs,
> Dreaming that life is a dream which is real,
> The river a reflection of itself in its own waters,
> Goya sketching Goya among the smoky mirrors.
> The industrial vista was my Mont Sainte-Victoire
>
> At the high window, shipping from all over the world
> Being borne up and down the busy, yet contemplative, river;
> Skylines drifting in and out of skylines in the cloudy valley;
> Firelight at dusk, and city lights in the high window,
> Beyond them the control tower of the airport on the hill
> —A lighthouse in the sky flashing green to white to green.

It is passages like these that give Ireland back to itself in the way that the inclusiveness of Ginsberg and Williams brought the prose qualities of America, pregnant with life, back into poetry. Durcan has been subject to the same recriminations as the good Beats have, by those who read with the eye rather than the ear. The eye notes only the absence of regular stanzas and assumes chaos. Not so, however. Durcan's breathing line, far longer than the iambic pentameter, is written for the ear (which does not mean it cannot be read off a page) and is the key to his inclusiveness. His irregular stanzas terminate when the ear, not the eye, says they should. Indeed, he is usually at his worst when he departs from his natural metric and tries to write in conventional measures. But I mention these things merely as an indication, in terms of style, of what I consider most important in Durcan—his comic inclusiveness, his openness to the social heterodoxy, the incongruity, the babel of Irish life in the past decade.

The ear, however, can be seduced as well as sated, and Durcan has not been immune to its temptations—rhetoric, longwindedness, the public stance. Once he was the unknown poet who speaks of himself in "The

Hat Factory," reading a newspaper in a quiet pub with an old man for company:

> He is the recipient of an old age pension
> While I am so low in society's scale
> I do not rate even the dole
> But I am at peace with myself and so is he,

a poet whose juxtapositions—and this was their power—were international but rooted in the local. Ireland was a landscape over which played an invisible web of facial and religious strands, in which the citizenship of the Irish in the larger world was registered intuitively, imaginative, as in "Fermoy Calling Moscow".

> She sells her sweetmeats and she makes her tea
> And when things get bad on RTE
> She tunes in to Radio Moscow while she irons:
> *O they'll not knock Mrs Crotty down.*

Now he is the recognized poet who travels on cultural missions to Russia and America and reads to large audiences in a style they have come to expect. The juxtapositions in his poems now are more in the nature of political assertions, and the language is showing signs of a corresponding degeneration into cliché, as in "Going Home To Russia":

> We Irish have had our bellyful of *blat*
> And *blarney*, more than our share
> Of the *nomenclatura* of Church and Party,
> The *nachastvo* of the legal and medical mafia.

> Going down the airbridge, I slow my step,
> Savouring the moment of liberation;
> As soon as I step aboard the Aeroflot airliner
> I will have stepped from godlessness into faith:

Where once he praised the language of journalism, in "To A Reporter" for its vivifying fidelity to the actual world, now he is in danger of deadening his own poetic with the easy opinionatedness of the newspaper editorial. I shall return to Durcan, but suffice it to say that he seems to

have come to a fork in his own particular road, with a mass audience
waiting in one direction, and a small, potentially more discriminating one
in the other.

If Durcan has reached a crossroads, so too, in a different way, has Paul
Muldoon. The mental traveller of "Immram" has now relocated himself
physically from Belfast to the monkey-puzzle of American life he so brilliantly exploited in that poem. Whether this will damage or enhance his
talent remains an open question, but it seems an appropriate moment to
consider a body of work almost more American than Irish in the eclecticism
of its myths, its imaginative homelessness. In a way, Muldoon is not so
much an Irish poet as a poet who happens to have been born in Ireland.
What is real about him is not his Irishness but the intensity of his imaginative synthesis, wherever it is applied.

Unlike Durcan, whose mediumistic trance is a listening in to the voices
that have room to breathe and populate his long lines, Muldoon is a cold
mathematician, measuring his effects to the last millimeter, controlling
the apparent pandemonium, the modern flux, with a hidden orchestration
of traditional stanzaic forms. As with Durcan, however, the key to his
inclusiveness is in his technique—not the open, aural line this time, but
a precocious mastery of traditional forms that seemed, even in the early
poems of "New Weather," to be able to ventriloquize contemporary modes
(Auden, Larkin) with almost casual ease. But the important thing is that
by the time of "Mules," when he had something of his own to say,
technique was already in harness to help him say it. Thus, the deceptive
simplicity of "Lunch with Pancho Villa," where the background might be
violence in Northern Ireland or political violence anywhere, and the
activist and contemplative in a man (or a poet) are expertly played off
against each other;

> "Look, son. Just look around you.
> People are getting themselves killed
> Left, right and centre
> While you do what? Write rondeaux?
> There's more to living in this country
> Than stars and horses, pigs and trees,
> Not that you'd guess it from your poems.
> Do you never listen to the news?
> You want to get down to something true,
> Something a little nearer home."

Having had this argument with himself, it seems to me Muldoon was free
to adopt a purely aesthetic position—to be, as Patrick Kavanagh once
put it, the man who simply states the position without caring whether his
words change anything or not. Thereafter, he could expand into his own
kind of inclusiveness, he could pick and choose from what he saw, felt,
heard and read around him, or extrapolated out of Ulster. His slices of
life are, therefore, amoral, but this is a sign of their poetic authenticity.
The perspective is often that of Frank O'Connor's knowing little boy, an
innocence deliberately maintained for the sake of purity of representation.
Muldoon has never claimed a moral position for himself, and stands apart
from the outrage of Durcan or the guilty heartsearchings of Seamus Heaney. His poetry has myths—Immram Mael Duin, The Trickster, for example—but no moral imperatives. And his myths, it seems to me, are
merely "conceits," pretexts for building great frescoes of contemporary
life, for the kind of living inclusiveness and network of correspondences
that excite his imagination. They do not have a moral dimension, but
they do have what Kavanagh considered necessary for the true comic
vision, namely abundance of life. Consider, for example, this scene from
"The More A Man Has, The More A Man Wants:"

> Into a picture by Edward Hopper
> Of a gas station
> In the mid-West
> Where Hopper takes as his theme
> Light, the spooky
> Glow of an illuminated sign
> Reading Esso or Mobil
> Or what-have-you—
> Into such a desolate oval
> Ride two youths on a motorbike.
> A hand gun. Balaclavas.
> The pump attendant's grown so used
> To hold-ups he calls after them:
> Beannache Dé ar an obair. [God bless the work.]

Here, the nihilistic violence is assumed onto an aesthetic level, and presented pictorially without being judged. The scene could be the American
Midwest or contemporary Ulster. The diction is colloquial to the point
of slackness, but underpinned by a sonnet form that scatters half- and
quarter-rhymes along its length, with "Hopper" and "obair" establishing

the basic irony, the basic correspondence. Not much more than a hint, really, but that, in essence, is the Muldoon approach—a dance of pure style in a void, where morally weightless phenomena are linked through the fortuitousness of rhyme. There are some who will feel such aesthetic detachment borders on cynicism, a failure of feeling. If they do, they can get their anger from Paul Durcan.

The best instance I know of the difference of approach of these two poets can be found by reading two recent poems on the same subject, Durcan's "The Anglo-Irish Agreement 1986" and Muldoon's "Meeting The British," in relation to each other. Both poems are about power and oppression, the relation of colonizer to colonized—but the handling of the subject is entirely different and characteristic of the individuals concerned. In Durcan, the position of the ordinary Irish is stated directly:

> The exclusive suburbs of Dublin city
> Are necklaces of Crossmaglens
> In which armies of occupation fester
> Behind fortified walls and electronically controlled gates.

In Muldoon, however, the Irish tragedy is implied from a situation remote both in place and in time, a meeting between American Indians and the British outside Detroit in the eighteenth century:

> They gave us six fishhooks
> And a blanket embroidered with smallpox.

Where Durcan is overtly judgmental, Muldoon states the facts and lets their resonances do the work. Where Durcan's idiom is the spoken, the vernacular, Muldoon's is consciously derived from the literary, a high style of civilized discourse making its own statement at gut level. Durcan's breathing line is open, while Muldoon's is governed, albeit loosely, by the formal principle of rhyme and pentameter. Where Durcan's contemporary Ireland smoulders under the burning glass of his *saeva indignatio*, the Ireland of Paul Muldoon is refracted at us coldly, indirectly, through the prism of allusiveness.

If these two have eaten up most of the available air between them of their poetic generation, it is worthwhile nonetheless to look at some others who exemplify, in their different ways, why Durcan and Muldoon are exceptional. Broadly speaking, the rest may be divided into those, such

as Thomas McCarthy and Peter Fallon, Medbh McGuckian and Nuala
Ní Dhómnaill, who work within the frame of certain Irish myths handed
down to them, and those, such as Michael O'Loughlin and Dermot Bolger,
who reject the myths but have nothing to put in their place. The myths
I have in mind are Irish Republicanism, Irish Catholicism, and the domestic ideal. All the above-named have written credibly within one or
other of these myths without, it seems to me, either challenging them
seriously or enlarging them, as both Durcan and Muldoon have done. It
is precisely this limitation, really a kind of failure of imagination, that
makes the difference.

I had said earlier that it seemed to me that in the Ireland of the past
decade such was the pressure of social change—call it disintegration if
you will—that the ordinary people had outstripped their own intellectuals
in imaginative grasp of reality: that is to say they were, and are, leading
lives not yet documented or expressed by their poets, who should, in fact,
have prefigured them. An example of this is the immersion of Thomas
McCarthy in a myth-Fianna Fail Republicanism with DeValera as its
implied hero—that the generality of Irish people have, with sighs of
boredom and relief, quietly outgrown. In his early poem "State Funeral"
about the death and burial of DeValera, McCarthy sets the scene:

> It was a landscape for old men. Today
> They lowered the tallest one, tidied him
> Away while his people watched quietly.
> In the end he had retreated to the first dream,
> Caning truth. I think of his austere grandeur,
> Taut sadness, like old heroes he had imagined.

Yet in his three books, McCarthy has continued to kneel before the altar
of this dreary phenomenon, against which every Irish poet worth the name
had, for decades, struggled to avoid asphyxiation of the spirit. Because of
his insistence upon this material, he has been called a political poet, yet
the life he describes, the life of electioneering, the decline of aging Dáil
members, the tending of party shrines, and so forth, is, I would suggest,
a peculiarly elitist one—certainly not political in the broader sense. In
McCarthy, there is a fatal confusion between political power and intensity
of life, as, for example, in "The President's Men":

> There's dust on Mr Dinneen's boots: Where has
> He been canvassing, I wonder? What house

Has unlatched a half-day of harvest work
To listen to his talk? My father knows
The Party poll, the roll-call of promise
The roads we shall take when I am older
In search of power . . .

In search of power! Even the language goes dead, rather than implicate itself. McCarthy is, in fact, a novelist in verse who has given us thumbnail sketches of certain period phenomena, but to describe him as a poet is a mistake. He has no ear, and his vision of "the long sorrow of Ireland" is a fatally sentimental one, an evasion of contemporary reality rather than an expression of it.

Another mythical Ireland, this time a Catholic agrarian one, defines the work of Peter Fallon. His vision is borrowed from Kavanagh, and his style from Frost, Heaney, and Paul Muldoon. But it is the Kavanagh of the 1930s, before he left rural Ireland for London, Dublin, and the ruinous years that led eventually to the redemptive vision of the late poems. Fallon, on the other hand, seems determined to root himself in the innocence of the first phase—as if Kavanagh had decided to run the Iniskeen farm as a going concern and write poems as well. On a practical level, this sounds like eminent good sense. On the spiritual level, however, I am not so sure that it is not highly disingenuous. Fallon seems to me a little too much in the market with a product, and innocent Catholic visions such as "Spring Song":

A new flock flowed
Through a breach,
A makeshift gate.
And this is heaven:
Sunrise through a copper beech.

have a borrowed air about them. The sheepfarming, the rural dances, the meet-you-after-second-mass matinees are all as in Kavanagh, but where Kavanagh paid a lover's sacrifice for such visions, Fallon's mind is cold, exploitative. He ranges over the same material like a folklorist, not a lover—his Billy McNamees and Phils seem like props in a carefully constructed idyll of Fallon's own, designed to keep out the pain of a deeper self-confrontation. There is hardly a single moment of real human intimacy in his three books, yet he is constantly insisting on how much he "belongs" in his rural community, as in "Madelaine":

> We were children together.
> We have our ways. We might drag out an "Aye"
> Or nothing, nod "I do and I don't"
> And know exactly what we mean.

As with Thomas McCarthy, the true angels and demons of poetry are kept safely at arm's length—except that where McCarthy wards them off by wrapping the green cloak of Republicanism around him, Fallon wraps around himself an even greener cloak of pastoral innocence.

If McCarthy and Fallon are in their different ways wedded to romanticisms that seem to me an evasion of either the truly political or the truly personal, then the counter-statement comes in the work of Dermot Bolger and Michael O'Loughlin. But is it in fact a counter statement? In spite of an initial impression of hardbitten urban realism, both seem to me fundamentally romantics. But they are *urban* romantics—their models are European decadents in the case of Bolger, and in O'Loughlin's case an idealized concept of the poet as politically crucial figure on the run from police—an idealization culled, I would suggest, from a too literal reading of texts by and about Osip Mandelstam. Bolger is a truer poet in his novels, where the breathing line of the prose sentence seems to be more naturally his voice, than in the stanzaic forms, where his ear fails him drastically and the music goes flat. In his work, society—by implication Irish suburban society—is oppressive and institutional (jails, hospitals, factories) and is viewed from the perspective of the alienated victim (drug addict, prisoner, illegitimate). As vision this is direct, honest, and true to the contemporary crisis, but the derivative romanticism of the language almost invariably vitiates it, as, for example, in "Frankenstein":

> the flickknife's steel wings unfurl in the man's palm
> as he slices the slab of hash on the swaying tabletop
> a nation of outcasts sown together by blazing eyelids
> in this market flat where a blazing autopsy never stops
> below in the street refrigerated lorries hum all night
> ambulances   spurt   blue   flames   down   shrunken
> passageways
> where whores on stilts are picked up in the headlights

One can see what he is trying to do, but the poems do not come alive, not through failure of vision but failure of technique, an inability to select from the influx of stimuli in the light of a leading idea. Nonetheless, the direction of his impulse, that of a betrayed generation turning away in disgust from the Ireland of DeValera and the blood sacrifice of 1916, is never in doubt:

> Gulls shriek as teachers drill us into step
> *We shall march forth to meet with destiny*
>
> We paraded in line towards the wooden
> desks
> Past a framed proclamation and a crucifix
> And begged God that our turn would be
> next
> *We shall march forth to meet with destiny*

Michael O'Loughlin works the same territory but more effectively because of his truer ear for line lengths in the stanzas, and because he has purged his language of romanticism. What is left is a stripped, ironic instrument adequate to the reality it is expressing, as in "The City":

> And no matter how you toss it
> It always turns up the same:
> The plastic sun of Finglas
> Squatting on every horizon.
> The squandered coin of your youth:
> The slot machines you fed have rung up blanks
> Not just here, but everywhere.

Yet he too is a romantic, though not in the sense Bolger is. Faced with the Irish urban nightmare, Bolger's romanticism takes the form of withdrawal indoors to worlds of monomania, paranoia,—whereas O'Loughlin's takes the form of going into exile. He too has dissected the DeValera legacy and found it wanting, as in "The Irish Lesson":

> When I got too old to fear them
> They appealed to a baser emotion;
> I was cutting myself off
> From a part of the nation's heritage

> but I didn't want to know their nation's heritage
> it wasn't mine

but in walking away from it, he has succumbed to another illusion, that
of exile in Europe as a move toward life and the future. For if anything,
the bourgeois museum that is contemporary Europe is even deader than
the crumbling society he has left, with its psychic emanations from the
ruins. Everywhere he goes he meets romantics like himself, leading disillusioned afterlives:

> I suddenly see him, poor Sean
> With his Aran sweater
> And second-class degree in History
> A pale-faced corpse
> Drifting like a dead fish
> Through a sea of foreign newsprint
> Red-bearded idol of a scattered army
> Of terylene shirts and expense accounts
> In half the capital cities of Europe

Having made the grand gesture, he is vaguely and disturbingly aware of
his own prosperity, of having been absorbed into the power complex he
sought originally to decry, as in "Concert-going in Vienna":

> I had not thought death had missed so many.
> This woman here in front of me, for instance
> In pearls and grey hair in a stately bun
> Nodding her head in time to Bruckner's Fourth.
> She is not dead, nor am I.

His insecurity, as I mentioned above, takes the form of seeking out exemplary models and / or situations that will authenticate his sense of
himself in advanced social systems that care for the poet as an economic
entity but ignore his spiritual message. Hence his identification with certain Russian poets, notably Mandelstam whose tone he borrows to excess,
or with the activist Frank Ryan, or with the Limerick Soviet—pinpoints
of authenticity in a sea of mediocre materialism. At the heart of his poems,
however, he is too honest not to acknowledge that he has traded one
death, that of DeValera's Ireland, for the deeper, more collective, death
of Europe.

If the political myths that engage these poets are ambivalent, so too is the private realm. A number of male poets, notably Aidan Mathews, have made it their own, but it is more or less exclusively the realm of the two female poets, Medbh McGuckian and Nuala Ní Dhomhnaill, who have gained most prominence in the last ten years. The poetry of both is grounded in private rather than collective experience—home, domesticity, sexuality—but the imaginative projections they have made of it are extraordinarily different. In McGuckian's case, domesticity is projected back into what appears to be the world of late Victorian fiction. Her work as a whole reads like moments of epiphany from a verse novel written in the first person singular, whose housebound heroine is variously an amateur at painting, poetry, and flower arranging, occasionally waiting for a suitor or "confined" by childbirth, and endlessly sifting such bric-a-brac—"my crested notepaper," "my edge-to-edge bolero," "my auburn-bearded anx-iete-du-soir"—as seem to define her daily existence. Here is an excerpt from "Sabbath Park" that gives the flavor of this closed, narcissistic world:

> . . . . Broody
>
> As a seven-months' child, I upset
> The obsolete drawing-room that still seems
> Affronted by people having just gone,
> By astonishing Louisa with my sonnets,
> Almost a hostage in the dream
> Of her mother's hands—that would leave them
> Scattered over their damask sofas after
> Some evening party, filled
> With the radiance of my fine lawn shirt.

Once, it should be noted, she "feels her age" and "sighs for liberation," but on the whole this is a congenial, if apparently claustrophobic, world in which the female is simultaneously trapped and manipulative, where sex is hinted at rather than stated, a powerful nuance rising through the decorous language. As one giant conceit of domestic life it is quite consistent. The question to ask is whether it is intended ironically, as an oblique comment on the lives of contemporary women. Or is it, instead, a compensatory fantasy the author actually wants to believe in? I see little, if any, evidence of irony.

Where McGuckian is coy and oblique, Ní Dhomhnaill is exuberant and elemental. In her love poetry and poetry of female experience she uses the Irish myths as though she owned them from time immemorial, rather than as something given to her by the Celtic Revival or the school system of DeValera's Republic. Instead, they are grafted in a living continuity with the most contemporary of experience, as in "The Race":

> Like a mad lion, like a wild bull,
> A wild boar from a Fenian tale,
> A hero bounding towards a giant
> With a single silken crest,
> I blindly drive the car
> Through the small towns of the west:
> I drive the wind before me
> And leave the wind behind.

or they are fused with the deeps of the modern subconscious, as in this lovely invocation before sleep;

> Down there there's ancient wood and bogdeal:
> The Fianna's bones are there at rest
> With rustless swords—and a drowned girl,
> A noose around her neck.

The sexuality is proud and direct, but behind it there is a sacramental vision that reminds me of Yeats's Ribh, a coming together of religious and sexual energies in a new synthesis—myth and fairytale on the one hand, biological and psychoanalytic awareness on the other, as prefigured in Yeats's "Ribh In Ecstasy":

> Godhead on Godhead in sexual spasm begot
> Godhead. Some shadow fell. My soul forgot
> Those amorous cries that out of quiet come
> And must the common round of day resume.

There is in Ní Dhomhnaill a wholeness of outlook: she seems to me the only one of her contemporaries, along with Durcan and Muldoon, not to have been deadened by working within the parameters of Irishness, to have made of it a wellspring rather than a historical blind alley.

The true artist, as Samuel Beckett once noted apropos his Irishness, is the one who comes from nowhere. Too many contemporary Irish poets seem to me to be making it their business to come from Ireland, mapping out smug little locales for themselves, riding political hobbyhorses, generating exportable myths with one eye on the Cultural Relations Committee and another on the Irish American Foundation. They are careerists who have found for themselves a way from the local to the international, but not, as for instance Kavanagh did, from the local to the universal—the true road of art. All of them without exception are carrying, by early middle age, a topweight of prizes, awards, and bursaries of dubious intrinsic merit. Not one of them, it would seem is unacceptable to a state that is simultaneously beggaring its people, alienating its young, and causing the kind of atomization and social misery I have alluded to at the beginning of this essay. Yet one looks in vain through their work for an admission of their own compromise. Their fingers are pointed elsewhere, never at themselves. Some of them, the more polemic ones like McCarthy and O'Loughlin, are showing signs of substituting prose for verse as their main mode of expression, as the opinionated self rises to supplant the lyric poet. The best of them, Paul Durcan and Paul Muldoon, are the ones with the strongest digestive systems for contemporary reality, the ones who exclude least from their democratic vistas. These, for all their faults, are the ones who will survive to name their age. The rest will have had their reward in the present tense, from an intelligentsia as interested in conferring fake laurels on each other as it is ignorant of the crisis of Irish life seething all around it.

Notes on Contributors

Anthony Bradley was born and raised in Ireland. He is a graduate of Queen's University, Belfast, where he was also a fellow at the Institute for Irish Studies (1982–83)). He teaches modern Irish literature at the University of Vermont. He is author of *William Butler Yeats* (a critical introduction to Yeats's plays), editor of *Contemporary Irish Poetry*, and has written numerous articles and reviews on Irish literature.

James D. Brophy has edited (with Raymond Porter) *Modern Irish Literature* (Iona: Twayne, 1972), a *festschrift* for William York Tindall, and *Contemporary Irish Writing* (Twayne, 1983). He has also written the critical studies *Edith Sitwell: The Symbolist Order* (Southern Illinois University Press, 1968) and *W. H. Auden* (Columbia University Press, 1970). He is a professor of English at Iona College.

Harry Clifton was born in Dublin and educated at University College, Dublin. He has published (with Gallery Press, Dublin) three collections of poems: *The Walls of Carthage* (1977), *Office of the Salt Merchant* (1979), and *Comparative Lives* (1982). He was the Irish representative at the Iowa International Writing Program 1985 and poet-in-residence at the Frost Place, New Hampshire, 1986. Currently he is working with the Irish civil service in Dublin.

John Engle is director of the Institute for American Universities in Aix-en-Provence, France. His doctoral dissertation at U.C.L.A. was written on contemporary Irish poetry, and he has written extensively on modern and contemporary literature.

Eamon Grennan has published his poems in *Poetry Ireland Review*, the *New Yorker*, the *Paris Review*, the *Irish Times*, and other American and Irish magazines. Two volumes of his poetry, *Wildly for Days* and *What Light There Is*, were published by Gallery Press, Dublin. He was educated at University College, Dublin, and Harvard University. Currently he is an associate professor of English at Vassar College.

Dillon Johnston lectures on modern Irish literature as a member of the English department at Wake Forest University. His *Irish Poetry after Joyce* appeared from the Notre Dame University Press and Dolmen Press in 1985. He is a director of the Wake Forest University Press, which for more than a decade has been publishing many of the best contemporary Irish poets.

Eileen Kennedy, professor of English at Kean College of New Jersey, also directs the graduate program, the M.A. in liberal studies. She has published previously on John McGahern, including an interview with him in the *Irish Literary Supplement* and an article on McGahern's novels in *Recent Irish Literature*. Her work has appeared in many journals, including *Éire-Ireland* and *James Joyce Newsletter*.

James McElroy has taught at St. Patrick's College, Maynooth. He has also taught at Iona College, the College of New Rochelle, and Pace University. Several of his articles and reviews have appeared in the *American Poetry Review*, the *Irish Literary Supplement*, and *Poetry Canada Review*.

John Mahon, associate professor of English at Iona College, coedited and contributed to *"Fanned and Winnowed Opinions"*: *Shakespearean Essays Presented to Harold Jenkins* (London and New York: Methuen, 1987). His earlier work has appeared in the *Evelyn Waugh Newsletter*, *Notes and Queries*, and *Hamlet Studies*.

Maureen Murphy is a dean of students at Hofstra University. She is president of the American Conference for Irish Studies, bibliographer of the International Association for the Study of Anglo-Irish Literature, and a member of the Executive Council of the American Irish Historical Society. She was a member of the faculty of the Yeats International Summer School in 1981 and 1985. She has written on Irish history, literature, and folklore, and on the Irish language.

Christopher Murray teaches in the Department of Modern English and American Literature at University College, Dublin. He holds a Ph.D. in history of theater from Yale University. He has written extensively on Irish theater and drama and is the author of the chapter on modern drama in the new edition of *Anglo-Irish Literature: A Guide to Research* (edited by Richard J. Finneran for the Modern Language Association of America). He is editor of the *Irish University Review*.

George O'Brien was educated at Ruskin College, Oxford, and Warwick University. He has taught at Warwick and Vassar College and is currently assistant professor of English at Georgetown University. He has written extensively on nineteenth-century and modern Irish fiction. His own short stories have won awards in Ireland. *The Village of Longing,* a memoir, was published by Lilliput Press in 1987, and his study of Brian Friel is due out from Twayne in 1989.

Daniel O'Hara, professor of English at Temple University, is the author of many essays on modern literature and criticism, including three previous pieces on Kinsella's poetry. His books include *Tragic Knowledge: Yeats's Autobiography and Hermeneutics* (1981), *The Romance of Interpretation: Visionary Criticism from Pater to De Man* (1985), and *Lionel Trilling: The Work of Liberation* (1988).

Charles B. Quinn is a professor of English at Iona College, where he teaches courses in Irish literature, history, and language. He studied at University College, Dublin, and has written an introduction to the language, *Irish for Everyone.* He has just finished a term as president of the Eastern States Celtic Association (ESCA).

Robert E. Rhodes, professor of English at the State University of New York at Cortland, has served on the American Conference for Irish Studies Executive Committee for twenty years, most recently as president from 1985–87. He has coedited three collections of Irish and Irish-American interest and has spoken and published widely on Irish and Irish-American topics, including a number of essays on William Trevor.

John Unterecker chaired the Graduate English Department at Columbia University before joining the University of Hawaii. He has published two books of poetry and numerous works of criticism, including *A Reader's Guide to W. B. Yeats* and *Voyager: A Life of Hart Crane.* He has held a Guggenheim for work on Yeats, and is general editor for the Columbia University Press series of books on twentieth-century American poetry. In 1985 he was given the Hawaii Award for Literature.